STREAMING MEDIA HANDBOOK

Eyal Menin

PRENTICE HALL PTR
UPPER SADDLE RIVER, NJ 07458
WWW.PHPTR.COM

ISBN 0-13-035813-4

Library of Congress Cataloging-in-Publication Data

Menin, Eyal.
    Streaming media handbook / Eyal Menin.
        p.   cm.
    Includes index.
    ISBN 0-13-035813-4
        1. Streaming technology (Telecommunications)   I. Title.
    TK5105.386 .M45   2002
    006.7′876–dc21

                                                    2002009487

Editorial Production/Composition: *G & S Typesetters, Inc.*
Executive Editor: *Mary Franz*
Editorial Assistant: *Noreen Regina*
Cover Design: *Bruce Kenselaar*
Cover Director: *Jerry Votta*
Marketing Manager: *Dan DePasquale*
Manufacturing Manager: *Alexis R. Heydt-Long*
Buyer: *Maura Zaldivar*
Full-Service Production Manager: *Anne R. Garcia*

Prentice Hall books are widely used by corporations and government agencies for training, marketing, and resale.

For Information regarding corporate and government bulk discounts please contact:
Corporate and Government Sales (800) 382-3419 or corpsales@pearsontechgroup.com

RealPlayer®, RealOne®, RealSystem®, RealSystem® Producer, RealSystem® Server, RealVideo®, and RealNetworks® are the registered trademarks of RealNetworks, Inc. QuickTime® and Darwin Streaming Server are trademarks of Apple Computer, Inc. Other company and product names mentioned herein are the trademarks or registered trademarks of their respective owners.

Printed in the United States of America

10   9   8   7   6   5   4   3   2   1

ISBN 0-13-035813-4

Pearson Education Ltd.
Pearson Education Australia PTY, Ltd.
Pearson Education Singapore, Pte, Ltd.
Pearson Education North Asia Ltd.
Pearson Education Canada, Ltd.
Pearson Educación de Mexico, S.A. de C.V.
Pearson Education – Japan
Pearson Education Malaysia, Pte, Ltd.

To my son, Idan, for his continued support

Contents

Part II
ENCODING AND STREAMING VIDEO   111

Chapter 6
Video Capture   113

Chapter 7
Encoding Workstation   125

Chapter 8
The Encoding Process   141

Part III
STRATEGIES   243

Chapter 12
Marketing Techniques   245

Chapter 13
Case Studies   265

Preface

Streaming Media Handbook will help many readers without technical experience add streaming media to their Web site. The book takes a basic approach, explaining the steps needed to prepare video or audio for streaming on the Internet or on private networks. I had the idea to write this book when I realized that most guides about streaming technology primarily addressed an audience that had extensive computer and network experience. Until now the exciting world of streaming video was a privilege only few could enjoy; one had to have technical knowledge of computers and basic video production skills. The purpose of this book is to simplify terms, share knowledge, and guide readers in choosing the proper tools to help them use streaming media technology in their day-to-day tasks.

Who Should Read This Book

This book is designed for readers of all levels, from the novice to the expert. *Streaming Media Handbook* is for everyone interested in learning how to stream media on the Internet, on a corporate local area network (LAN), or on a wireless local area network (WLAN). The book covers basic setup procedures that apply to every industry. Whether you work in the entertainment industry, you want to post media on your small-business Web site, or you are planning to add rich media to an enterprise network, this book shows you the steps necessary to reach your goal.

First-time users of streaming technology will find that this book uses simple terms and is easy to read. An illustrated guide leads you step-by-step through the installation of hardware and software, making it a task anyone can perform. Advanced readers will find useful information in the chapters explaining the latest software and streaming media tools on the market as well as detail configuration tips to operate media servers behind firewalls. Experienced users can apply the examples and case studies to their environments, helping them identify similarities and apply solutions to situations previous streaming guides did not address.

How This Book Is Organized

Streaming Media Handbook is divided into three parts. The first part (Chapters 1–5) provides a comprehensive overview of the preproduction process, which makes your video ready for streaming. The second part (Chapters 6–11) explains the various hardware and software products on the market. This part compares core streaming technologies such as QuickTime, RealMedia, and Windows Media, and helps you select the appropriate technology for your needs. This part also provides a step-by-step guide to setting up encoding workstations and to setting up media servers for the distribution of media on-demand or live webcasting. The last part (Chapters 12–13) has useful resources for all readers. It includes a list of streaming media providers, hardware and software companies, and online marketing techniques to promote media on the Internet. This part also has three case studies in which streaming media technologies were used.

A Companion Web Site

With the purchase of this book you are eligible for free online technical support from the author. Log on to *www.streaminghandbook.com* and enter the necessary information. After doing so, you will be eligible to receive instant access to updated resources that cover software upgrades, and to receive more information about products mentioned in the book.

Tools You Will Need

To further your knowledge of streaming media technology, I recommend that you create a laboratory environment where you can practice setting up streaming media. This laboratory environment will let you practice with hardware and software installations before you do the real thing. You can learn how to configure a dedicated encoding workstation and distribution media server. These computers can be part of a local area network or placed on the Internet. As described later in the book, some software installations are available for Windows, UNIX, and Macintosh operating systems. *Streaming Media Handbook* is addressing installations only on the Windows operating system. Read Chapters 6–10 to learn how to configure encoding workstations and media servers. These chapters are a useful guide for the preparation, storage, and display of streaming files.

Conclusion

The streaming media industry is growing rapidly. From a small jerky image streamed over a dialup connection to a global solution that provides enhanced communication tools, streaming technology has taken our world by storm. Streaming media has become widely used by small businesses as well as large enterprises. Today, companies that provide streaming media services are traded on the open stock market. The ability to instantly deliver a message in a cost-effective way across cities, states, and countries has changed our world. A technology that belonged to few is now used by many, opening up the world to an exciting and promising future. I hope this book helps you to better understand streaming technology and its potential. As you read you will notice that the book debunks the myth that has clouded streaming technology since its early days. In many ways the ability to stream video is similar to keeping fit at your local gym. You cannot stay in good shape simply by paying your monthly dues. You must also exercise. The information in this book gives you the equipment to train with; it offers you the knowledge to compress analog or digital video and to distribute streaming media on the Internet or on your local area network. Once you have this tool it is up to you to exercise it.

Acknowledgments

I thank Mary Franz, my publisher, for her encouragement and guidance. Thanks also to John Townley, Barbara Roeder, and Julie Nemer for an excellent job straightening out my tangled syntax, and to Mark Haefeli and Scott Harmolin, who gave their permission to publish two of the case studies in Chapter 13. And I can't forget the dedicated individuals at Microsoft, Packet Video, Palm, Monster Cable, Apple Computer, and RealNetworks who prefer to stay anonymous but who went out of their way to help me gather the necessary materials and examples I described. Your help and support was much appreciated.

Part I

STREAMING VIDEO PRODUCTION

1

Streaming Media Basics

What Is Streaming Media?

Streaming media is a technology that delivers large digital audio and video files in real time across computer networks. The evolution of streaming media has had a tremendous impact on the development and acceptance of the Internet as a new communication medium. Today, tens of millions of Internet users depend on streaming media technology to deliver information through Internet radio, live webcasts, and media on-demand archives. From leading news networks to global record companies to top Hollywood Studios to corporate executives, a growing number of companies and individuals are using streaming media technologies.

How does streaming media work? Prior to the invention of streaming media, visitors to a Web site had to download large files to view them on their local hard drive. The download process was very slow and not efficient because most computers at that time used dial-up modems to connect to the Internet. Streaming media technology changed the way we listen to audio and watch video on the Internet. Instead of downloading a whole file, a computer uses a streaming media player to connect to a streaming media server to request transmission of a live signal or play back prerecorded content. The software player then acts as a display device on the computer. The server does not permit the entire file to download; rather it chops the digital file into tiny minipackets and transmits them over the Internet. The packets travel to the computer that has made the request for audio or video and are reassembled for local playback. Streaming files are transmitted over computer networks using special protocols that enable the transmission of the files without the need to download them. Two of these protocols are the Real Time Streaming Protocol (RTSP), which is an application-level protocol for control over the delivery of data with real-time properties, and the Microsoft Media Server (MMS) protocol. RTSP is used to deliver Real Video and Apple's QuickTime Streaming files. A growing number of vendors use RTSP for the development of new technologies that deliver streaming content to mobile devices. More information about these protocols can be found in Chapters 5 and 11. The use of streaming protocols has significantly improved the way moving images and sounds are transmitted over computer networks. Streaming media technology has evolved and become a well-known technology. The purpose of this book is to guide you, the reader, to an understanding of streaming technology. After reading this book you will be able to use the technology for your own projects.

Before beginning with an overview of streaming technology, let us stop for a moment and consider how certain events change our lives. Before September 11, 2001, companies and individuals looked at streaming media applications as a technology aimed at supplementing or compensating for other media, but, after the terrorist attack on World Trade Center and the Pentagon, this view changed. In the days following the attack, because the commercial airlines had been used as a weapon, many companies revised their internal travel policies. Individuals were diverted to other means of transportation. Air travel suffered major losses. The government and the public raised questions about airline security and the ability of the existing security programs to prevent future attacks on the airline industry. In North America, many companies have offices in multiple states and cities and company employees are used to traveling among these offices. In addition, companies often send employees to visit vendors and clients. Employees consider such travel part of their job description. After September 11, fear of future attacks and the risk of increased corporate insurance premiums forced companies to restrict travel of executives and staff. These cultural changes helped technologies such as videoconferencing and streaming media gain attention again and become hot commodities.

The streaming media and videoconferencing industries had been hit badly during the dotcom fall. The new reality, as bad as it was, changed the way companies evaluated streaming technology. During the weeks following September 11, vendors and service providers specializing in video communications geared up to fulfill the growing demand for corporate applications that enhanced communication between one to one and one to many.

The events of September 11 had an incredible negative effect on the U.S. economy. Market analysts claim that more than 1.5 million people lost their jobs during the months following the attacks. The United States launched an unprecedented campaign against terrorism and went to war with the ruling party in Afghanistan after blaming the Taliban for harboring Al-Qaida—the terrorist group responsible for the attack on America.

In October 2001, the New York chapter of the Media Communications Association (MCA-I), formerly known as the International Television Association (ITVA), gathered for their monthly meeting, titled "Where Do We Go from Here?" The topic was a discussion of the impact of September 11 on the video industry. Executives from companies affected by the attack on the World Trade Center came to share their experience. Panelists included representatives from Merrill Lynch, Jack Morton Productions, Verizon Communications, and March Incorporated. All these companies had used streaming media before the event, and all were in agreement that they would be using it much more after the event. The meeting was recorded and is now available through a link from the book companion Web site at *www.streaminghandbook.com/go/itvany_sept11/*.

History of Streaming Media

At least once a year I visit the American Museum of the Moving Image in Astoria, New York. The museum is dedicated to educating the public about the art, history, technique, and technology of film, television, and digital media and to examining their impact on culture and society. The American Museum of the Moving Image has assembled the nation's largest and most comprehensive collection of moving image artifacts, one of the most important of its kind in the world, numbering more than 83,000 items. For example, the collection includes photographed studies of locomotion made by Eadweard Muybridge in 1887; an early mechanical television created in 1931 by C. Francis Jenkins; the chariot driven by Charlton Heston in the epic film *Ben Hur* (1959); Computer Space, the first coin-operated video arcade game (released by Nolan Bushnell in 1971); a character puppet of Yoda created by Stuart Freeborn for *The Empire Strikes Back* (1980); and many other items.

Moving images have helped us shape our world. They were created from storyboards that took us out of our daily life and into the wonderful world of celluloid. We laughed during the black and white scenes of Charlie Chaplin's movies, cried during the tragic endings of Greta Garbo's movies, and cheered in joy when Judy Garland won the fight against the wicked witch of the West in *The Wizard of Oz*. Moving images have became part of our lives and a central monument to modern-day technology.

The video industry went through many stages of development that paved the way for streaming media technology. In the early 1980s, video became mobile with the introduction of portable video recorders and a public product with the introduction of home videocassette recorders (VCRs) and, later, home video cameras. In the early 1990s, linear video editing systems were replaced by nonlinear digital video systems. From editing video on a VCR player and sending it to a VCR recorder, the industry developed computer-based editing solutions. At this stage, video content was captured by a computer, edited, and sent out again to be taped for distribution. Prices dropped, and capture and storage technology improved. After the Internet was made available to the public, it was just a matter of time before media was transmitted over computer networks. In 1994, the old world of cameras, tapes, and tube-based video display changed forever. Kevin Kelly describes this phenomenon in his book *New Rules for the New Economy*. The distribution of digital media has officially evolved from hardware distribution to software distribution. What does this means? Companies used to distribute their media on vertical helical scan (VHS) tapes, or on read-only-memory compact disks (CD-ROMs). Now that more than half a billion people have a connection to the Internet, companies can store their media on a network and deliver it to their audience faster and cheaper. Today, the most popular method of distributing news is over computer networks. The world has moved from distributing news to the masses using traditional TVs to distributing news over computer networks. It does not matter if the news is sent in the form of an email or a streaming audio file. The fact is that the Internet has become an effective and inexpensive method to share information among people all over the globe. This has changed the way we think about media, the way we process media, and the way we will distribute media in the future. Welcome to the streaming video age–the world in which digital media is processed in a blink of an eye, a world in which media stored on computer networks moves at the speed of light from the Web server of the *New York Times* Web site to your desktop computer, regardless of whether you live in Frankfurt, Tokyo, or Buenos Aires! Welcome to the new age of digital media–the age in which software applications operate on computers to produce sound waves and moving images!

Many aspects of the history of streaming media technology are similar to the development of television. After film, television was the most significant technological achievement that improved communications in the 20th century. Since its introduction in the early 1950s, the medium expanded and is now used worldwide by TV stations, satellite systems, cable operators, corporate departments, the military, and individuals using videoconferencing systems. Every industry has modified television technology to its own needs, but all have one thing in common: the need to transmit moving images and sound from one location to another. In much the same way, streaming media may become the most significant achievement in communication of the 21st century. How can I make such a sweeping statement? The answer lies in the potential explosion of streaming media as a tool to transmit moving images over an Internet Protocol (IP) network. The technical information needed to achieve this task is discussed in more detail in the following chapters. Here let us review how streaming media can achieve all that it is expected of it and much more.

Until the introduction of IP-based networks and before the introduction of individual personal computer (PC) systems that store data locally and not on a centralized mainframe, the notion of sharing data was limited. There were no multiple points of access. Limited access to information limits the ability of individuals to get to information and share it anytime and from anywhere they want. The introduction of IP-based networks and the growing ability of individuals to access information using multiple devices (mobile phones; laptop computers; personal digital assistants, or PDAs; Internet appliances; and so on) have increased productivity and lowered operations costs. How is this growth measured? More access points on the network increase individual productivity. Increased individual productivity (ability to share information more often and more effectively) generates higher productivity. Higher productivity generates better sales. Better sales generate higher revenues. Higher revenues help offset the costs of network expansion. Lowering the costs of network deployment enables more individuals to gain access to the network. This economic cycle is the reason for the success of many companies relying on information technology. How can streaming media affect this cycle? Individuals on the Web or on networks often move information as text and images to convey a message. To speed up their response, many companies have started using videoconferencing. For example, a company executive located in Chicago can communicate with another executive in another city or to several executives located in several other cities. A video and audio signal is generated by the videoconferencing systems and that signal is transmitted between these video sites. However, a videoconferencing system enables point-to-point connectivity. If more than two video sites wish to connect, they must use a videoconferencing bridge, which acts as a hub delivering the audio and video signal among the videoconferencing sites. Such systems are widely available to companies through company-owned equipment or independent vendors. Real-time communication over videoconferencing systems has both high operational cost and limited distribution. The first videoconferencing systems were designed to connect one or more video sites together, using Integrated Services Digital Network (ISDN) and T1 (an ISDN line that transmits data at 1.5 Mbits per second) lines to deliver video. Protocols used by videoconferencing systems were different from the protocols used to deliver video over computer networks. The key to establishing a large distribution base is to send the video signal over computer networks. In mid-2001, newly released systems started shipping with support for Ethernet connectivity. Some of the latest systems even include a webcasting device that takes the system-native H-320 signal, converts it to streaming format, and transmits it with an IP-supported protocol over computer networks. People say that "one image is worth 1,000 words." If this it true, how many images is one minute of video worth?

Streaming media technology uses conversion methods that transform an analog or digital clip of media into a digital format that can travel from one location on the network to the other. Because streaming media technology transfers content in digital form, data is sent by chopping the content into little bits of information called packets. These packets of information travel at an enormous speed across the network. Once they have reached their destination they are assembled again and displayed on the recipient computer. Chapter 2 describes how streaming technology works. It is essential to mention here that this method represents a revolution in the way we will transfer information in the future. Streaming media technology opens the door to endless possibilities for improving communication in the near future. As companies rally to support Microsoft's .NET initiative (a plan to connect all information and services available on the Web through shared computer servers), more information is revealed about plans to enable new ways to serve digital media over computer networks. Some of these ideas include ways to distribute new music releases streamed from company servers to .NET-enabled servers. These .NET servers will deliver their content to home PCs, handheld devices, cars, or mall-based kiosks, allowing users to select music, sample it, and make a purchase. All these devices will support e-commerce and will be able to process online payments in real time. The very same advantage can help modern salespeople retrieve fresh data to close a deal. What could be more efficient than salespeople with wireless laptops, showing a presentation they have accessed on their network using a wireless modem? The salespeople will provide their clients with an electronic contract and be able to verify additional information (credit or company background) before opening a line of credit. Once credit has been approved, the salespeople show in real time how to manage the product and the clients receive access to the product immediately. This type of service is not a scene from the Sci-Fi channel but rather an example of a sales tool available today on the Web. Add a touch of streaming video and the sale is closed.

A handful of start-ups and more established companies introduced new streaming media technologies as early as 1995. Progressive Networks (known today as RealNetworks) released its RealAudio product in April. Xing Technologies followed with StreamWorks. Whereas RealAudio delivered audio-only streams to 14.4-kilobit-per-second (kbps) modems, Xing's StreamWorks distributed Moving Picture Experts Group (MPEG) files at low frame rates in small windows over 64 kbps ISDN links. Other players included Vosaic Corporation, which came up with a way to deliver live multicast, on-demand, and other forms of video programming over the Internet at 45 times the bandwidth efficiency of standard IP transport; the Israeli-based VDOnet, which released the first true scalable system capable of generating 15-frame-per-second (fps) video-audio content at rates ranging from 14 to 512 kbps; Geo Emblaze (another Israeli company), which delivered streaming content without the need for a plug-in; Vivo Software (acquired by RealNetworks in spring 1998), which was a popular media on-demand solution; and VXtreme, which designed the first synchronized, rich media presentation on the Web. The race began and all start-up companies rushed to distribute players and close contracts with new customers. Microsoft was a late-comer and joined the race only in early 1997. The Seattle-based company had underestimated the potential hidden in the Internet. First, Microsoft had miscalculated the explosive growth of the Internet, limiting resources for the development of Internet-related products. This policy gave Netscape a competitive advantage with its browser; gave America Online (AOL), CompuServe, and Prodigy a free hand to expand their dial-up Internet Service Provider (ISP) businesses; and kept Microsoft away from the streaming arena until summer 1997. In a short period of time, the giant software maker made some strategic investments in a few streaming media companies, including, surprisingly, in its 20-year-old competitor Apple Computers (enabling Macintosh computers with Office applications and the Microsoft Internet Explorer browser). All this was done with the goal of gaining a market share. Other investments included the acquisition of VXtreme, an investment in Progressive Networks (later named RealNetworks), an investment in VDOnet, and an announcement that Netshow version 2.0 (the company's new streaming platform) would be compatible with all leading streaming protocols (VDOnet, VXtreme, and RealVideo). These investments were a typical Microsoft strategic plan to speed up software development. By investing in VDOnet, Microsoft gained access to a scalable technology that later became Intelligent Streaming (the ability to encode video for a range of different modems). The investment in Progressive Networks gave Microsoft access to Real-Network's RTSP proprietary technology and the ability to play back Real-Network content from a Microsoft media server. When RealNetwork realized what had happened, it quickly released a new version of its encoder with codecs (short for compressors/decompressors) that were not part of the business deal with Microsoft. The complete acquisition of VXtreme gave Microsoft an advantage over RealNetworks in the deployment of full screen video. The investment in VXtreme was related to Microsoft investments in Comcast (a cable operator) and Web TV (a developer of an interactive Internet-television platform).

Rob Glazer, RealNetworks CEO and an ex-Microsoft executive, was familiar with Microsoft business practices. RealNetworks announced in February 1998 the acquisition of Vivo Software (the makers of the Vivo player, which had at that time presence in over 5,000 Web sites), and Xing Technologies. These acquisitions increased RealNetwork's distribution base (the Vivo sites migrated their content to RealVideo platform) and helped Real's engineers develop a new platform for a newly emerging broadband market (using Xing core platform).

During the first months of 1998, the tension between Microsoft and RealNetworks grew. It soon became a personal war so intense that Rob Glazer testified in July against Microsoft in its antitrust Senate hearing. Microsoft followed suit and announced that it had started selling the

$30 million investment it had made in RealNetworks in July 1997. Microsoft had originally paid the company a $30 million licensing fee and another $30 million for 3.3 million shares of stock, worth approximately $9 each at that time. The investment had appreciated nicely, closing at $41 at the time of sale.

Who Should Use Streaming Media?

Streaming media technology enables companies and individuals to broadcast media over IP networks. Streaming media, as we know it, is used today in very few areas, divided into two major sectors: enterprise applications and consumer products. People use streaming media where before they used traditional media such as radio, public television, internal television, satellite networks, phone conferences (video or audio), video tapes, CD-ROMs, and print brochures.

The enterprise candidates for the use of streaming media are departments that will experience significant savings through their use of streaming technology. Departments such as sales, training, and human resources have a steady need for communication tools. These departments will see immediate savings by comparing existing methods of communication, expenses related to travel, and the actual cost of using print or satellite networks to deliver news and information to employees. The use of streaming video in these cases will prove to be affordable and productive. As with every other new technology, there is a risk factor. Without the complete support of all parties involved, projects deploying streaming media on corporate networks will not succeed. Companies must allocate all available resources and coordinate all relevant departments to successfully deploy streaming video on their internal network. The streaming media enterprise will include a few basic scenarios, discussed in the following sections.

Live Executive Broadcasts

Company executives use video to convey messages to employees or colleagues. These messages consist of, for example, information about company policies, presentations covering new business engagements, the introduction of a new health plan, the demonstration of a new product, or long-distance learning. In this model, streaming media would be used to transmit these presentations as live broadcasts or as simulated live

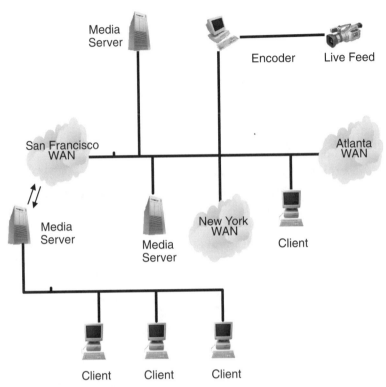

Figure 1–1
Live executive webcast

broadcasts (see Figure 1–1). Attendees would be notified in advance and asked to join the webcast at the specified time.

Most of the live broadcasts today are accompanied by synchronized slides that presenters use to emphasize details of their presentations. These slides can be presented during the webcast or afterward as part of a rebroadcast or as a media on-demand option. Slide synchronization in real time is a new feature of Windows Media Encoder 7.1 or higher. By inserting text event commands into the stream, preloaded slides are inserted into the Web page interface that users see. Synchronization of slides is available for RealMedia and QuickTime technologies as well, but only after the event, as media on-demand. Live executive webcasts encourage attendees to submit questions on the phone or via the Web. An interactive application can be designed to support the submission of questions to the presenter. Third-party applications enable Web-based chat that allows viewers to ask questions during the broadcast and receive feedback in real time. A moderator fields questions from the audience and reads them to the executive. The executive then responds to the questions during the live broadcast.

On-Demand Video Archive

The same company wants to make its chief executive officer's (CEO's) presentation available on-demand to all employees in the company. Business needs dictate that all content must be available to all users within 24 hours of the live event. During the broadcast, a digital copy of the event is saved to a disk for later on-demand encoding. The company has a streaming archive application with multiple servers clustered across the network (see Figure 1–2). This system would use Network Load Balancing to provide load balancing and fault tolerance to the cluster and to allow the cluster to be scaled up if needed during both live webcasts and high-peak media on-demand times. The media on-demand content

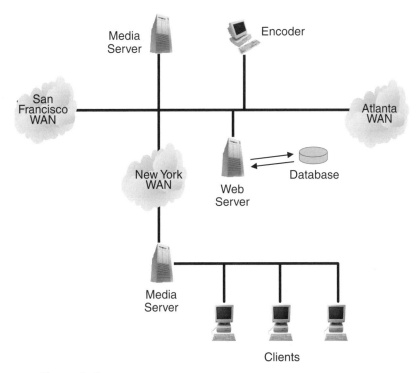

Figure 1–2
On-demand webcast

would be replicated to all clustered servers overnight, when network use is lowest. The system would identify computers by their IP number, locate the nearest media server, and redirect them to the media server closest to their locations. By directing users to the nearest media server, the network will not suffer from congestion at peak time, when too many employees attempt to view the webcast.

Live Broadcasts for Mix Users

If the company wants to make its live executive broadcasts available to the company's Local Area Network (LAN) users, as well as to their off-site dial-up and Virtual Private Networking (VPN) users, when the onsite executive does a presentation the video and audio signal generated onsite needs to be divided during transmission in two or more directions (see Figure 1–3). First, an encoding workstation is set up onsite. The video and

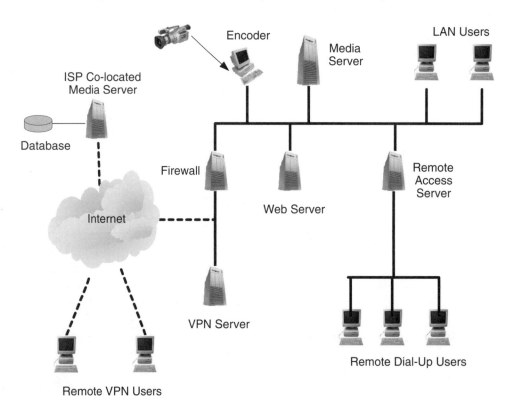

Figure 1–3
Live executive webcast to Intranet and Internet users

audio sources are connected to the encoder. Then, the encoder transfers an encoded streaming feed to both the media server located on the company's internal network and to the media server located on the public Internet. Depending on the configuration of the company's LAN, the signal is available as a Multicast or a Unicast webcast. Due to the condition of public networks and the limitations listed in Chapter 2, the live webcast on the Internet will be available to company employees outside of the company's LAN in the form of a Unicast webcast.

Because VPN users in this example can access the Internet from any number of local ISPs, the company has an ISP host the live event for them on the Internet. This allows the company to support remote users while not revealing the webcast link to the Internet. To prevent unauthorized access to the live streams from the Internet, the ISP's media servers are configured to use authentication against a membership database service. Users connecting via the Internet must supply their username and password to gain access to the live stream.

Business Communications

An increasing number of companies are using digital media to enhance their business communications. Corporate CEOs can get critical information to employees and partners quickly, efficiently, and cost-effectively using streaming media. Employees receive the same message at the same time without leaving their desks. Businesses can then store these presentations, making them available for on-demand viewing to anyone, anywhere, anytime.

In other fields, sales managers can educate their sales force quickly and easily by using streaming media to communicate information about products, initiate product presentations, or provide sales and marketing materials and videos from corporate events. In addition, sales representatives can use their laptops and handheld devices to show appealing marketing presentations or video product demonstrations to their clients.

In recent years the functionality of corporate networks has been degraded because of streaming media's bandwidth demands. This has resulted in unsatisfactory experiences for users of digital media and reduced the productivity of all network users. Fortunately, advances in storage and network technologies are now making digital media a much more viable option for enterprise-wide communications.

In addition to the typical features of project planning, such as establishing a vision and goals, identifying plans and requirements, acquiring executive support, identifying Intel users, and creating a project schedule, plans for implementing digital media must also address network topology and financial constraints.

Streaming media applications are suitable for any type of content. To better understand what streaming media technology can do, first think about it as another channel of distribution for audio or video content and then compare the cost of producing and distributing streaming media with the cost of producing and distributing video over satellite or traditional radio and television. The efficiency and cost savings that streaming media technology has to offer are its major strengths. Digital imaging has reduced the cost of production tremendously. The fact that today we can edit images (still and moving images) on our desktop computers is a tremendous advantage. Ten years ago, to edit a short media clip or to resize an image we had to find a company that specialized in image processing. The cost of labor was high, and the rendering of a 30-second clip took a very long time. Streaming media technology enables the fast processing of moving images and easy distribution across computer networks that are not bound by laws or borders.

In live webcasts, a content creator sets up an encoding workstation to capture a real-time event that will create the digital media for the media server to stream. A Web page includes a link to the live event, and everyone who clicks that link sees or hears the same content at the same time; they join the event as it happens. Streaming live content is much the same as streaming static content, with one difference: the encoder sends encoded material immediately to the media server.

Live webcasts should accommodate the production and distribution of content that is time-sensitive, including live concerts, news events, financial presentations to stock holders, executive speeches to corporate employees, live fashion shows, interactive sessions in which audience participation is required, and many other events in which broadcasting in real time is more important than making it available as media on-demand.

Media on-demand files are first created from live or recorded sources; then they are copied to a media server. Everyone who clicks the link to a live stream sees the same material from the beginning; on-demand files always begin playing at the beginning. Good uses for on-demand streaming are archives of live broadcasts, information that is not time-sensitive, and interactive presentations that do not require immediate response. We can also create simulated live events by recording an event in real time, and, instead of broadcasting it, recording it to disk.

Later, an announcement is made about the availability of this content at a certain time and the event is then released to the public as a live webcast. This is called "live to tape," meaning the content was recorded in real time to tape and played back later as a live webcast.

Advantages of Using Streaming Media

When streaming media was first introduced, people believed that there were more disadvantages than advantages to using streaming technology. Because bandwidth was limited and computers at that time used 14.4-kilobyte-per-second (kBps) modems, the only streaming files that could travel the Web were audio files. In the past four years, network infrastructure has improved significantly in North America, Europe, and Asia. Most workplaces provide high-bandwidth capacity and employees use their office networks to access the Web on a daily basis. In North America, over 25 million homes are connected to the Internet via Digital Subscriber Line (DSL) or cable modems averaging data transfer rates of approximately 400 kBps. This enables the delivery of audio and video in an acceptable quality. True, the window size is limited to 320×240 pixels, but as compression technology improves we will be able to enlarge the window size to fit the full screen.

Although four years ago people dismissed streaming media as a young technology delivering jerky video in a one-square-inch window, today streaming media has earned respect and become a helpful tool used by individuals and companies worldwide. The main advantages of streaming media are:

- The ability to produce low-budget video and audio broadcasts. This includes both production tools to create content and distribution tools to deliver media.
- The ability to replay broadcasts at nominal cost.
- The ability to make these broadcasts media on-demand on corporate networks or the public Internet.
- The ability to "pay per use." Companies that use streaming media pay their ISPs for storage and data transfer. This use is calculated per MB stored or transferred.
- The ability to generate better statistics for marketing and budget calculation. Because streaming files are in digital format, new software tools can provide both better measurement of use patterns

and better data about the actual audience that watched the streams.

- The ability of the audience to access live or on-demand webcasts from any place in the world at no special cost, except the cost of connecting to the Internet.
- The ability to archive media in an organized manner for search and display over secured or public networks.
- The ability to have faster 24/7 administrator access to stored content for adding, modifying, or deleting files.
- The ability to protect digital media and permit access to live broadcasts or to media on-demand only by authorized or licensed audiences.
- The ability, unlike radio and television, to facilitate interactive presentations in which audiences participate in events and interact with presenters via audio conversation, videoconferencing, or submitting questions in chat rooms.

The advantage of using digital files supersedes any benefits of using analog source material. By converting analog media to digital format, streaming media uses enhanced methods for creating, storing, managing, and displaying content over computer networks. With the growing popularity of portable devices, streaming media is expected to reach handheld devices such as PDAs and cellular phones. The extension of existing systems that are already implemented in streaming media in desktops to portable environments will advance the ability to track digital-file performance. These methods will provide valuable information to content owners, indicating audience purchasing preferences. Advertisers have been waiting for this for a long time. In the enterprise arena, such technologies could be heaven-sent for corporate executives seeking increased productivity and faster response.

Disadvantages of Using Streaming Media

The main disadvantage of streaming media is that the playback quality depends on the network bandwidth. Poor network conditions and bandwidth fluctuations easily result in annoying disruptions to the end-user. The problems with using streaming media are blamed more on the technology itself or on the methods associated with its use. But like any other new technology, streaming media must first learn to crawl and then walk before it can learn to run. This is the way we humans develop, and this is the way we create the technologies that improve our world. Streaming technology is limited primarily by bandwidth and compression-quality constraints.

Here is an example how bandwidth limitation restricts the throughput of a webcast: We cannot transmit a live webcast from a remote location if the only way to access the Internet is via a phone line. A phone line provides no more than 40 kBps output; with such a limited amount of bandwidth we can only transmit an audio webcast.

Another example of bandwidth restrictions that limit the technology is a webcast transmitted on a corporate network. Many corporations use their networks for the transmission of data related to mission-critical applications. Network administrators prioritize financial transactions and applications, handling group communication before webcasts. This situation limits their ability to use the network to its full capacity.

Also, multiple users pulling streaming files at the same time can abuse the network. This method, known as Unicast streaming, is a technology that sends a unique stream to each member of the audience. The disadvantages of Unicast streaming appear when content is sent to large audiences. For example, if the content bandwidth is 100 kBps and there are 1,000 viewers, the total network bandwidth needed from a single server is 100 megabytes per second (MBps). There are not many corporate networks that can support such a large capacity.

Leading Technologies in the Market

As a result of mergers and acquisitions, mentioned earlier, the face of the streaming media industry has changed. Two main competitors dominated the new market during 1998–2000: Microsoft and RealNetworks. The only streaming player to survive this market fluctuation was Geo Emblazed. This streaming technology required no plug-in (i.e., there was no need for a streaming player on the recipient's side) and used Java to push moving images to browsers. When it became clear that Microsoft and RealNetworks would reign in the desktop streaming market, Geo Emblazed changed its name to Emblaze and shifted its focus from the Web to mobile devices.

After summer 1998, Microsoft released two more versions of its old Netshow server, naming them Windows Media Technology. Real-

Networks renamed its technology RealSystem and released three more versions. In summer 2000, a new streaming player emerged–Microsoft's old rival Apple Computers, known for many years for its QuickTime player. The software was well respected among video professionals and was mainly used for playback on editing systems and CD-ROMs. On the Internet, the technology was limited to only progressive downloads. This limitation forced users to download the file first and then play it back on their computers. Because of this process, media files had to be short and window sizes small. Long files in large windows required long waiting periods to download. With the introduction of QuickTime Server and its Windows brother the Darwin Streaming Server (DSS), Apple officially entered the streaming war. Before the release of its streaming technology, Apple signed an agreement with RealNetworks–an agreement that would corner Microsoft's market. Because both companies used RTSP as their streaming protocol, RealNetworks agreed to support Apple's QuickTime files in live and on-demand applications from its RealSystem servers. Apple relied heavily on its reputation, a move that proved to be correct. After the introduction of QuickTime streaming player version 4.2, the software reached an almost 10% market share. The later QuickTime player version 5.0 provided wide support for SMIL technology, giving developers the ability to stream rich media presentations synchronized with images and text.

Here is a comparison of the leading streaming technologies.

- With QuickTime streaming technology (Figure 1–4) we can stream content for live and on-demand applications. QuickTime streaming technology was initially designed to support streaming content on Macintosh-based computers. Since version 4.0, the QuickTime Streaming architecture has been available for Windows as well. QuickTime uses a client-side player requesting content from a QuickTime Server. The player can only be installed on Macintosh and Windows operating systems. The same applies to QuickTime servers. The Macintosh version is called QuickTime Streaming Server; the Windows version is called Darwin Streaming Server (DSS).

- RealNetworks claims to distribute over 200 million copies of RealPlayer (Figure 1–5). The competition between RealNetworks and Microsoft is fierce. Both companies are trying to create a presence for their players in every possible PC. It is expected that the battle

Figure 1–4
QuickTime Player interface

will roll over next to mobile devices. RealNetworks has the largest support for various operating systems, for its software player, streaming content producer, and media servers. Since the release of RealOne Player in December 2001, which use technology similar to that of Microsoft, RealNetworks has added XML (Extensible Markup Language) language to the limited SMIL technology (used before to enhance presentations) and offered new ways to synchronize multimedia presentations from within its player.

- After the introduction of Windows Media Player version 7.0 (Figure 1–6), Microsoft committed to enabling the playback of multimedia content on all desktop PCs and handheld devices that use

Figure 1–5
RealPlayer (RealOne) interface

Windows-related software. With an exception of only a few operating systems, today Windows Media files can play back on almost every desktop and PDA and will be able eventually to play back on cellular phones and Internet appliances. Windows Media technologies are embedded in new .NET initiatives, as well as in every Windows operating system. This strategy gives Microsoft a big advantage because it ships its operating systems and all Office products with components to serve and display streaming content over IP networks. Microsoft streaming technology is divided into three groups: Windows Media Tools (supporting the creation of enhanced rich streaming media content), Windows Media Services (serving live broadcast or media on-demand content), and Windows Media Player (supporting playback of live broadcast or media on-demand content on desktops, laptops, and mobile devices).

Figure 1– 6
Windows Media Player interface

The market today is divided among (in alphabetical order) Quick-Time, RealVideo, and Windows Media technologies. There are advantages and disadvantages of using any one of these technologies over another. In the next chapters we learn about these three formats and become familiar with many aspects of their components. It is likely that in the future the market will demand a universal streaming format. MPEG4 is a good candidate for consolidating all streaming technologies into one single method of recording and playback. Will MPEG4 have the same impact on the film industry as MPEG3 (MP3 or MPEG-1 Audio Layer-3) had on the music industry? How soon will vendors adopt the format and how will streaming leaders such as RealNetworks and Microsoft cooperate to enable the creation of universal distribution players using MPEG4? This would permit RealMedia files to play on Windows Media players and vice versa, and it is indeed a challenging task. In past years, vendors formed special alliances to address technological tasks. For example, when the popularity of Napster (and the file-share concept) went sky high, companies such as Sony, BMG, and Warner Brothers gathered with Microsoft, IBM, and RealNetworks in an attempt to develop a copyright mechanism that would protect their content from Web piracy. The rapid development of technology depends on stiff competition. As competition drives companies to excel, additional resources are made available to developers. The development of digital copyright management solutions has been dictated by a business model driven by record companies and Hollywood studios with concerns about the illegal distribution and copyright violation of content on the Internet. These alliance groups are working hard to protect their assets, developing encryption systems to manage digital files and permit playback only in an authorized environment. Due to the various groups and their technological preferences, the consumer will be hurt again. Each group is making efforts to create the ultimate software solution to stop illegal copies of content, and part of the plan is to include hardware manufacturers to produce special devices that will play back the encrypted content. Such cooperation between software and hardware vendors will result in the appearance of new playback devices—again, not one device, but multiple devices supporting multiple encryption systems. Does this sound like a visit to our local electronics store? Are we heading back to a VHS, S-VHS, 8-mm, Hi8, VHS/C, and Mini-DV format discussion? No doubt the consumer will suffer the most. For example, users with Windows Media players supported by Microsoft's Digital Right Management (DRM) solution can download music content or convert music CDs to a Windows Media format. The files are encrypted in a few variations so they can be played back by a specified rule (to protect the copyright and avoid content duplication). At this time, the new media file can be played back only with Windows Media software. The same applies to content encrypted with RealNetworks's DRM solution; it can only be played back with RealNetworks software. This creates a big problem of incompatibility among multiple devices. For example, users sign up on an online movie site that streams full-length movies to broadband users. They purchase a license to see a movie, but they want to display it on their home TV. With the current plans to combine PCs and television screens, we might think that this would be possible. But it is not, and it will not be possible as long as televisions and PCs use separate playback devices. Technically, we need to transfer the signal from the PC to the television. If both are using a digital storage solution (Sony's TiVo or Panasonic's ShowStopper) and that device is connected to a home network, theoretically this should be possible, but no! The hard drive must first have a software solution that verifies that it is allowed to play back the secured file. And because Microsoft was not in the group that developed the Sony or Panasonic copyright protection system, files that are licensed on the Web cannot play back on your television. The bottom line is that incompatibility and lack of a universal system to encode, encrypt, and stream media will slow down the development of a reliable and secure system that is accepted and widely used in the market.

Summary

- Streaming media is a technology that delivers large digital audio and video files in real time across computer networks.
- The events of September 11 gave the streaming industry a boost, encouraging companies to use the technology more and to replace live group meetings with online video applications.
- Streaming media has evolved since its early days and today has the capability to deliver video of acceptable quality to desktop PCs and portable devices.
- Individuals and companies use streaming media to deliver compelling messages and interactive presentations over computer networks.
- There are many advantages to using streaming media. The main disadvantage of streaming media is that the playback quality depends on the network bandwidth.

2

Networks

Networks—Basic

Network computers and intranet environments based on individual personal computers are relatively new to the public. Widely used for more than 25 years by governments, large business, and universities to share information among many computers located in various locations, networks have reached small to mid-size business and home users in recent years. At the most elementary level, a network consists of two computers connected to one another to share data. All networks, no matter how sophisticated they are, are based on this simple system. Although the idea of connecting a computer to another computer with a cable seems simple, it represents a major achievement in communication.

Networks are designed to share information in a timely fashion. Personal computers are great business tools because they use innovative software solutions to speed up the way information is created and processed. Without a network, individuals with valuable and important information cannot share it quickly and easily with others. At best, they can go through the slow process of copying their data to a floppy or ZIP disk and then sending the disk. A network allowing workers to share information from their computers is shown in Figure 2–1. In such a network, computers can share information at a transfer speed of 100 megabits per second (Mbps). Individual users can also print their files using the network printer; there is no need to connect a printer to each computer. Computers that are part of a network share data, messages, graphics, printers, fax machines, other hardware resources, and, most significantly, media.

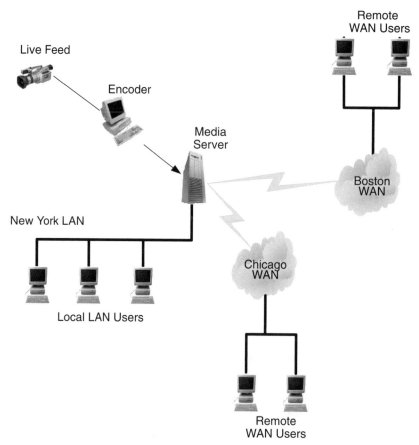

Figure 2–1
Centralized architecture

There are two types of network architecture: local area network (LAN), computers connected to one another in one location, and wide area network (WAN), computers connected to other computers in different locations. Newly emerging wireless technologies offer new ways to connect to networks, but in general they fit into the WAN category. Today, most businesses rely on network computers to deliver information and crucial data. Filing cabinets and typewriters have been replaced by disc storage and computers. There are many issues relating to maintaining networks, keeping them safe from unauthorized visitors, and storing their data for disaster recovery. These are serious concerns that apply to data of all types, including streaming media.

All networks have certain general components, functions, and features that are similar. These include computers that provide shared resources to network users (servers), computers that access shared network resources provided by servers (clients), hardware resources provided by servers (printers and other peripherals), and the actual media (documents, images, video or audio, and applications). Networks can be divided into two categories: peer-to-peer networks and server-based networks. The distinction between peer-to-peer and server-based networks is important because each has different capabilities. In a peer-to-peer network, there are no dedicated servers or hierarchy among the computers. Normally each computer acts as a client and a server, and sharing and printing capabilities are defined on an individual level. The user at each computer determines the type of data he or she is willing to share with the rest. In a server-based network, computers act as clients and a dedicated server acts as a leader that provides permission to individual computers, dictating sharing and printing capabilities. The decision to deploy one network over the other depends on the size of the organization, the level of security needed, the level of administration support needed, the amount of network traffic, and the budget. Organizations that wish to deploy a streaming media solution on their networks should choose the second option; streaming media architecture works better on a server-based network.

A server-based network includes at least one dedicated server (a computer used as a server and not as a client or workstation), client computers, and shared hardware resources. As the network increases in size and traffic, more than one server will be required, as well as, of course, more clients and network resources. A server is a computer with significant random-access memory (RAM) and central processing unit (CPU) power to handle multiple applications on a network. There are many specialized servers that perform tasks on a network. For example, file and print servers manage user access and the use of file and printer resources (users can store data in a centralized depository and share it as if it were stored on their hard drive), application servers make the server side of client-server applications and data available to clients (databases are a good example; they are stored in a centralized location and can be modified and viewed by users), and mail servers manage electronic messaging between users on the network or with external users. Software plays a significant role in the deployment of new networks. No matter how powerful or advanced servers or client computers are, without the proper software they will not be able to perform even the simplest task.

Another significant feature of networks is the ability to transfer data between computers in an efficient and secure way. Most networks today are composed of hybrid technologies (hardware and software) that were used in past years to rapidly expand the growth of business and public networks. This situation represents a challenge to many network administrators. If only one standard had been implemented from the start, network upgrades would have cost less and could have been achieved faster. However, inconsistent deployment in past years has created a web of resources that must be reconfigured or totally upgraded before data can flow seamlessly. To understand these obstacles, we review a variety of network topologies existing in the market.

Local Area Networks

Token ring is a network topology that uses a token-passing mechanism to pass information. Computers in a token ring network pass information to one another in a cycle, meaning that when one computer sends data to another computer, this data flows through many other computers linked between the two that are communicating between one another. Token ring networks first used a data transfer rate of 4 Mbps and have been upgraded to 16 Mbps. Token ring, although technically feasible, is not a supported topology for streaming. Because in a token ring topology data packets must travel from one point to another passing through many different clients (computers), if even a single client is not operational all the data transmission stops and if even a single client is using its allocated bandwidth to run other applications, the transmission of data slows down significantly.

Ethernet (also called IEEE 802.3) is a widely used base for network technologies. Ethernet normally operates with a transmission rate of 10 Mbps. Ethernet uses a Carrier Sense Multiple Access with Collision Detect (CSMA/CD) algorithm.

Fast Ethernet is technically composed of two separate standards. The 100BaseT standard is an enhancement of the IEEE 802.3 standard. It uses a transfer rate of 100 Mbps instead of the original transfer rate of 10 Mbps. The second standard is the 100VG-AnyLan. Unlike Ethernet, which uses the CSMA/CD algorithm, this standard uses a new method to negotiate the transmission of data in a segment. Instead of broadcasting to all members of the network (and creating multiple collisions with data packets from other members), 100VG-AnyLan uses a demand priority mechanism controlled by the network switch or hub. This method generates fewer transmissions and fewer collisions and therefore maintains a calmer network.

Gigabit Ethernet operates with a data rate of 1,000 Mbps. It is used primarily as a server connection and a backbone connection. Gigabit Ethernet uses the CSMA/CD algorithm for arbitrating data for the transmission of a given segment.

Fiber Distributed Data Interface (FDDI) is an enhanced networking alternative to other network topologies. It operates with a data transmission rate of 100 Mbps. FDDI uses dual ring architecture to provide redundancy in case of failure. FDDI is used for backbone links in corporate LANs.

Asynchronous Transfer Mode (ATM) is a broadband network topology designed to transfer high volumes of data within LAN and WAN networks. ATM standards include provisions to accommodate faster data rates as technology progresses. Common data rates used by ATM today include OC-3 (155 Mbps) and OC-12 (625 Mbps). ATM is perhaps the best networking topology, but it is not widely used because it requires socialized configurations that add to the total cost of deployment. Instead, it is used for connecting various segments of a network together.

Wide Area Networks

WANs connect individual LANs with one another. WANs also connect users and the Internet backbone.

Digital Subscriber Line (DSL) is a new WAN topology that takes advantage of existing copper voice lines that connect homes and businesses to the local phone company. The total bandwidth data transfer speed of DSL lines ranges between 56 kbps and 14 Mbps, depending on the configuration and type of DSL compression technique used. Some versions of DSL support concurrent voice and data, making it a perfect solution for a place with a single home line. An important factor in DSL deployment is that it is a dedicated line between the end-user and the phone company. Many businesses have replaced their T1 lines with dedicated DSL lines, which provide the same reliability as T1 lines at a fraction of the cost.

Asynchronous Transfer Mode (ATM) is also used in WAN environments. Many of the new backbone segments added to the Internet use ATM topology, making it capable of seamlessly handling both WAN and LAN architectures.

Integrated Services Digital Network (ISDN) is an all-digital technology that takes advantage of existing copper-pair phone wires used to connect homes and businesses to local phone companies. ISDN is composed of three channels, called B channels. Two B channels are capable of 64 kbps each, and they are used for voice and data. The third channel is called the D channel, and it is used to provide signal control for the two other B channels.

X.25 is an international standard developed for point-to-point transmission of data. X.25 was used to connect terminals to mainframe computer systems. The technology performs constant error checks (for data loss) and creates overhead on the network. Due to these problems, X.25 is no longer used in new installations. However, many segments on LAN networks still use X.25.

Frame relay is packet-switching architecture similar to X.25, but it provides better stability and less error checking, making it a favorably fast technology. It is widely used by organizations to connect point-to-point segments on a WAN.

Cable modems are a new technology that offers high-speed Internet access over traditional cable television systems. Cable modems share bandwidth among many customers using the same fiber optic line. As more end-users connect to their cable modems, less bandwidth is available. Cable companies are currently addressing this issue by improving line distribution and increasing compression schemas. Most cable modems use an asymmetrical design, meaning the downstream is greater than the upstream. This should be taken into consideration when planning to generate a streaming signal from a location with cable modem connectivity.

Analog modems use standard plain old telephone service (POT lines). Analog lines have a speed between 28 and 56 kbps, depending on the phone line connection. A relative large number of Internet users connect to the Internet using analog modems. When planning a webcast you must take this into consideration.

T1 lines are digital circuits used by many companies. T1 is a standard digital line that carries both voice and data at equal up- and downstream rates of up to 1.54 Mbps. T1 lines are used by enterprises to connect WANs or internal LANs in multifloor buildings.

Internet Protocols

Now let us take a look at the protocols that move data on these networks. Streaming media technologies use the very same protocols that are used to transmit documents and images. They all rely on the Transmission Control Protocol/Internet Protocol (TCP/IP) architecture. Since 1969, TCP/IP has been an industry standard and is designed to provide high-speed communications on network computers.

Internet Protocol (IP) is a network-layer protocol responsible for transmitting blocks of data called datagrams from sources to destinations. Sources and destinations are identified by fixed-length addresses divided into five major classes (range A, B, C, D, and E). IP also provides for the fragmentation and reassembly of long datagrams, if necessary, for transmission through small-packet networks. Every machine on the Internet has a unique identifying number, called an IP address. A typical IP address looks like this: 216.27.61.137. Each of the five IP classes has a different meaning:

- Class A covers IP numbers in the range 1.0.0.0–127.0.0.0. It is mostly used by large networks, for example, by ISPs such as Qwest or Sprint.
- Class B covers IP numbers in the range 128.0.0.0–191.255.0.0. It is mostly used in mid-size networks such as a college campus.
- Class C covers IP numbers in the range 192.0.0.0–223.255.255 .255. It is mostly used in enterprises. Small workgroups in a corporation use different subnet mask numbers that permit the replication of the same range of IP numbers (up to 255 per group) to extend network capacity.
- Class D covers IP numbers in the range 224.0.0.0–239.0.0.0. It is mostly used for Multicasts.
- Class E covers IP numbers in the range 240.0.0.0–248.0.0.0. It is used for experimental purposes and is reserved for future use.

User Datagram Protocol (UDP) is a standard, low-overhead, connectionless, host-to-host protocol that is used over packet-switched computer communications networks and that allows an application program on one computer to send a datagram to an application program on another computer. The main difference between UDP and TCP is that UDP provides connectionless service, whereas TCP does not. Connectionless service allows the transfer of information among subscribers without the need for end-to-end establishment procedures. Such procedures generate constant authentication and verification signals that overwhelm networks.

HTTP is Hypertext Transfer Protocol. This protocol facilitates the transfer of hypertext-based files between local and remote systems. It is the protocol used to transmit Web pages across the Internet.

All three streaming technologies (Windows Media, QuickTime, and RealSystem's RealVideo) use these protocols to transfer data packets of their media between the host server and the client media player. All three technologies have developed a rollover mechanism that attempts to maximize the users' experience by providing three levels of transfer. First, all three players default to UDP as a preferred mode for transferring data packets. If UDP cannot be used, due to firewall blocking, for example, the player attempts to use TCP. Only the Windows Media player rolls over from TCP to HTTP. QuickTime players and RealPlayers need to be manually configured to accept HTTP as a delivery option.

How Computers Connect on a Network

Network administrators use a combination of hardware and managed software to connect computers together in different segments of the network. Table 2–1 illustrates the level of connectivity and its purpose.

Networks—Advanced

Companies have been slowly converting their networks to support multimedia protocols such as plain data, voice-over IP, and video. In the future, these networks will deliver content to desktops, laptops, and wireless handheld devices regardless of their physical distances from the company. This approach will increase user interactivity and overall company performance because information will travel in a more efficient and cost-effective way.

Table 2–1
Levels of Connectivity

Device	Used In	Connects
Router	Connects between company sites	Links a local network to a remote network, for example, the Internet; can be used to connect a LAN to a LAN, a WAN to a WAN, or a LAN to the Internet
Switch	Connect between floors; office level	A device to segment networks into different subnets; segmenting the network into different subnets keeps one network from overloading
Hub	Connects computers on the same floor or in the same office	A connection device for networks; allows multiple segments or computers to connect and share packets of information

Network architects recognize that the deployment of streaming media over IP will vary from site to site, depending on a combination of internal business requirements and the unique conditions of the network to be used for content distribution. Here I introduce general methods for planning and enabling a network to stream media. I include descriptions of a test to help determine if the segments of the network are capable of delivering streaming video. However, product configurations and other elements of network architecture that are not covered here may require the network manager to seek additional resources that may affect the design, such as network audits, before streaming technology can reach the entire network.

Before investing in products and services to stream media over IP, information technology (IT) executives and representatives of departments that will use the technology should form a team to prepare a plan to define objectives, seek available resources, and implement the strategic deployment of streaming technology on the corporate network. This group should review corporate communications objectives as well as other relevant business goals (e.g., moving to e-business practices, retaining valuable knowledge workers, and increasing productivity). A needs-analysis phase should also survey one or more user groups about how they perform their functions today and their willingness to change behaviors to maximize the impact of the new technologies on their productivity. In this process, it is important to distinguish clearly the level of interactivity users expect to have with the new multimedia content to be streamed over the network. First, determine how users will benefit from streaming media on their network. Second, proceed with planning how to deploy these solutions. And last, gather together all resources needed to create the desired application. This will include concept planning, team gatherings (internal staffers and external vendors), role designation, budget approval, and the creation of a timetable.

Only after completing these tasks should the team proceed with the actual deployment. In traditional enterprises, users make use of content delivered by the following groups:

- Human resources–related topics concerning employees
- Corporate communication messages corresponding to corporate rules of conduct, company policies, executive addresses, and general company overview
- Training department materials that concern individuals or groups within the enterprise
- Sales department communications covering new product releases, product maintenance, and communications with company distributors

Return on Investment

It is important for the multitask team to identify how the introduction of streaming technology will impact the enterprise and how this impact can be measured. For example, savings on travel is the first measurement that most companies target. High-value employee and client or customer retention, especially among professional service providers, is another common business metric that benefits as a result of expanding visual communications in the enterprise to include streaming video. Another area where streaming media can improve productivity is the introduction of products and the provision of technical support for them. Streaming media can be used both to display various aspects of a product and to replace technical support to some degree by providing visual training in how to use or troubleshoot a product. This can result in increased sales (by incorporating a product video tour on the company Web site) and increased productivity and savings in the product support department because employees do not have to repeat explanations of basic functions and solutions to problems that can normally be covered by simple instructional videos.

Typically a return on investment (ROI) calculation begins with the measurement of basic and advanced activities or processes in place before the introduction of new technologies. Once the measurement has been done on the baseline activities and postdeployment activities, a project may show significant improvement that can be easily measured.

In the analytical phase, the business process managers identify the applications that will best leverage streaming media service in the enterprise's LAN, WANs, or public Web site. A "service" is a network-based, managed capability that provides value to the day-to-day operations of a group of people or a capability that increases effectiveness when presented to customers of the enterprise.

Planning and Deployment

When deploying streaming media architecture on a corporate network, you, the corporate multigroup task force, will define the needs and priorities. The following provides guidelines for both the technical team that facilitates a streaming media-enabled network and the creative team that prepares and serves streaming media files. Marketing issues are described in detail in Chapter 12. I encourage readers in all groups to become familiar with these terms and concepts.

The first step in deploying media servers on an enterprise network is to plan carefully before the actual installation. Enterprise networks consist of various segments. Network computers have experienced extremely fast growth in the past few years. Technology has evolved rapidly, pushing aside old configurations and ideas and bringing efficiency and savings by building wider and more productive networks. As a result, many companies have networks that consist of one or more topologies, as mentioned earlier. For example, network segments that were constructed in the late 1980s have token ring–based hardware. Segments built more recently have fast Ethernet-based hardware. This mix of hardware and software will create problems of incompatibility. These can consist of mixed networks (token rings and Ethernet), networks that make excessive use of hubs and not switches (having a large number of packet collisions), and networks that have fast Ethernet connectivity to the desktop but T1 capacities among their WAN segments. To avoid complications that will result in the loss of time and resources, you must design a strategic plan identifying what has to be done to the network, to the client computers, and in your company before you begin the streaming solution installation. The following checklist will help clarify the steps needed to deploy streaming media technology on an enterprise network. Chapters 9 and 10 cover how encoding workstations and distribution servers are configured, and you need to read them thoroughly. This checklist is not intended to replace the professional network analysis performed by your network administrator; instead it is a guide to determining in a general way if your network can stream video.

- Select a section on your LAN to test the delivery of streaming media from a media server to client computers.
- Set the following minimum requirements for a multimedia computer that is capable of receiving streaming media. All the computers that participate in this test must meet these requirements:
  - 233 MHz CPU with MMX or higher
  - 64 MB of RAM (for Windows 9x; Windows NT/2000 requires 128 MB RAM and Windows XP 256 MB RAM)
  - Sound Blaster–compatible sound card
  - Speakers
  - Ethernet card, 10 or 100 Mbps
  - Internet Explorer or Netscape Navigator browser, 4.0 or higher
  - Basic network configuration to support TCP/IP protocols
- Start mapping Ethernet connections to every client. List all models, manufacturers, and serial numbers of hubs, switches, and routers in the LAN and between segments of the WAN. You will need this information later in the event that you have to contact the hardware vendor's technical support.
- Carefully draw a map of bandwidth segments on your network, listing the capacity between all points.
- Find out which applications are used in your network, what their use pattern is, where they are hosted, and how much bandwidth they normally use during peak and off-peak times.

• Select a streaming media format to be deployed on your network. Refer to Table 2–2 to determine which technology best suits your needs.

• Based on the architecture of your network, and after you have identified the weak spots that may generate bottlenecks, select the appropriate place to install one or more media servers. The media server must be in a location that will have the most bandwidth allocated for streaming media files. If there are firewalls between the location of your media server and the clients, refer to the fire wall section in this chapter to properly configure your network before performing this test.

What streaming protocols does each technology use? QuickTime and RealVideo use the RTSP protocol, an application-level protocol that provides a framework to enable the controlled, on-demand delivery of real-time data, such as audio and video. Sources of data can include both live data feeds and media on-demand. This protocol is intended to control multiple data delivery sessions; provide a means for choosing delivery channels such as UDP, Multicast UDP, and TCP; and provide a means for choosing delivery mechanisms based on Real Time Protocol (RTP) (RFC 1889). Microsoft uses its own MMS protocol. MMS is the default method of connecting to the Windows Media Unicast service. Both RTSP and MMS contain a control mechanism to handle client's requests, such as Play, Stop, Fast Forward, or Rewind. Both protocols ensure that media packets arrive in a format recognized by the player. Control requests are always carried over TCP; data packets are carried over UDP, TCP, or HTTP.

When connecting to a uniform resource locator (URL) listed on a hypertext markup language (HTML) page, both protocols practice a rollover procedure to achieve the best connection. First, the player uses the TCP protocol to place a call to the server and request a data connection. The server confirms the data connection and then attempts to send out data packets in the following order. First it attempts to send packets over a UDP port. If network congestion or firewalls are blocking proper data flow, the player then communicates to the server that it wishes to try another connection using TCP ports; if data can be sent and reach the client using a TCP port, the server then streams its content properly. If network congestion or firewalls are blocking proper data flow, the player

Table 2–2
Streaming Technology Client-Server Compatibility List

Function	QuickTime	RealSystem	Windows Media
Client default settings include support for UDP and TCP	Yes	Yes	No
Client default settings include support for UDP, TCP, and HTTP	No	No	Yes
Server settings include support for UDP, TCP, and HTTP	Yes	No [a]	Yes
Server transport protocols	RTSP PNM HTTP	RTSP PNM	MMS HTTP
Client O/S [b] supports:			
Iris	No	Yes	No
Linux	No	Yes	No
Macintosh	Yes	Yes	Yes
Palm	No	No	No
PocketPC	No	Yes	Yes
Solaris	No	Yes	Yes
Unix	No	Yes	No
Windows	Yes	Yes	Yes
Encoder O/S [b] supports:			
Iris	No	No	No
Linux	No	Yes	No
Macintosh	Yes	Yes	No
Palm	No	No	No
PocketPC	No	No	No
Solaris	No	Yes	No
Unix	No	No	No
Windows	Yes	Yes	Yes
Server O/S [b] supports:			
Iris	No	Yes	No
Linux	No	Yes	No
Macintosh	Yes	Yes	No
Palm	No	No	No
PocketPC	No	No	No
Solaris	No	Yes	No

Table 2–2
Streaming Technology Client-Server Compatibility List (*continued*)

Function	QuickTime	RealSystem	Windows Media
Unix	No	Yes	No
Windows	Yes	Yes	Yes
Administrator access via browser	Yes	Yes	Yes[c]

[a]RealSystem server does not support HTTP streaming. However, streams can be forced to enter through a firewall by using specific ports. Note the order in which the other ports are mentioned. The player will attempt to get media in this order: first RTSP port 554, then PNM port 7070, and last HTTP port 8080. Use the following syntax in your RAM reference file to force streams to enter through port 8080 of your firewall:

```
rtsp://real_server_name:8080/file_name.rm?cloakport="554, 7070, 8080"
```

[b]OS, operating system.
[c]Requires Windows Media Administrator program to be installed and proper network permissions.

next communicates to the server that it wishes to try another connection, this time an HTTP port. QuickTime and RealVideo clients must be configured manually to use HTTP incoming ports; the Windows Media client is preconfigured to roll over to HTTP ports in the event that UDP and TCP ports are blocked. The unavailability of preconfigured settings (to roll over to HTTP ports) on the QuickTime and RealVideo clients represents an additional time-consuming task when deploying streaming media clients on corporate intranets. RealNetworks offers a custom player that can be configured in advance (to include proper HTTP rollover) when deploying streaming media on an enterprise network; the IT department must install the player on all clients and desktops. Windows Media Player is a default software on every Windows operating system. Table 2–3 illustrates rollover procedure for the three technologies.

A significant factor in facilitating streaming video in a healthy network is to properly map a network topology and determine the capabilities of your network. Knowing where users connect to the network using a shared hub versus a switch, for example, may help you limit the media use on that network segment. Hubs often suffer increased collisions from traffic patterns that introduce a consistent stream of data onto network, the way streaming does. Because each user is in his or her own collision domain, switches often do not suffer from the same problem. Switches

Table 2–3
Client and Server Ports Use

Client attempt to connect	QuickTime[a]	RealSystem[b]	Windows Media[c]
Client connects to server on the Internet			
Port used to communicate with server	554 TCP	554 TCP	1755 TCP
Port used to receive media	6970-6971 UDP	6770-6799 UDP	1024-5000 UDP
Client connects to server on the Internet with network congestion			
Port used to communicate with server	554,7070 TCP or 80 HTP	554 TCP	1755 TCP
Port used to receive media	6970-6971 UDP or 80 HTTP	6770-6799 UDP HTTP[d]	1024-5000 UDP
Client connects to server on the intranet			
Port used to communicate with server	554 TCP	554 TCP	1755 TCP
Port used to receive media	6970-6971 UDP	6970-6999 UDP	1024-5000 UDP 80 HTTP
Client connects to server on the Internet through a firewall			
Port used to communicate with server	554, 7070 TCP or 80 HTTP	554 TCP	1755 TCP or 80 HTTP
Port used to receive media	6970-6971 UDP or 80 HTTP	6970-6999 UDP HTTP[d]	1024-5000 UDP or 80 HTTP
Client connects to server on the intranet through a firewall			
Port used to communicate with server	554, 7070 TCP or 80 HTTP	554 TCP	1755 TCP or 80 HTTP
Port used to receive media	6970-6971 UDP or 80 HTTP	6770-6799 UDP HTTP[d]	1024-5000 UDP 80 HTTP
Encoder connects to server to initiate a live stream			
Encoder call out	10000-65635 UDP	4040 TCP	1755 TCP or 80 HTTP
Server listen	10000-65635 UDP	554 TCP 6770-6799 UDP	1024-5000 UDP
Server will stream through	554 RTSP 7070 TCP or 80 HTTP	554 TCP HTTP[d]	1024-5000 UDP 80 HTTP

[a]Data applies to QuickTime Player 5.0, and QuickTime Streaming Server or Darwin Streaming Server 4.0 or later.
[b]Data applies to RealPlayer version 6.0 and Real Server 8.0 or later.
[c]Data applies to Windows Media Player 6.4 and Windows Media Services 4.1 or later.
[d]RealSystem server does not support HTTP streaming. However, streams can be forced to enter through a firewall by using specific ports. Note the order in which other ports are mentioned. The player attempts to get media in this order: first RTSP port 554, then PNM port 7070, and last HTTP port 8080. Use the following syntax in your RAM reference file to force streams to enter through port 8080 of your firewall:

```
rtsp://real_server_name:8080/file_name.rm?cloakport="554, 7070, 8080"
```

also perform better in Multicast traffic handling because they can prevent a Multicast signal from running on every port; rather, they transmit the signal only to designated IP addresses. IP Multicast is an extremely useful and efficient mechanism for multipoint distribution of information. At layer three, IP devices are able to understand and participate in distinct IP Multicast sessions based on the use of unique IP class D group addresses. Switches and routers supporting layer three Multicastings can broadcast Multicast signals only to those parts that request it. A hub, on the other hand, broadcasts to every port, requiring every connected desktop to respond to the broadcast, thus overwhelming the network and reducing its throughput.

Here is an overview of how streaming media is created, who handles it, and where it is stored. To see digital media, audio and video content must be captured, converted to a computer format (encoded), and distributed to viewers and/or shared on corporate networks for rebroadcasting or on-demand viewing. To capture the content, existing videotapes or audiocassettes can be used as input for streaming media. Large companies can use existing video production facilities to capture content or outsource the production of their live or on-demand content.

Encoding–Video or audio content is first converted into a computer format. This is called encoding. Encoding uses mathematical algorithms to compress the information into a smaller media format so that it can be streamed live or stored on a computer for on-demand viewing or scheduled rebroadcasting.

Distributing and streaming–Once the content has been converted into a digital format, it can then be distributed over a network. It can be stored in one or many media servers. It can be streamed live to many employees or stored for on-demand viewing in the corporate digital archive. More and more companies are using Web-based interfaces to pull rich media synchronized with text and images, creating the ultimate interactive experience for their end-users.

New culture–For digital media to be effectively implemented in your organization, you must take into consideration new behavioral and cultural issues that are related to streaming media technology. The challenge is to help people feel comfortable being videotaped and recorded, process the information using new media tools, create applications that will be both appealing and easy to use, and encourage users to start using these applications to replace conventional phone calls, faxes, videoconferencing, and face-to-face meetings.

People tend to be nervous when appearing in front of cameras. They are often tense and react differently, and the results may be poor. You as a video professional must take these facts into consideration to avoid a disaster for you and the executive you have just filmed. Enterprises must provide basic training for their video and IT personnel in the process of creating and delivering digital media. Standards and workflow templates should become part of your routine production; they will create consistency in the appearance of the final product and will confirm the quality of delivery in a proper way.

New roles—New business roles must be created, not only to develop and maintain the content of and new infrastructure for digital media, but also to maintain an environment that promotes and supports the use of new media. These new roles include:

- Digital Media Support, a team of people who assist users and departments in the creation of streaming media content. This team understands audio and video technologies as well as network systems. They create the templates to be used in the daily production of digital content for the enterprise. They encode live streams, prepare them as video on-demand, and create interactive applications to display this content on the corporate network.

- Producer or coordinator, a person who produces or coordinates the production of video and audio content. This person receives prerecorded content from various departments. His or her role as a mediator is to ensure that the media are properly converted and submitted into the newly designed corporate digital network.

Content distribution—Because most streaming products were initially developed as Internet applications, they require TCP/IP as a transport protocol. Most streaming media services will not work with other protocols, such as IPX, AppleTalk, or NetBEUl. Ethernet (IEEE 802.3) is the preferred LAN topology under which both Unicast and Multicast are supported.

Choosing a Streaming Architecture Model

Two main streaming architecture models are used, centralized, and distributed. Table 2–4 describes which types of applications each model is used for.

Table 2 – 4
Applications and Architecture

Centralized Architecture	Distributed Architecture
Network consists of few remote sites or low user concurrency in those sites	Network consists of many remote sites and/or high user concurrency at those sites
Network consists of a relatively high WAN bandwidth between remote users or sites and server position	Network consists of low WAN bandwidth availability between clients and server position
Normally serves live or "scheduled live" content with little or no on-demand content	Normally hosts media on-demand content
Multicast enabled between the servers' position and remote sites	Multicast not enabled within or between the sites

Centralized Architecture

A centralized architecture involves hosting a farm of media servers at a single location (see Figure 2–1). This location supports users on the entire network. Depending on the use patterns in the enterprise, this method may be preferred when there are few remote sites or the user concurrency in those sites does not exceed the available bandwidth on the network. It is also appropriate in Multicast situations in which the entire enterprise is Multicast-enabled.

The advantages of centralized architecture are:

- It allows simple content management. It is easier to distribute content among multiple servers at the same site. This allows the sharing of technologies, such as shared storage in the form of a storage area network (SAN), to provide a single high-performance and fault-tolerant volume across all of the server's onsite clients. In this model, all servers are clustered and look as if they were one device. If one server fails, content is available for playback through the other servers.

- It allows a more efficient use of hardware. Servers are added only when needed to increase capacity.

- It allows single-site management. There is no need to redirect users to different servers based on their network location.

However, there are also disadvantages to using a centralized architecture model. First, this model does not scale well in very large enterprises. It also increases the load at the central location where the distribution media servers are hosted. In addition, a centralized model does not make efficient use of WAN bandwidth. For example, if there are 100 users in the same remote site watching a live Unicast presentation (in which each user gets access to one stream of 100 kbps), and each is consuming 100 kbps of bandwidth, they will require a true consistent output of approximately 10 MB over the WAN. If one of the network segments between the users' location and the host server is only a T1 line (1.5 MB), a distributed model may be more appropriate.

Distributed Architecture

A distributed architecture involves placing several servers known as splitters, reflectors, or stations in strategic locations throughout the network to serve users. User requests are then directed to the server closest to them to view the stream (see Figure 2–2). Using the previous example, if 100 users are watching a live stream at 100 kbps each, with a distributed architecture, only one copy of the stream is transmitted over that same T1 line and is stored at the nearest media server. Users then retrieve the stream from the nearest local server to their site. The local server retrieves the original stream from the central server on the other side of the WAN. This preserves the more costly WAN bandwidth between the central and remote sites and ensures that the impact on other critical line-of-business applications is minimized.

The advantages of distributed architecture are:

- It may create a more fault-tolerant, scalable media on-demand solution.
- The same servers can be used for live webcast transmissions after proper configuration and advance testing.
- It can extend Multicasts to parts of the network that are otherwise not Multicast-enabled. For example, if a router that separates two sites has not been configured to pass Multicasts, you can set up a tunneled Multicast, linking the two parts of the network. Identifying where these Multicast islands are and how to connect them should be a concern of network administrators in an enterprise design plan.

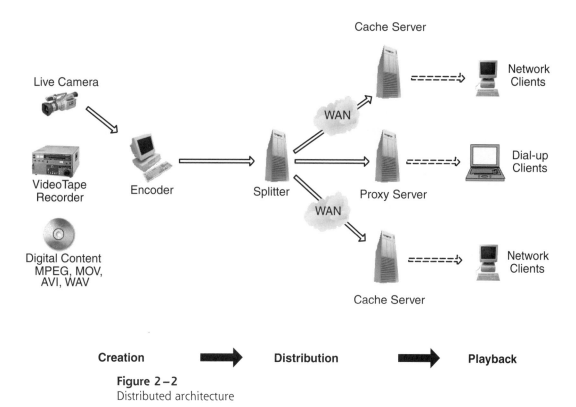

Figure 2–2
Distributed architecture

Distributed architecture introduces technical challenges that should be addressed before this model is chosen. First, a strategy for redirecting user requests to the media server closest to them must be implemented by the network IT department. User location is defined by either a static or dynamic IP assigned to it. Based on a corporate table of IPs, it is possible to determine the users' geographical areas and to redirect their requests to the media server closest to their site. This calculation should be derived from your network design and must be flexible enough to automatically adjust to changes in this design. Redirection can be achieved in a number of ways, using various hardware and software techniques. Knowing where to strategically place servers to achieve the optimal configuration for performance and cost should be a major part of any design of a streaming media infrastructure. New Content Delivery Networks (CDNs) for enterprises promise to resolve known issues pending in the successful deployment of a distributed architecture.

Content Delivery Networks

CDNs emerged as a result of the poor delivery of content on the public Internet. A CDN provides an architecture of Web-based network elements, arranged for the efficient delivery of digital content. CDNs leverage a strategically arranged set of distributed caching, load-balancing, and web request redirection systems (see Figure 2–3). They ensure that, based on user proximity and server load, content is served up in the most efficient manner to the user requesting it. This arrangement benefits the end-user (and the content provider), as well as network connec-

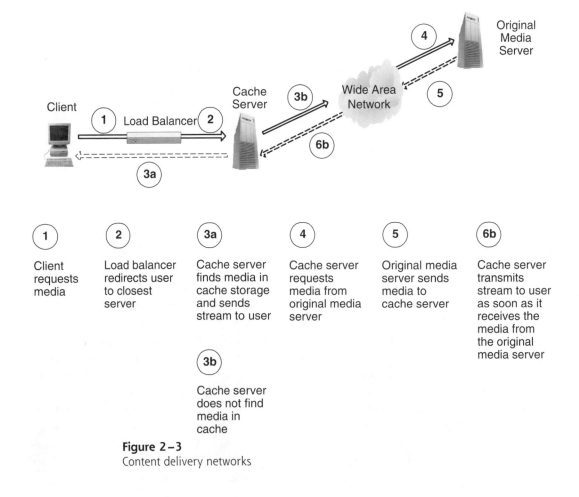

Figure 2–3
Content delivery networks

tivity providers, who leverage the operational rewards of streamlined bandwidth consumption.

At the present time, there are no case studies available of successful deployments of CDN solutions for streaming media within enterprise networks. Streaming service providers such as Akamai, Williams Communication, and Cable & Wireless have successfully deployed CDN on the public Internet. Using a CDN network on the public Internet allows the reduction of response-time delays by minimizing the number of Internet stops a Web request must make from the content source. One way the service providers do this is by hosting replications of the content of the CDN service provider's data center in cache servers, also called surrogates, located within points of presence (PoPs) along the edge of a network, one to five hops (step connections) away from the user. This enables CDN service providers in many cases to deliver content stored in cache servers just from one hop away from the user. This setup enables CDN service providers to deliver, on behalf of their content provider customers, the best possible experience to end-users, who are notoriously intolerant of response-time delays.

CDNs bring order and quality of service (QoS) to the Internet's IP backbone to eliminate or minimize the wait time before media is displayed. Network delays or inconsistent response times go almost unnoticed when the requested media are text-based email or static Web pages. But in the multimedia world of entertainment services, gaming, live videoconferences, and streaming broadcasts, which are sensitive to response-time delays, extra steps must be taken to ensure the delivery of a quality experience to end-users.

A user request to a content provider's Web site is redirected to a data center of the CDN provider. Typically, the content provider must set up this redirection itself using the tools and encoding methods dictated by the CDN service provider. The CDN contains a lookup service that steers a content request to the content surrogate that is closest (geographically or shortest travel time) to the user or is the least busy.

To determine the content server most available to a user at the time of a request for content, CDN service providers make use of load-balancing technology. Load balancing can be facilitated by the CDN service provider; it directs traffic to the least loaded server.

In addition, in recent months CDNs have made use of Web switching, also called content switching or application-layer switching, to further enhance QoS levels. These software capabilities enable the network connectivity elements in a CDN (routers and switches) not only to examine IP address information when determining a best path through the network, but also to calculate the specific response-time requirements of the application or content being requested. Using all this information, a CDN can deliver content to end-users in the most efficient way.

What Is Quality of Service?

QoS refers to the performance of a specified set of rules to deliver high-quality transmission over a communications channel or system. QoS is indicated by channel- or system-performance parameters, such as signal-to-noise ratio (S/N), bit error ratio (BER), message throughput rate, and call blocking probability (the formatting of data into blocks for transmission, storage, checking, or other functions).

QoS has received considerable attention in data network journals for years, yet it remains poorly understood and, due to lack of consensus in the industry about which of the several QoS strategies is superior, many network managers have hesitated to implement one QoS measure over another.

RSVP, the Reservation Protocol, is one of the mechanisms available for QoS on most routers on the market today. Two other more popular prioritization schemes are Diff-Serv and IP Precedence. The bottom line is that implementing QoS in a LAN helps to protect the integrity of service-sensitive applications and does not require major upgrades. Most of the leading network equipment vendors already support common QoS standards, such as RSVP. These settings are included with most new routers and switches. They need only to be enabled by the network administrator.

There is one drawback, however. If the protocol or scheme chosen for QoS in the local loop is not the same as that implemented in the backbone, the enterprise network needs to put QoS translation software in place for QoS requests to operate end-to-end during its use. Even when QoS protocols are in place, more is needed for interactive video applications to take advantage of the mechanisms without significantly affecting mission-critical data applications. When video is prioritized over data, data application performance is sacrificed. To avoid this, the network manager should segment and manage the bandwidth on each switch and router to limit the total prioritized video traffic and balance it with other applications running at the same time on the network.

How Does Streaming Video Work?

The following illustrates how streaming media works in different environments. Regardless of the technology used or the protocols that deliver video packets (RTP, RTSP, or MMS), all streaming technologies use a schema such as the one shown in Figure 2–4. The source media either is located in a tape (and plays back from a videocassette recorder, VCR) or is captured live by a camera. Video and audio cables transfer the audio-video signal from the source device to a capture card connected to encoding workstations. The capture card converts the analog video signal to a digital signal that the computer can recognize. The software encoder detects the digital signal coming from the capture card and converts that raw video to a streaming format. The encoder either sends the signal to a distribution server (for further distribution on the Web) or it encodes and captures the media as a streaming file (for storage in the media storage bin for future on-demand playback). The media server is the source of media that responds to requests coming from Internet or intranet users. Internet or intranet users request the video by logging in to a Web server and clicking on a HTML page with information about

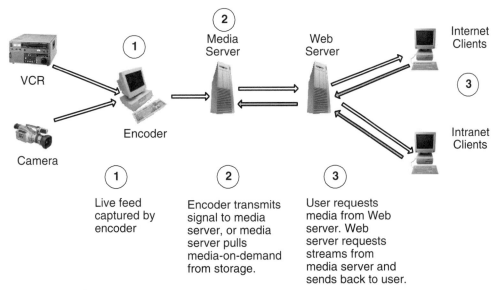

Figure 2–4
General overview of streaming media schema

the streaming file. When these users click on the HTML link, they generate a call to a reference file that points to the media server. Depending on the syntax links listed in the reference file (reference files are ASX, RAM, or MOV files that redirect user requests to the media server), the media will be pulled either from the live encoder or from its permanent storage space in the media storage bin. This applies to all types of live or on-demand streaming topologies. What vary from setting to setting are the components that are added to this schema.

Figure 2–5 illustrates in detail a scenario in which the media server is located on a corporate intranet. The live webcast is generated by a camera that sends the video signal to an encoder workstation. The encoder workstation transmits the video signal to an internal media server that distributes the webcast to local LAN users. The same server distributes the

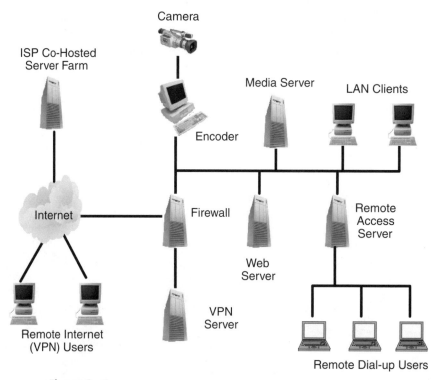

Figure 2–5
Streaming from behind the firewall to both Internet and Intranet users' schema

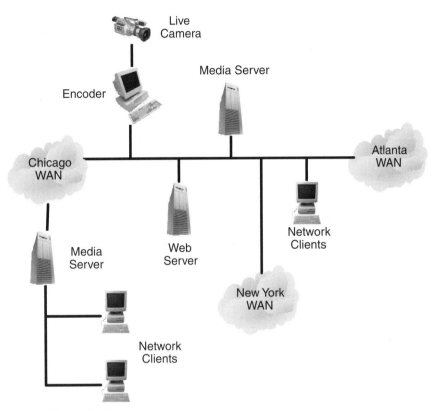

Figure 2-6
Streaming on the Intranet schema

media through the network firewall, over the Internet, to another media server. All users log on to the webcast through a secure network supporting dial-up modems, internal LAN connections, and a VPN for accessing the media over commercial networks such as DSL or cable modem. A VPN server gives users access to the corporate intranet through the firewall. Dial-up users dial in and join the webcast by authenticating with a remote access server (RAS). Note that the streaming signal penetrates the firewall using HTTP streaming over port 80. This complies with default firewall settings that normally block UDP or TCP ports. This example uses Windows Media technology.

Figure 2–6 illustrates an example of a live broadcast recorded by a camera and sent over an intranet. The video signal is sent to the encoder workstation. The encoder workstation transmits the streaming signal to

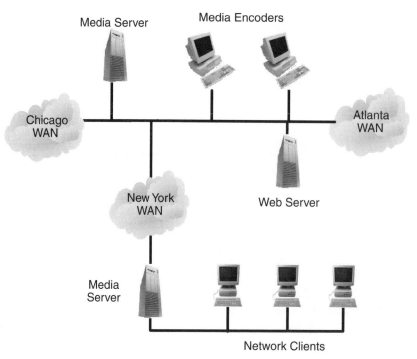

Figure 2–7
MOD Intranet streaming schema

the media server on the LAN. The media server does two things: It distributes the webcast to local clients on the same LAN segment and it acts as a publishing point for another media server that pulls the feed over the company WAN and redistributes it on its own LAN. Users from both locations access the webcast by logging in to the Web server on the LAN and pointing to the media on it.

Figure 2–7 illustrates an architecture that provides a step up in design from the previous two schemas. In this case, media on-demand is created and stored on a local media server. Users from a few remote locations access the media through a Web page and an active database. Once stored, it is immediately available for viewing. Note the position of the replication media server, which copies all the media that is on the first server. This is a good example of using caching techniques to help play back a better quality video. Users are directed to watch content from the nearest media server, minimizing hops, and avoiding potential network bottlenecks. Users log on to the company Web server and request the media stored on the network. Upon request, the media is pulled and sent to the requester.

Firewall Issues

A firewall is hardware, software, or a product that combines hardware and software that provides security to computer networks. Firewalls act as an interface between two networks (e.g., the Internet and a private network) and regulates traffic between these networks to protect the internal network from electronic attacks originating from the external network. The firewall is capable of handling the following tasks:

- Isolating internal and external traffic (a bridge service)
- Making internal addresses invisible and directly inaccessible from outside and passing through authorized traffic after proper checking (a proxy service)
- Facilitating protected (encrypted) connections to cooperative parties over public networks (a tunneling service)
- Filtering outgoing traffic for security and network use rules (filtering or monitoring service)
- Filtering incoming traffic for rogue data, for example, viruses, spam, inappropriate data (filtering service), or improper actions (port scanning or overload prevention service)
- Blocking forbidden external services or addresses (blocking or "network nanny" service)
- Providing log-in services for authorized outside users and allowing the approved outside user to simulate an inside user (proxy or log-in service)
- Caching network traffic (cache service)
- Converting between different network protocols on different protocol levels (bridge service, when handling lower level protocols; gateway service, when handling higher level protocols)
- Diverting traffic for cost optimizing, accounting, network planning, monitoring, and so on

- Providing consistent, open entry to the internal network (portal service)
- Facilitating public network address and connection sharing (proxy service)

In short, a firewall is a system designed to defend against unauthorized access to or from a private network. How is streaming media performance affected by firewalls? Most problems with streaming media are due to using the wrong network configuration. The following are some problems that affect streaming media on networks and suggestions for solving them.

- Wrong firewall settings–Make sure that the firewalls on your network are properly configured to allow the protocols, ports, and addresses required by your streaming media architecture. Refer to Table 2–3 for reference.

- Wrong router settings–If you are attempting to Multicast on your network, make sure your routers support Multicast protocols. Check the IP ACLs (Access Control Lists) on the routers to find out which protocols, ports, and addresses are allowed. If necessary, set up Multicast tunneling. See the router manual for details.

- Network congestion due to problems with the bandwidth allocation–You need to use special network traffic analysis tools, such as Network Monitor, included in the Windows NT 4.0 operating system. Because we are facilitating streaming media for a Windows-based network, for best results use the complete version of the tools included with Microsoft Systems Management Server. See the Network Monitor documentation for details. You may have to take some special action to avoid network congestion (including the use of QoS-enabled equipment) or even redesign the network.

- Lost packets–Use the same technique as for bandwidth analysis. Tracing with Network Monitor (or other network analyzers) enables you to find the faulty devices (such as hubs, switches, or routers).

- Multicast issues–If you are planning to locate your media server behind a firewall and stream content to media players on the other side of the firewall, reconsider the server location. A media server behind a firewall does not make much sense. All media servers need to open a TCP connection based on the player request. Most firewalls permit TCP requests if they are initiated behind the firewall (and if these requests are going outside). Based on the TCP request of a media player, the media server will open a UDP channel or port so it can send out data packets. The firewall will block any attempts to open a UDP port from inside the network. The solution is to move the media server to a perimeter network known as demilitarized zone (DMZ), a perimeter network outside the main internal network but still secured by the firewall. This will also apply when configuring an encoding workstation to transmit a streaming signal to a distribution server. All streaming encoders offer the possibility of choosing a port number and protocol to be used for webcasting a video feed between an encoder workstation and its corresponding media server (see Chapter 8).

All enterprises use firewalls to protect their network from unauthorized entries. Network administrators block most ports on the firewall and permit entry only through a few ports. To view Web pages, for example, port 80 must be open on the firewall. Deploying a large number of streaming media clients on an enterprise network is a time-consuming process. QuickTime has not addressed this issue yet. RealSystem provides an automated way to custom-configure clients. Windows Media comes with a default rollover mechanism that routes media requests to UDP, TCP, and, if not successful, to HTTP. This function is favored by many IT managers when deploying streaming solutions behind firewalls.

Firewalls and/or proxy servers sometimes introduce problems with certain types of protocols, especially those used by streaming. A careful review of the firewall's capabilities as well as the ports used by the streaming applications will help establish a streaming network that performs well while providing network-level security.

Summary

- Networks consist of two types of architecture: LANs and WANs. The first normally serves groups of employees in one location; the second connects between two locations.
- Networks use different topologies to achieve smooth transport of data packets between computers on the network. Networks are

the pipes that deliver data from one location to another. For this data to move properly across networks, it must use certain protocols that are known by both client and server.

- The task of successfully deploying a streaming media solution on a company network must be addressed by a team of representatives from major departments: IT, human resources (HR), training, corporate communications, and sales.

- Enterprises should select a centralized or distributed streaming media architecture that best fits their network needs. Large-scale deployment of a distributed architecture should use CDN and QoS technology to maximize distribution and network efficiency.

- Firewall issues often determine whether streaming media can be seen on corporate networks. Careful planning and good implementation will determine if you will be able to stream media or your network in a cost-effective and secure way.

3

Source Material

Definitions of Video and Audio

Video is a means of reproducing moving visual images by representing them with an analog electronic signal. The images are decomposed into a series of horizontal scan lines. In this way, the signal can be stored, transmitted, and reproduced. Different countries have adopted different standards for video signals and equipped their broadcast and nonbroadcast facilities with supporting equipment; today there are three major standards for video systems used in the world: NTSC, PAL, and SECAM. NTSC is used in the United States and also in many other countries.

Audio is sound within the acoustic range available to humans. An audio frequency (AF) is an electrical alternating current within the range 20–20,000 Hz (hertz or cycles per second) that can be used to produce acoustic sound. Audio plays an important role in the delivery of a successful video presentation. If audio were not included in video transmissions, audience would have the same experience moviegoers had in the beginning of the 20th century during the time of silent film, when moving images included titles describing the events on the screen. In computers, audio is the sound system that comes with or can be added to a computer. An audio card contains a special built-in processor and memory for processing audio files and sending them to speakers in the computer. An audio file is a record of captured sound that can be played back. Sound is a sequence of naturally analog signals that are converted to digital signals by the audio card, using a microchip called an analog-to-digital converter (ADC). When sound is played, the digital signals are sent to the speakers where they are converted back to analog signals that generate varied sound.

Audio files are usually compressed for storage or faster transmission. Audio files can be sent in short stand-alone segments—for example, as files in the WAVE format. In order for users to receive sound in real time for a multimedia effect, to listen to music, or to take part in an audio- or video-conference, sound must be delivered as streaming sound. More advanced audio cards support wavetables, or precaptured tables of sound. The most popular audio file format today that is not part of a video file is MP3.

Because computers recognize only digital format for playback, content must be captured (converted from an analog to a digital format) and stored on a computer before it can be transferred to another computer or played back over a network by visitors to a Web site. Many people confuse digital tape formats such as DV or Digital Beta with digital file formats stored on a computer. All digital formats have some common traits. All digital video formats use binary code (signals that are made up of a series of ones and zeros); and all digital video formats, from the least expensive to the most expensive, share the enviable capability of unlimited generations (of editing) without a decline in quality. The differences between digital files stored on tape and digital files stored on a hard drive are the media used for storage and accessibility.

To encode streaming files you must point your encoder to an audio or video source on your computer (or on your network). Therefore, I recommend that you capture content and store it as an AVI (Audio Video Interleaved video file) or a WAVE file (audio file) on your computer before you start encoding. To capture your source of media you need:

- A media source (a camera, microphone, VCR, or another computer)
- A capture card, as described in Chapter 6
- Software to convert the digital feed into a digital file or a streaming file

A variety of audio and video formats are available in the market that play back media on compatible devices. Become familiar with different video and audio formats before proceeding with the actual production of content (Chapter 4).

Video Formats

A video format is a standard that determines the way a video signal is recorded by an analog or digital camera onto a videotape and the type of playback system that is used to play back that tape. Some standards are DV, Digital 8, 1-in Type C, ¾-in U-Matic, ¾-in U-Matic, 8-mm, Beta, Beta ED, Betacam, Betacam SP, SP, D-1, DCT, D-2, D-3, D-5, Digital Betacam, Hi8, M-II, VHS, and S-VHS.

When the television produces a color picture from light, the system starts out with three channels of information; red, green, and blue (RGB). This is one form of component video. In the process of translating these channels for use in distribution, they are often first converted to Y (luminance signal), R-Y (first color difference), and B-Y (second color difference) or Y Pb Pr (a version of component video). This is another form of component video. Component video is considered to be the highest quality analog video because its signal is broken down to maximize its video levels. The term "component" refers to the elements that are needed to make up the picture. It could be argued that an S-Video signal is also a component signal. A composite video signal, on the other hand, contains all the information needed for the color picture in a single channel of information–luminance, color, and synchronization information. It has a much lower program production quality than component video. Analog compression is used to place the three channels of component information into the single channel of composite information. Once that compression takes place, it is extremely difficult to get back the original quality of the component signal. One of the advantages of using digital versatile disc (DVD), for example, is that playback can be maintained as RGB and it does not need to be converted to composite. When we capture video to our computers we convert the video signal to a composite or component video depending on the type of input connection we use and the codec we use (YUV 4:2:2, YUV12, or YUV9). New capture cards such as the Osprey 500 support RGB input. NTSC, PAL, and SECAM are all examples of composite video systems.

Audio Formats

In the past 20 years, audio has moved from analog recording using LPs (long-playing records) and tape cassettes as the playback media to digital recording using computers with digital surround sound playback. At one time, music could only be recorded from a live group of musicians. Each audio source (sound source) was recorded onto a separate audio track and the complete output resulted when all the tracks were mixed and recorded onto a master tape. This analog process was slow and expensive.

Table 3–1
Digital Audio Formats

Extension	Origin/name	Remarks
AU, SND, ULW	Sun Microsystems	Sun/NeXT/DEC/UNIX sound file
AIFF, AIF, AIFC	Audio Interchange File Format	File format for storing digital audio (waveform) data on Macintosh computers
GSM	GSM audio file	Audio file used for GSM-supported devices
MIDI, MID, SMF	Musical Instrument Digital Interface	Protocol designed for recording and playing back music on digital synthesizers
MP3	Moving Picture Experts Group	MPEG-1 audio layer-3, compresses to $1/12$ of file size
WAV	Microsoft	Audio file that has become a standard PC audio file format for everything from system and game sounds to CD-quality audio

The recorded mixed media could not be modified and the only way to correct mistakes was to record a complete new session. Today, the Musical Instrument Digital Interface (MIDI), sequencers, sound cards, and synthesizers allow anyone to create music right on his or her desktop computer. Even a modest setup can create surprisingly realistic audio tracks. You probably have many of these tools in your computer already.

Even if you are not a musician, the technology surrounds you. Songs can be downloaded as MIDI or MP3 files that will play back on your computer's sound card. Computer-based audio files can now deliver your favorite songs over the Internet. You can download a group of your favorite songs as MP3 files and then create a custom CD to listen to at your next party, create a collection of your favorite tunes to share with your friends, or add a soundtrack and sound effects to your latest video recording. Streaming files promise a wider, faster, and more secure distribution of digital media in the years to come.

How do you create your own music and audio files? If you are a budding composer, the most basic setup includes a keyboard and some MIDI sequencing software. Using this combination, you can play individual piano, bass, drum, and horn parts right from your desktop, using the computer's sound card to play back the sounds of your "band." You can edit the parts with off-the-shelf software, save the file as a standard MIDI file, and send your composition to your friends over the Internet so that they can play the same piece of music on their PCs.

What is the difference between this modest setup and a professional setup? As your personal music studio starts to grow, you expand the sound-production possibilities, the palette of sounds, and the recording tools. A music studio is an expanding set of tools. Only one thing is essential: good ideas. Without them, no amount of expensive gear can make you a pro.

Many digital audio formats have been introduced. Table 3–1 lists these formats, their origins, and what they are used for.

Video Equipment

The purpose of video is to tell a story to many people without the need to re-create the event every time. Telling a story involves the design of a stage where the story takes place and the use of tools that help deliver it. Shooting video has many components of aesthetics and balance that drive the message in the right direction. Props must be located in comfortable places, light simulates atmosphere, sound helps create an ambience, actors provide action, and the videocameras record what they see. At a later stage, a video editor spends hours or days assembling the raw video clips to make a complete story with a beginning, middle, and end. Producing video content for the Web or for distribution with streaming technology does not require broadcast-quality equipment. Streaming technology uses Internet protocols to deliver content over computer networks. Streaming servers distribute the signal (similar to television or radio broadcast transmitters), and desktop computers or new Internet devices (see Chapter 11) receive the signal and play it back (similar to television sets and radios, which are receivers). Commercial audiences can receive a signal that ranges from 14 to 1,000 kbps (1,000 kb equals 1 Mb) sent from the distribution server. Video transmitted within this range is not close to traditional broadcast quality, which ranges from 8 to 25 Mbps. Therefore, using broadcast-quality equipment (videocameras and recorders) to record the signal is not essential for a successful Web video production. Of course, the highest level of recording generates the best picture for playback, but not every organization or company can afford to purchase or rent high-quality video equipment for its production. Digital prosumer (short for "professional consumer") equipment has become very popular in recent years. Cameras such as the Sony VX2000 or the Canon XL1 and industrial videocameras such as the Sony DVCAM series offer superb recording quality for streaming video applications at a moderate price. Desktop editing systems such as Adobe Premiere (*www.adobe.com*) and Final Cut Pro (*www.apple.com*) provide low-cost nonlinear editing solutions for new media production.

If your organization has mid-level to high-end production gear (analog or digital video and editing equipment), use it to record video and then capture and convert your media to digital format. Purchasing new equipment can be a very costly process. If you do this, carefully calculate how soon you will see a return on your investment. Remember that, in addition to equipment, you need the knowledge to operate it. More difficult, you need experience in creating suitable content for your needs. Organizations or individuals that produce video only a few times a year should consider renting equipment or outsourcing production to subcontractors. If you feel confident in your ability to produce video content and plan to purchase new gear, here is what you need to start producing digital video:

- A portable light kit supporting three-point lighting
- A digital camera that operates on both batteries and electrical power
- A tripod for your camera; use a tripod with a fluid head
- Microphones
- An audio mixer
- A set of headphones
- A portable color monitor
- Extension cables for power and audio
- Stock tape (Mini-DV or DVCAM)
- Carrying cases to safely transport your equipment

In 2000, Centerseat.com, like DEN.com and Pseudo.com, launched a site that promised to webcast original and licensed programming to Internet users with broadband connections. The site delivered video presentations synchronized with contextual text, images, and e-commerce opportunities. (The Centerseat story is presented as one of the case studies in Chapter 13.) In my previous occupation as Director of Streaming

Services at Centerseat.com, I conducted several internal seminars for our company employees, covering video production techniques for the Web. As I was explaining different techniques to our producers, assistant producers, and video editors, I realized how hard it was for them to draw on their years of experience in the television broadcast industry and adapt this knowledge to the production of streaming video programs. When you are producing for the Web, you are creating content for a totally different medium. For this reason, I encourage every producer to read the following section before attempting to produce video Web presentations.

Light

Most people think that a camera is all they need to shoot a video. This assumption is completely wrong. Any videocamera, no matter how advanced, will produce poor results without proper light. Lighting for video is a complicated task that requires knowledge of both videography and general lighting techniques. Different scenes require different lighting. Two people sitting on a sofa require different lighting than a group of students sitting in a classroom. A man running in a corridor requires different light settings than a man swimming in a pool. Lighting for video requires components and planning that are not used when lighting for film. Lighting for the Web relies heavily on the very same techniques as lighting for video, but the nature of streaming video delivery is different from traditional broadcasting. When lighting a scene for a webcast, keep in mind that the wrong lighting will produce a poor-quality image and that the image will look even worse after the encoding process.

The primary job of lighting is to bring the level of light up to a point at which an image can be produced on a piece of film or digital video-camera chip. It is important to provide adequate lighting for your subject. A television is capable of displaying a poorly lit image, but for transmission over the Internet or an intranet, the video compression codecs used in streaming video may not produce a useful image if the subject is poorly lit. Although most camcorders can produce an acceptable image at low light, professional studio lighting helps produce images with sharper edges, lower contrast, richer color, and less video noise. Images that have these qualities are more likely to compress well. To maximize your video output (from the camera to the capture card to the encoder), use soft diffused light. Use a diffusion sheet or reflective umbrella to soften the light source, remove heavy lighting contrast, and reduce harsh shadows. Add a background light to help separate the subject from the background and to improve the definition of line edge. Try to avoid using direct light on the subject, but if you have no other way to light your subject use the following guidelines to maximize the quality of the video:

- Use a tripod.
- Avoid camera movements.
- Avoid movement in the background.
- Use the gain function on your camera to add light to the subject.
- Use a close up or a medium shot (face or mid-body picture) to minimize the amount of information the encoder must process later.
- Do not zoom in or out; provide stable footage.

A video in which the subject is not properly lighted or is not lighted accessibly will require extra processing when it is encoded and converted to streaming files. If you are familiar with encoding streaming media try this exercise. (Beginners who are not familiar with encoding software and techniques are encouraged to read the second part of this book before trying this exercise.)

- Mount your camera on a tripod and connect it to your workstation capture card. Launch your software encoder. Use any of the three encoders mentioned in Chapter 8. For this test, configure your encoder to encode at 100 kbps; the window size should be 240×180 pixels. Use 16 kbps for audio. Open the statistics windows of the encoder to monitor the quality of the encoded stream.

- Put your subject in a dark area of the room and ask him or her to move continually. Start encoding. Notice that the image becomes pixilated and that the number of frames per second decreases. Now add light. Ask your subject to make the same movements as before. Notice that the image becomes more visible, pixilation decreases, and the number of frames per second increases.

- Now try camera movements. Turn off the light and use the natural light of the room. The subject should not move. Use a handheld camera and move it around the subject. Look at the statistic levels. You should notice the same degradation in quality as before. Now turn on the light and move your camera around the subject as before. Watch the player statistics carefully. You should notice a better performance when the light is on.

The performance is poor when you use low light because the encoder is attempting to compensate for the poor image. This results in low output and eventually a poor quality image.

The art of lighting for video is covered extensively by Bill Holshevnikoff in his videotape series and mobile workshops. Since 1989, Holshevnikoff has been educating film and video professionals across the United States and Canada. Backed by some of the industry's major manufacturers, including ARRI, Chimera, Lowel, GamColor, Schneider, and Kino Flo, his workshops and lighting seminars have set a new standard for film and video education. The *Power of Lighting Video Series* contains the first four programs of Holshevnikoff's educational video series. These tapes provide comprehensive lighting techniques and theory that can be applied to all levels of videography and film making. To purchase Bill's tapes, log on to *www.power-of-lighting.com*.

Lighting a set for a video shoot requires a basic knowledge of the way a camera processes light and translates it into video. You may not be satisfied with just any random lighting of your subject for a number of reasons. When showing a video clip to your audience you are trying to catch their attention. Multiple camera viewpoints and good composition help generate an attractive presentation, but poor lighting creates only damage. Lighting conditions can vary considerably. You may not be able to shoot using some natural conditions. Fortunately, today lighting kits provide good resources to compensate for most situations.

Videocameras can shoot under a remarkable range of lighting conditions. Unfortunately, the camera always lies—what you will see in your camera viewfinder is not always what is being recorded. To stay as close as possible to the original light conditions of your subject, use the camera's manual configuration option and use the manual iris and shutter. Monitor the available light through a black-and-white viewfinder, or set your color monitor to display black and white. Lighting aspects are more noticeable when observed through a black-and-white or shaded environment. Table 3–2 lists examples of traditional lighting conditions that can be found in daily life.

When a production crew is asked to shoot video they normally first visit all the locations. This preproduction visit determines what components of audio, video, and light they need to bring and set up before the shoot starts. Because proper lighting of the subjects is essential to generating good images for video, most lighting engineers use artificial lights on a set. For example, if the crew is asked to shoot an interview in a room

Table 3–2
Traditional Lighting Conditions

Day Exteriors	Day Interiors
Strong sunlight	Large windows
Sunless sky light	Direct into subject
Evening light	Reflected into subject
Dawn, dusk, and sunset	Daylight with add-on artificial light such as tungsten or fluorescent

Night Exteriors	Night Interiors
Street lighting	Illuminated ceiling (fluorescent)
Shop window lighting	Pole lamps
Car headlamps	Wall fittings
Firelight	Table lamps
	Candlelight

with a lot of windows, the lighting engineer will cover all the windows and create a three-point lighting set with artificial light.

Sound

As every video professional knows, there is a significant difference between broadcasting video with audio and broadcasting audio only. When broadcasting a video and audio signal, your target audience pays more attention to the video. We first react to a moving image and only then associate it with a sound. For example, have you ever watched a thunderstorm? First the light appears, and afterward the accompanying cracking noise is heard.

Creating an audio-only broadcast challenges us to do two tasks: to attract the audience's attention, generating interest in the subject without showing moving images, and to keep their attention with high-quality sound. Because people listen to audio while doing other things at the same time (such as driving, working, or taking care of domestic chores), radio broadcasting has become a specialized industry in which behavioral patterns are carefully studied to achieve the maximum impact of delivery despite limited conditions in the field. The same applies to audio web-casting on the Internet. Audio stations rushed in the late 1990s to facilitate live webcasts of their stream to loyal listeners and potential new audiences. Today most radio stations operate live webcasts that are Internet replications of their airwave signal. If you listen carefully, you will find that the signal is pretty good, even at low bandwidth settings. Net radio is a successful business and many advertisers find it a good platform for reaching new customers in ways that did not exist before.

If you plan to deploy an audio-only webcast or if your audio feed is part of an audio and video webcast, you must use all possible resources to ensure the good capture, processing, and distribution of your audio feed. Audio is an analog source and in order to capture and process it you need to use a combination of analog and digital devices.

Live audio is captured using microphones. Microphones are devices that convert sound energy into electrical current or digital data. Different microphones create different effects of sound. All microphones have a diaphragm, or membrane, that vibrates in response to sound waves and converts them into electrical energy. There are three kinds of micro-phones: condenser, dynamic, and ribbon. Dynamic microphones are uni-directional, relatively large, and suitable for handheld operation. They are often used to record voices or musical instruments, and they pick up sound that is nearby. Condenser microphones must be amplified extensively in order to be useful. They tend to be small and are used as clip-on microphones to capture voices or sound coming from musical instruments. Ribbon microphones are bidirectional and have 180-degree coverage. They are mostly used to record voices, for example, in a conference room. They are very sensitive and can capture wind noise if they are not protected properly with a wind flag. The nature of your production will dictate which type of microphone you use.

After you have selected the proper microphone, you must connect it to a mixing board. Microphones placed in different places will pick up different sounds. You must balance the sounds to emphasize the ones you want the audience to hear. To do this, you use a sound mixer. The sound mixer must have multiple input options (tracks) for microphone connections (XLR or Plug input), playback line devices (Plug or RCA input), or camera outputs (XLR or RCA input). Microphones produce different output levels than other devices; "level" here refers to the relative strength of the signal measured in decibels (dB). Line level signals are more amplified than microphone level signals. Line level signals are usually between −10 and +4 dB in strength, whereas microphone levels range between −30 and +60 dB. Use extension cables or plugs sold by Monster Cable (*www.monstercable.com*); the necessary cables and connectors can be purchased online or from one of their resellers listed on the Web site. Input all the sound sources into your mixer and monitor their levels. Most video professionals prefer the low-cost high-efficiency Mackie Mixers. For an investment of approximately $350.00, you can purchase the Mackie 1202 VLZ, which accepts 12 incoming audio sources. Mixers accept microphone connections, playback devices, camera feed, and computer line-out signals. Use good-quality headphones so that you cannot hear external noise when you balance the levels of your incoming audio signals. Connect the line output from the mixer to the capture card on your encoding workstation and you are ready to start a webcast.

Cameras

Videocameras are electronic devices that capture and document life as it appears on the camera's optical lens. Camera manufacturers try to produce cameras that replicate the accuracy and quality of the image seen by the human eye and record the very same experience to tape. The technology is not there yet. Until this is possible, there will always be a discrepancy between what we see in life and how it looks on the wide screen or on our desktop. Digital cameras have introduced a new level of accuracy that was not available with analog cameras. The best way to choose a digital camera for your production needs is to find a local reseller and ask him or her to compare some of the digital cameras available on the market. There are three types of digital cameras: consumer products, prosumer products, and professional products. Videocameras cost from $1,000.00 for a home videocamera to $40,000.00 and up for a studio-broadcast-quality camera. Streaming video files play back nicely if you have recorded the media with a Mini-DV or DVCAM camera.

A good camera that can produce decent content must have the following functions:

- White balance—Controls that strengthen the blue or red colors so that neither overpowers the other, allowing white objects to appear pure white, not tinted, and color to be reproduced accurately

- Manual zoom—The ability to enlarge an image by manipulation of the lens elements to increase the size of the subject
- Manual focus—A control that helps the user select and focus certain subjects in the frame
- Manual IRIS—A control that helps the user control the amount of light that enters the camera
- S-Video output—A connection that maximizes the camera output signal while capturing media on a computer
- Color viewfinder—A control that helps the camera operator balance color levels, more common in prosumer equipment

How you plan to use your media is important in the selection of a videocamera. For example, if you are planning to record media, edit it, and output it back to tape for distribution on VHS tapes, you need to purchase a high-end camera using Beta SP, DVCAM, or DVCPro format. If you are planning to shoot video, edit it, and encode it to streaming media, a DV camera will do the job. There are two types of DV cameras: DVCAM and Mini-DV formats. Most camera manufacturers have recording and playback products supporting these formats.

Sony and Canon have introduced a line of prosumer cameras (Sony VX1000/2000, the DCR PD-150, or Canon XL1) that have quickly become very popular among production companies that create streaming content. Consumer DV Reviews (*www.consumerdvreviews.com*) provides an accurate and detailed comparison of a variety of consumer and semi-pro cameras on the market. Table 3–3 lists a comparison of the most interesting features of the Sony DCR PD-150 and Canon XL1.

Both cameras have a list price of below $4,000.00, making either an affordable investment. Both produce a clear digital image. I favor the Sony DCR PD-150 because it brings a new dimension to low-cost semi-professional cameras. Built on the core features of the VX2000, the DCR PD-150 has a black-and-white viewfinder, settable time code, a built-in XLR audio adapter, switchable 4:3 or 16:9 aspect ratio, switchable Mini-DV or DVCAM recording, and switchable 12-bit or 16-bit audio recording. Time codes can now be set by the user. And you can choose between Drop Frame (DF) and Non-Drop Frame (NDF). Many video professionals stay away from the Mini-DV format because its tapes tend to be fragile. The option of recording both formats on the same camera adds extra value to the Sony DCR PD-150.

Table 3 – 3
Comparison of Canon XL1 and Sony DCR PD-150

	Canon XL1	**Sony DCR PD-150**
Recording mode	Mini-DV	DVCAM/Mini-DV
CCD	3	3
CCD size	$\frac{1}{3}$" (270,000/250,000 pixels)	$\frac{1}{3}$" (380,000 pixels)
Shutter speed	1/15,000 max	1/10,000 max
Lines of resolution	500	500
Audio	XLR input	XLR input
	12 bit/16 bit PCM Digital Stereo	12 bit/16 bit PCM Digital Stereo
Lens	F/1.6–2.6, 5.5–88 mm (interchangeable)	58-mm aspherical lens
Notable features	XL Interchangeable Lens System (16x zoom supplied)	2-position neutral density filter
	Magnesium alloy body	USB Memory Stick Reader
	XL Interchangeable Lens System (16 x 200 m [supplied]: f/1.6–2.6, 5.5–88 mm)	Analog-to-digital conversion and pass through using i.Link
	Pixel shift technology	DV cable (Requires Firewire board on host computer)
	Four-channel digital audio system	

Action

It is easy to learn how to shoot quality video for streaming when you understand how streaming works. To maximize the transmission of streaming video and minimize buffering or quality degradation during transmission, you must take in consideration the encoding process performed before the packets are sent to the media player. Streaming media encoders take video and audio signals from a local digital media source or from a capture card. The capture card acts as a mediator, taking the video signal from its original analog or digital format and converting it to a specified size and level of compression. Streaming media encoders take the feed created by the capture card and compress the streaming file. Because the capture card copies what the camera or VCR sends to it, there is no degradation of quality during this process (the only loss is a result of resizing and compression depending on the codec used). Once the streaming encoder receives its feed, it proceeds with the conversion of the digital media to streaming format. The specific format has special characteristics such as a new window size and new limitations on the bandwidth to be used for the creation of audio and video streams. Figure 3–1 shows the process.

What affects the quality of video processed through the diagram in Figure 3–1? There are four factors that have an effect on the ability of streaming video to play back properly. First, the production process– the light conditions, camera movements, audio levels, and editing concepts–affects how the video is encoded. Second, the encoding process has many configurable options–audio and video codecs, window size, assigned frames per second, pixel formats, and audio video filters. Third, the network that moves data packets between the media distribution servers and the software client player can be overwhelmed with data traffic or just paired in a wrong way. This is true whether the network is public (the Internet) or private (your company's intranet). And last, the computer that plays back the media must be configured to play the streaming media. I have heard complaints from people who have tried to play back Windows Media streaming files on a QuickTime client, people who have tried to play back broadband video through a dial-up modem, people who have tried to play streaming files on a Pentium computer with Windows 95 and 32 MB of RAM, and so on.

I recommend that every producer take the time to become familiar with streaming software encoding tools. The more you are familiar

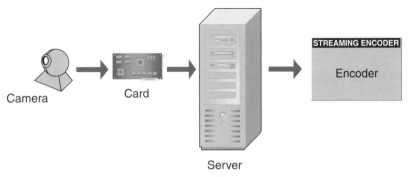

Figure 3–1
Capture media technique

with the limitations of these tools, the better you will be able to adapt and produce raw footage that will work smoothly with streaming encoders. Here are three rules to help you produce better content for distribution as streaming video.

The first rule to keep in mind is to minimize changes and movement from frame to frame. The transmission of large video files over the Internet is still a problem. Most Internet users rely on their company networks to help them access the Web at speeds greater than 300 kbps. In years to come, broadband connection through DSL and cable modems will increase the number of broadband-connected homes. Until then, you must keep in mind that the majority of your audience cannot see video properly. Because of this, streaming software developers minimize the amount of information that is passed from the distribution server to the client player. The technology sends out only the information describing pieces of the image that change from one frame to the next (these frames are called delta frames). Occasionally, an entire frame is sent (these frames are called key frames). If you use a portable DV camera to tape a steady subject, you will produce a streaming file consisting entirely of key frames. When captured and encoded into a 56-kbps streaming file, the content will look extremely jerky because there is not enough bandwidth to send (or present) all the required information. However, if you put your DV camera on a tripod and focus it on the same steady subject you will get an ideal streaming file (even at low bandwidths). Why? When the camera is on a tripod, the delta frame size is minimized because the background is static. When the camera is handheld, you are moving and the background changes all the time—the light changes, the focus changes, and the distance between you and the subject changes. This translates into changes in every frame, and the delta frames become the size of key frames. To improve the quality of streaming video at low bandwidths, plan to shoot common shots, medium and close-up shots. Remember that your audience will view this video in a small window. If you shoot landscapes or wide-angle shots, the subject will be lost when the large picture is shrunk for the Web. Minimize both camera movement (tilts and pans) and the use of fast zooms. Instead shoot steady shots and connect them later when editing.

The second rule is to minimize the use of bright whites, blues, and yellows. Use the same rules that are used in shooting traditional broadcast video (e.g., avoiding hot colors, patterns in backgrounds, and glare from the subject or the surroundings). Advise your subject to wear solid colors; dark solid colors on a bright solid is your best choice. Any type of pattern on the subject or around the subject requires extra attention from the encoder, resulting in the degradation of quality during playback.

The third and last rule is to get your audio levels correct. Audio is a very important component of your video presentation, so use a mixer to mix and control the audio levels before they reach your sound card. Try to find any artifacts or image distortions, which often appear while transferring a video signal between video devices, and correct these problems before recording. Remember that you are producing for a different medium, using different equipment and technology. Any attempt to make changes to an audio or video setting on a capture card during a live webcast (or capture session) may result in the corruption of the digital file or in a computer-processing overload. If the latter happens, the system will crash and you will need to reboot. This is the last thing you want to do during a live webcast. Streaming video production should not be approached in the same way as television or film production, not at least until streaming technology reaches the level of stability of other technologies.

Summary

- Video and audio techniques are used to capture real-time events and to transmit them or record them on tape. Video and audio signals can be captured with analog or digital equipment. If the signals are captured or recorded with analog equipment, they must be converted to a digital format before they can be recognized by a computer.

- There are numerous video and audio formats on the market. The industry needs to standardize these formats to one global format. This standardization will help developers create better technologies to capture and deliver digital media in a cost-effective and efficient way.

- To produce streaming video, you need to be familiar with the new hardware and software used to create digital media. More important, it is imperative that producers understand the process of converting digital video or audio to streaming media before they start producing video for the Web.

- Pay attention to proper use of light, camera, and sound during production. Streaming video production requires the use of different techniques from traditional television or film production.
- Remember the three rules of thumb that will help you produce better streaming video: minimize camera movements and use tight shots, avoid hot colors and patterns, and get your audio levels right.

4

Stock Library Media

When Not to Produce Video

Stock libraries are a perfect solution for producing a cost-effective project. Most stock libraries offer on their Web site samples of media in streaming or downloadable formats. From news to educational to health-related to entertainment footage, companies specializing in the restoration and distribution of media through stock libraries have created online solutions that are easy to navigate and search and that make it easy to preview content before licensing it. Look for online stock libraries that specialize in the content that you need. For example, Historicfilms.com stores a large inventory of film covering over 80 years of news and industrial film and video. Sekani.com has a large collection of royalty-free footage, as well as traditional footage ranging from animals and wildlife to clips about transportation or medical news. Artbeats.com has a collection of art-related video. You can find on their site background and effects videos that can help you save time creating postproduction segments. Webmovie.com hosts a detailed guide to stock libraries Web sites.

The big advantage of using stock library media is savings. The cost associated with licensing stock library media is much lower than the cost of producing original media. This is a key benefit when you evaluate plans to produce content. For example, to license a 30-second clip about the undersea life of sharks might cost you $1,000 per week, but to send a crew to shoot video of sharks under water and then edit it will cost much more.

The task of every media producer is to find the best way to deliver his or her message properly using the latest tools available and at the same time to avoid running overbudget. When you produce or distribute media content (video or audio), you first determine your objectives and what you need to achieve these goals. Obviously, most readers of this book have a need to process analog or digital media and convert it to streaming media. This need is driven by corporate needs, marketing needs, or plain production needs. To produce original content you must have certain skills not all of us have. (Chapter 3 describes the process of producing original videos.) Not everyone is able to put together a multi-camera package with audio and live video recording. Not everyone can transmit video signal from one location to another. When necessary, we subcontract or outsource our production needs to experts. After you determine the objectives of your production and basic needs to generate video or audio, you must decide whether to outsource or to do the job in house.

The biggest disadvantage of using stock library media is that they tend to be very general so they can be used for many purposes and licensed to many customers. In addition, stock libraries often store media that are outdated. The media are often public domain; content that is in the public domain is not copyrighted because its authors intended to share it with the public. Media in the public domain can be used without restriction, as one piece or as components of other content. (Such media are also called royalty-free media.) The problem with using public domain media is that people have used these media before. When they were used before, the media might have been associated with a message, and when you use these media you might retain a residual echo of this message in your message. Also, the fact that the same footage has already been used in another piece of media takes away from the strong impression you want to make on your audience.

Because producing new content is a challenging and expensive process, most producers rely on a combination of the two, producing original content and also using stock library media. Stock libraries catalogs list video and audio content divided into categories, for example, entertainment, educational, and industrial categories broken down further into subcategories, making it easy for customers to search for their specific interests. Subscribing to a media catalog can save the cost and time of producing original content. News catalogs, for example, are very successful in selling their news reels for other uses. After the news becomes old, the media are stored and licensed again for documentary-style reports or for new news segments dealing with the same topic. But unlike news producers, who tend to use stock footage to complete their assignments, most other content producers prefer to rely on original content that better serves their needs.

Legal Aspects of Content Distribution

In the early days of the Internet, video and other content was a gray area that the legal community had failed to address. Compared to other traditional media, the growth of the Internet was unprecedented. Figure 4–1 compares the time it took 10 million people to adopt various technologies. For example, it took 36 years for 10 million people to use telephones as their main means of communication. It took 20 years for 10 million people to send electronic messages over their fax machines. However, it took only 4 years for 10 million people to embrace the Internet. Unlike other mass media technologies, the Internet introduced numerous benefits. Some we have found and learned to use; others are yet to be discovered. The Internet provides us with instant access to information and

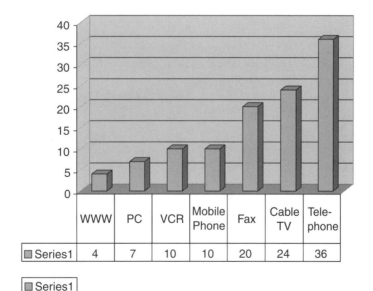

	WWW	PC	VCR	Mobile Phone	Fax	Cable TV	Tele-phone
■ Series1	4	7	10	10	20	24	36

■ Series1

Figure 4–1
Years to reach 10 million customers

with real-time communication tools that appeal to people of all ages, races, and religious backgrounds. If indeed the Internet contains such promising areas of exploitation, why was it not noticed by legislators in its early stages? In the mid-1990s, the legal community along with governments in many countries saw the Internet as a global email system designed to deliver electronic documents or data. The exploitation of the Internet was so fast that most governments had no legal infrastructure in place. A good example of this slow legislation process is the ongoing attempt to establish new Internet tax rules in the United States.

But the most famous legal battle belongs to the music industry. The music industry failed to envision the hidden potential of the Internet as a major distribution channel for music content. In late 1999, legislative task forces across the globe started a process of eliminating the free distribution of media in violation of copyright laws over the Internet. It was essential first to write and pass statutes for online copyright laws, before they could restrict Web entities. In November 1999, during the first MP3 conference in New York City, Chuck D., a musician under contract with an established record label, announced the first online distribution of a commercial CD in MP3 format on the Web. The revolutionary statement was loud and clear. Record executives were shocked to realize the threat to their revenues if the market changed and the artists themselves started distributing their original music online. Many other musicians followed suit. Record companies sent their troops of lawyers to court. After almost one year of fierce public battle in court, the era of free music online came to an end. A U.S. court ordered MP3.com, Napster (*www.napster.com*), and other Web sites distributing illegal media to comply with U.S. copyright laws and pay fines to the record industry or face a complete shutdown. The copyright laws state that any means of media distribution (music, images, or moving images) must be authorized by the copyright owner. Such permission normally involves a financial settlement between the copyright owner and the distributor. In the case of Napster, media were distributed, actually shared for free, by Internet users—an act viewed by the legal system as a clear violation of copyright laws.

The moral of this story is simple. You must have permission to use media for presentation, distribution, or resale. Copyright laws are complicated and rely on over 80 years of experience distributing content through radio, television, and cable channels. In 1998, people posted video and audio content on their Web sites without permission from the content owner. Today, such actions would result in an immediate lawsuit.

Individuals and companies that wish to use media on their Web sites should rely on original content they themselves have produced (and have copyrights on) or license content that grants them permission to distribute the media on different platforms. Marketing or business development managers must include a clause in their contracts related to content distribution, emphasizing that the Internet is a distribution medium like radio, television, or the newspapers. Most lawyers refer to the Internet as electronic distribution. A good resource for possible questions about online copyrights can be found at *www.publaw.com*.

Digital Media Formats

The first step in entering the digital video world is to understand the difference between analog and digital formats. In a digital format, electronic technology generates, stores, and processes data in terms of two states: positive and nonpositive. Positive is expressed or represented by the number 1 and nonpositive by the number 0. Data transmitted or stored with digital technology is expressed as a string of 0s and 1s. Each of these state digits is called a bit; a string of bits that a computer can address as a group is a byte. Prior to digital technology, electronic transmission was limited to analog technology, which transmits data as electronic signals of varying frequencies or amplitudes that are added to carrier waves of a given frequency. Digital media technology is primarily used with new physical communications media, such as satellite and fiber optic transmissions. The digital signal travels across networks and reaches user computers through a dial-up, DSL, or cable modem. The modem converts the digital information in your computer to analog signals for your phone line and converts analog phone signals to digital information for your computer.

Here is an exercise that illustrates how wide the current market selection of digital formats is. Walk into any electronics superstore in your neighborhood and look for the video section. Suddenly, you will be facing a large range of devices that capture and process media in many formats. Ten years ago, we had only 8-mm and VHS cameras. Today, some devices process analog media as Hi-8, 8-mm, super-VHS (S-VHS), S-VHS-compact (S-VHS-C), or VHS-compact (VHS-C); they process digital media as DV, Mini-DV, and digital-8 (D-8). And this does not include professional-grade devices. The variety alone is enough to make your head spin without the sales representative explaining each format's many features. Due to competition among the companies producing digital equipment, consumers as well as professionals are facing constant changes to video formats. What the market desperately needs is a single standard.

In terms of quality, convenience, and ease of use, digital video is the most viable choice for users who want to process video. Digital video provides 500 lines of resolution or more, the highest quality picture you can get. When you work with digital formats, editing and dubbing do not decrease video quality. And you can easily transfer digital video into a computer for editing, especially with increasingly popular IEEE 1394 (FireWire) and USB connections. The two basic digital formats, DV and D-8, both provide 500 lines of resolution, but they have subtle differences. DV is considered the original digital format; all the leading manufacturers offer these camcorders. DV machines record onto a Mini-DV cassette. On average, a DV camcorder costs more than a D-8 model, but the price gap is narrowing.

Most new DV machines come equipped with analog-line inputs to transfer older formats into Mini-DV or use the camcorder as a pass-through device or a recorder. If you need to input a clip of analog video into a computer, you can either run it into the DV camcorder and record it to a Mini-DV cassette or use the camcorder as a video-input device, running the output to a computer. For those who already have lots of analog tapes, this is an attractive feature, solving the backward-and-forward compatibility issue.

As digital formats emerge and storage concepts evolve, entertainment companies and corporations alike are exploring the possibility of converting their existing and future media to a digital archive. Storing media in digital format has both financial benefits and value in preserving media quality. In years to come, new software solutions and long-term planning will reduce the cost of production and improve our ability to retrieve media from the digital archives. Even the U.S. government has recognized the benefits of upgrading to a digital archive system. The federal government is in the process of converting the Library of Congress from analog to digital format. The contents of the entire library will be accessible through a computer interface for both library administrators and the general public.

What is a digital media archive? It is a system for managing, preserving, and providing online access to a wide variety of digital collections, from documents to images to sound and video files. With the exploitation of broadband Internet, individuals can perform search queries in a browser, display the search results, and retrieve media over VPNs in a secure and efficient way.

There are many advantages to using digital media as source for content. For example, an AVI file can be easily transformed into a QuickTime movie, or a QuickTime movie can be transformed into a WAVE file or a MP3 file. Most digital media–processing software provide an Export or Save as option to a variety of digital outputs. As long as the original source is properly captured using the best specification, and with compatible audio and video codecs (acceptable by the software conversion package), the process of resizing and compressing the output media is not difficult anymore. In short, digital media can be easily converted to additional digital formats to accommodate your various needs. Digital media can be packaged by processing it with a DRM. DRM solutions attach to the audio or music file digital bits that permit the playback of the file under certain conditions. The files are programmed to contact the DRM database for license verification. DRM solutions can program files to play only once or only on one PC or mobile device. This new exciting feature grants content owners full control of the distribution of their media over the Internet. It provides streaming media with the ability to stream within pay-per-view models or as part of a tracking system that monitors the life cycles of media files and their ability to play back only in an authorized environment. For more information about DRM solutions, refer to this book's companion Web site, *www.streaminghandbook .com.*

Analog Media Formats

An analog signal is a nominally continuous electrical signal that varies in some direct correlation with another signal impressed on a transducer. For example, an analog signal may vary in frequency, phase, or amplitude in response to changes in physical phenomena, such as sound, light, heat, position, or pressure. An analog signal has a continuous nature rather than a pulsed or discrete nature; it is a continuous electrical signal. Your television and VCR are probably analog video devices. To be stored and manipulated on a computer, analog video must be converted to digital video.

Analog formats have been used for years in professional broadcast facilities and in homes. Analog formats refer to media stored on tape or media stored on tape and transferred at a certain quality (of image and sound) from one tape format to another. From the clumsy heavy-weight tapes used in television stations during the 1950s to the one-half-inch VHS home videorecording systems, analog formats were used to capture and store news, educational, entertainment, and corporate events on tape for decades. Analog-based media were often replicated by connecting two analog machines (two VCRs of the same type or two VCRs of different types) and copying the signal of the source tape to the new tape. Signal loss, or degradation, referred to as generation loss, was always a concern to professionals. The loss started after the raw media was recorded on a high-end camera and stored on broadcast NTSC tape. The media would suffer first-generation loss during the editing process, second-generation loss during the dubbing process (to create copies of the master tape), and third-generation loss during the transfer to other distribution formats (VHS tapes). In the best case scenario, a television program that was recorded on video would be transferred four times before it reached the rental shelves of a video rental store. Film converted to analog tapes suffered larger generation loss because it had to be converted from 35-mm to high-grade video, and then to VHS.

Analog formats consist of audio tapes, old audio reels, and various formats of audio-recorded tapes. On the video front, analog formats include 16-mm and 35-mm film; old VHS, 8-mm, and Beta tapes; and professional formats such as three-quarter U-Matic or Beta SP format. In short, analog formats are all media recorded on tape, media that are not captured in digital format, and media that need to be captured and converted before they can reside on a computer. A digital format is any format that can be played on a computer and has characteristics that computers can modify. Looking at analog and digital media formats this way will allow you to better understand the concept and the advantages of the new media and their distribution over computer networks.

Today, most professionals prefer to create content in a digital environment rather than in an analog one. The reason is that conventional analog video must be converted to digital format (captured and stored as a digital file) before it can be loaded into a computer. This method is often more costly and complex than having a digital-to-digital conversion. Digital-to-digital conversion means that the source media are stored on a computer hard drive (e.g., as MPEG or AVI files), and you need to use a software conversion tool such as Cleaner to convert that media to another digital format. All manufacturers of video equipment today produce professional, semi-professional, and consumer versions of digital video equipment. The same evolution has happened in the audio world.

The analog-to-digital conversion process is slow, expensive, and time-consuming. The reality is that most organizations hesitate to convert their content from analog to digital because they fear that the current digital formats in the market will be soon obsolete. The large video manufacturers are not in agreement about which digital format to use as a standard. MPEG 2 is a good choice, but recent development in MPEG4 and MPEG7 compression makes use of additional data layers in the stream to deliver meta tags, adding interactivity to video presentations. These new exciting components are creating new possibilities for the deployment of the long-awaited features of interactive television.

In the interim, when you are faced with the need to convert some of your content from analog to digital format, the best way to proceed with the task is to first determine your target audience. To convert your source media to streaming files, use an encoding workstation, as described in Chapter 8. First, capture the media and convert them from analog to digital. Try to avoid compressing the captured files. Uncompressed files provide better quality raw media. Analog media is stored at a resolution of 640 × 480 pixels, 30 fps. Audio samples are stored on tape at 48,000-kHz 16-bit stereo. To save space on your hard drive, resize the captured files to 320 × 240 pixels, and your audio to 44,100-kHz 16-bit stereo or to 22,050-kHz 16-bit mono (for voice-only audio). Store the new media files as WAVE files (audio files) or AVI files (video files). When you work on a Windows PC, use Microsoft Video 1 codec with a 75% compression ratio. Cinepack or Intel codecs are not compatible with all streaming software encoders. In addition, note that some capture devices use proprietary codecs that are not installed on every computer. If you use these codecs during any part of your digitization or encoding process, the media may not play back on other computers. Use uncompressed YUV2, YV12, I420, or YVU9 capture format methods to supply your software encoder with the best possible uncompressed digital signal. AVI files recorded with this codecs are large. You will need a workstation that can support files larger then 2 GB. Windows 98, 2000, and XP support files larger than 2 GB in size.

Table 4–1
RAID Configurations

RAID 0	Block striping; fast read/write, but no fault tolerance
RAID 1	Disk mirroring; high-speed read/write; high cost
RAID 0 + 1	Mirroring and disk striping
RAID 3	Block striping; one drive is dedicated to parity; fast read/ slow write
RAID 5	Multiple-BLOCK striping; fast write/slow read; parity distributed across all disks in the array

When the process of digitizing your analog content is complete, transfer the media to another computer. Because you are now dealing with digital files, just copy and paste the file into the proper directory. It is recommended that you store digital media in a safe environment. Computer hard drives are not 100% bulletproof. They tend to lose their integrity and develop bad cluster problems with time. To avoid corruption or loss of your digital media, store important files on a computer with an array of hard disks (Redundant Array of Inexpensive Disks system, or RAID system). RAID systems are used to enhance the reliability of media stored on server systems. There are various RAID system configurations; RAID can be planned as non-RAID, RAID 0, 1, 0 + 1, 3, or 5. Table 4–1 lists some differences among the various RAID configurations.

Summary

- The main advantage of using stock library media is the reduction in the cost of production. The use of footage from stock libraries has its limitations because the material has been used before.

- There are many legal issues involved in the distribution of content over the Web. Become familiar with your state's or country's laws regarding the distribution of audio and video over the Internet.

- Digital media formats are widely used, but the industry is far from agreeing on a digital standard. To preserve quality and simplify the distribution of media, digital storage systems were invented and are becoming very popular.

- Digital media archives provide real-time tools to search for media, retrieve results, and play back samples on user desktop computers across corporate LANs and the public Internet.
- Analog formats are fading away because digital-supported equipment is being used more and more by professional and home users alike.

5

Mobile Networks

A Wireless World

Some people argue that the world was better without computers. For over 30 years computers were used only by governments, corporations, and universities–then we entered the information age. An evolution started and the average consumer was invited to access the World Wide Web with brand-new affordable personal computers. They found that computers have the power to process information in a faster and more efficient way. Today, preschool children learn how to type on keyboards before they learn to write. Computers consist of a brain (a motherboard and peripherals), a display (a large computer screen; the newest are flat monitors), a keyboard (used to give the computer instructions), a modem device (used to connect the computer to the Internet; modems are dial-up, DSL, or cable), and cables (used to connect all the parts together). Computers have become an essential part of our living space, much like a refrigerator or a kitchen stove. Without computers, we would need to use a typewriter to type a letter, we would need to physically visit the public library to search for information, we would depend on mail delivery services and faxes for the transfer of documents and images, and we would rely on phones for other communication. In short, without computers we would face a much more uncomfortable life than the life we have today. Many people do not realize how much the world as we know it depends on computers. We have become so used to working with computers that they have become integrated into our lives.

First there were stand-alone computers that worked independently and processed multiple tasks for us. Then we realized the importance of connecting these individual computers so we could share information. Networks allow us to use the same information and applications in different places and on different machines. Because computers are bulky and heavy, people prefer to replicate their computing capabilities in multiple locations rather than carry them around. Many of you have a desktop computer at work and another one at home. In the past two years, software developers have changed direction and started developing Web-based applications instead of desktop stand-alone computer solutions. As the Internet expands its reach, we will see how all the information we create or search for will be found or delivered through the Web. To increase productivity, many companies today allow access to their internal networks over secure browser interfaces. Employees are encouraged to access their email or exchange files with one another by logging on to their company's secure VPN.

The need to mobilize the workforce has shaped the way computers are designed. Laptops have become standard among students and corporate employees on the move. In 1998, Microsoft and 3COM introduced the Windows CE and Palm operating systems for portable devices. Hundreds of software developers have developed applications supporting the management and delivery of information in various formats from and to these devices. PocketPC and other Palm-based devices can read and write compatible Word documents or Excel spreadsheets. The memory size and the quality of display have been improved significantly to accommodate the growing demand for portability. Devices such as the Palm M series or the Casio PocketPC can store hundreds of contact names, a personal calendar, documents, games, and more on miniature flash cards that hold from 4 to 340 MB of memory.

As the demand for portability flourished, so did ideas for connecting these portable devices to networks to check email, collecting information, and transferring files—that demand creates supply. At the moment, mobile devices can be divided into two groups: voice and data devices. In the near future, we will see more products integrating phone capabilities and mobile computing. Today travelers carry a Palm or PocketPC device in one hand and a cellular phone in the other. Contact lists are duplicated and so are notes and schedules. Many ISPs target business travelers by installing Internet- and fax-enabled phones in airports. As a frequent flyer, I have noticed often these empty booths. Travelers on the run have little time to sit down, open their laptops, and connect them to phone terminals. These Internet stations are more likely to attract bored passengers who are not willing to pay for service.

A mobile wireless solution would be a better investment, preferably a wireless device combining both voice and data. The first companies to introduce this in the United States were Compaq with their iPAQ Bluetooth or Global System for Mobile Communications and General Packet Radio Service (GSM/GPRS) add-on packs and Samsung with its I300 Palm/Cellular phone device. Of these two devices, only Compaq's iPAQ is capable of delivering streaming media (more about iPAQ and other PocketPC devices that stream video can be found in Chapter 11).

How did wireless networks start? Early wireless LAN products were first introduced in the late 1980s. They were primarily created as a cheaper alternative to wiring an entire building. However, today's buildings are constructed with the cabling already installed; it turns out that wiring a building with unshielded twisted-pair cables does not cost that much. So, wireless LANs have not overtaken wired LANs in popularity. However, due to their mobility and accessibility, they have become quite prevalent.

Wireless data technology was driven first by the need to mobilize phones. In 1995, Ericsson initiated a project whose purpose was to develop a general protocol for value-added services on mobile networks. The protocol, called the Intelligent Terminal Transfer protocol (ITTP), handled the communications between a service node, where the service application is implemented, and an intelligent mobile phone. During 1996 and 1997, Unwired Planet, Nokia, and others launched additional value-added services on mobile networks. Unwired Planet introduced Handheld Device Markup Language (HDML) and the Handheld Device Transport Protocol (HDTP). Similar to HTML for the Internet, the new languages were optimized for wireless Internet access from handheld devices. In March 1997, Nokia introduced Smart Messaging, an Internet access service technology specifically for handheld GSM devices. The communication between the mobile user and the server containing Internet information used Short Message Service (SMS) and a markup language called Tagged Text Markup Language (TTML). SMS allows short alphanumeric messages to be sent to and received from mobile telephones. SMS can also be used as a transport for binary payloads and to implement a Wireless Application Protocol (WAP) stack on the top of the Short Message Service center (SMSC). (See the section on the WAP Consortium.) SMS was created as part of the GSM Phase 1 standard. It allows users to directly transmit messages to one another without the use of an operator. There are two types of SMS–Point-to-Point and Point-to-Omnipoint (or cell broadcast), which is used to transmit the same message from the originator device to a list of recipients within a given cell, area, or network. Both messaging options are limited to messages with fewer than 250 characters and are used primary for short, immediate communications.

Wireless local area network (WLAN) technology was adapted from cellular phone technology. Its evolution was driven by gains in superconductor performance. There are four generations of WLAN. The first generation (1G) uses the 902- to 928-MHz band (unlicensed band for Industrial, Scientific, and Medical uses, or ISM), which became increasingly crowded with interference from appliances and industrial machinery. It was originally developed for the military and allowed WLANs to operate at 500 kbps. The second generation (2G) was enabled by further semiconductor advances. It uses the 2.40- to 2.483-GHz band (ISM). This is a frequency called for by the 802.11 standard; microwave ovens use the same frequency and are a major source of interference. 2G uses spread-spectrum techniques, allowing data transfer rates up to 2 MBps. The third generation (3G) uses the 2.4- to 2.483-GHz band (802.11 standard). Cordless telephones have begun to use this band, increasing interference. More sophisticated modulation formats allow 7 MBps throughput. The fourth generation (4G) uses the 5-GHz band (5.2, 5.3, and 5.775 GHz); the 5-GHz band is also called the Unlicensed National Information Infrastructure (U-NII). The U-NII is dedicated solely to high-data-rate communication systems. It uses the 802.11 standard as well and boasts data transfer rates of 10 MBps and higher. The 5-GHz band has a 350-MHz bandwidth (compared to a 83-MHz bandwidth at 2.4 GHz and a 26-MHz bandwidth at 900 MHz). Table 5–1 lists the technical details of the four WLAN generations

1G WLANs are analog-based systems that handle only analog 3-kHz voice transmission. 2G WLANs focus on digitization; many digital

Table 5–1
WLAN Generations

Name	Type/ frequency	Transmission rates	Bandwidth
1G	Analog/RF	902–928 MHz	500 Bps
2G	Digital/RF	2.4–2.483 GHz	2 MBps
3G	Digital/IP	2.4–2.483 GHz	7 MBps
4G	Digital/IP	5 GHz	10 MBps

systems are in place today around the world, transmitting voice and data at rates of 8–14.4 kbps. These systems are based on GSM, time division multiple access (TDMA), and code division multiple access (CDMA) standards.

3G WLANs are IP and multimedia-services networks that provide customers with far more than just narrowband voice services. They will satisfy the demand for more sophisticated wideband and broadband services requiring higher speed data transport. 3G systems will include not only wideband multimedia mobile networks, but also broadband fixed wireless access systems.

Fixed wireless systems have a long history. Point-to-point microwave connections have long been used for voice and data communications, generally in backhaul networks operated by phone companies, cable television companies, paging companies, and government agencies. They use frequencies that range from 1 to 40 GHz. The technology has continued to advance, allowing higher frequencies and thus smaller antennas to be used, resulting in lower costs and easier-to-deploy systems for private use and for a new generation of carriers that will use wireless access as their last mile of communication. The terms "wireless broadband" and "broadband wireless" are not used consistently, but generally both apply to carrier-based services in which multiple data streams are multiplexed onto a single radio carrier signal. Some vendors also use these terms to refer to privately deployed networks. Both types of wireless systems provide cost-effective ways to deliver high performance and high-bit-rate services. Broadband fixed wireless technology can support services requiring peak bandwidths of greater than 10 Mbps. And next-generation mobile systems will provide a wide range of bandwidths: 144 kbps for full mobility while driving or flying, 384 kbps for pedestrian traffic, and up to 2 Mbps inside buildings. At these rates, you can have videoconferencing capabilities while on the move.

How Do Wireless Networks Work?

WLANs are one more step toward achieving the full potential of computers and networks. They can provide immediate access to programs and information without having to connect a cable between computers and the network. WLANs use radio links or infrared light to replace the cables in a traditional wired LAN. Once a device is an approved member of the network, there is no need to install and configure a cable connection to exchange data between it and the network. Wireless links can be set up quickly and easily (especially on a laptop or other portable computer). WLANs extend the benefits of traditional wired networks to places where physical cable connectivity is difficult or impossible and are thus the preferred approach in many situations. For example, a wireless network may be the best way to meet the needs of the following users:

- People who carry their portable computers to more than one location within an office or campus, including doctors who want to monitor patient data or search centralized records while making hospital visits, factory workers who need access to product specifications and other documents, and business people who attend meetings outside their offices
- Businesses that do not want to spend a lot of money on hardwired networking
- Businesses that want to add users to their networks quickly in locations where network cables do not exist.
- Managers who want to provide temporary service to a large number of potential users
- Network managers who want to extend a common network between two or more buildings without digging trenches or running overhead cables
- Home computer users who want to extend their Internet connections beyond a single location without cutting holes in their walls and ceilings

In other words, WLANs can often extend an existing LAN or create a new one more quickly and at lower cost than a conventional wired Ethernet.

WLAN hardware costs more than comparable wired equipment, but prices are dropping fast. The real cost of installing a WLAN is very close to (or possibly even less than) the wired alternative because it is not necessary to pay for the labor and materials involved in laying a dedicated cable to every network location. WLANs, once installed and configured, are easy to maintain. At the same time, a WLAN is not the best solution to every networking problem. Many IT professionals have been trained and understand perfectly how to install and maintain conventional LANs and WANs. With the growing demand for WLANs, IT professionals need to become familiar with their advantages ad disadvantages. The current generation of WLANs is still significantly slower than a 100-MBps Ethernet, and interference from other services that use the same radio bandwidth (e.g., the short-range Bluetooth data exchange standard) can drop data-transfer speeds significantly.

In many situations a hybrid network that includes both wired and wireless elements may be the best approach—computers are connected in fixed locations, peripheral equipment such as printers with cables are added, and wireless links are used to extend the network to portable devices. A hybrid network offers the best economy, speed, and the simplicity of wired LANs where cables exist, and it adds the benefits of fast setup, mobility, and the convenience of wireless access for users with portable equipment.

The software that interfaces between the wireless network interface card (NIC) and the computer can be either part of the operating system itself or separate files that are loaded onto the computer. NICs are hardware devices that connect desktops, laptops, and handheld devices to networks; they use traditional Ethernet cables to connect to the networks. With recent improvements in wireless connectivity, NICs have been introduced that support wireless antennas acting as receivers connecting with the network transmitter and allow the exchange of data at rates up to 11 MBps. Beginning with Microsoft Windows XP, all Microsoft desktop operating systems will recognize a wireless NIC without the need for external software drivers. The previous versions of Windows (e.g., Windows 95, 98, ME, NT, and 2000) require external drivers. Incorporating drivers into the operating system makes installation easier and also provides additional features such as the ability to connect automatically to different WLANs as the user roams instead of having to manually configure the settings. Some wireless NIC vendors include software drivers for other operating systems such as DOS, Windows 3.x, and Linux. In the future, operating systems for PDAs are expected to include this interface. Microsoft's PocketPC 2002 does not recognize a wireless NIC and requires the external drivers.

From a user's point of view, there's not much difference between working on a computer connected to a network through a wireless link and one that uses a conventional Ethernet cable; both must be configured in order to communicate with the network. Either way, the computer uses the network to exchange data with another computer through the network interface.

WLAN Protocols

It is imperative to separate the infrastructure and concepts used for mobile phones from those used for mobile computing. In the near future, both networks (voice and data) will merge and become one single network. Some vendors are using 2G devices to accomplish this goal. In the section on the WAP consortium I explain how voice and data are delivered to cellular phones; Chapters 5 and 11 cover the infrastructure and applications that stream video to portable devices. At the present time, only PDAs accept streaming video as an official product. Cellular phones are expected to follow suit within 1–2 years in Asia and Europe and within a few more years in North America.

Several sets of standards have emerged to define WLAN operations. The most popular protocols among technology WLAN vendors are the IEEE 802.11b specification and the Wireless Ethernet Compatibility Alliance (WECA) WiFi standard (short for Wireless Fidelity). All WLAN equipment that meets the 802.11b specifications, even parts from different suppliers, operates together. It should be possible to use any manufacturer's hardware as long as that hardware carries a WiFi certification (but it is still a lot easier to set up a network when all the nodes are from the same manufacturer). Several competing wireless network standards also exist (see Table 5–2). The most notable is HomeRF, but the 802.11b or WiFi standard seems most likely to become the accepted wireless Ethernet standard. 802.11b data uses a radio technology called Direct-Sequence Spread-Spectrum (DSSS) in the frequency range between 2.4 GHz and 2.483 GHz. Within this range, the United States Federal Communications Commission (FCC) has specified 11 overlapping channels. The number of channels is different in other countries. To compare, AM broadcast radio operates at frequencies near 1 MHz, FM broadcast stations operate near 100 MHz, and cellular telephones use frequencies near 850 MHz. DSSS transmits a signal over a relatively wide-frequency bandwidth in order to reduce the amount of potential interference and thereby increase the likelihood that it will be received accurately. It also allows a large number of signals to share the same set of frequencies.

With a multitude of possible solutions, there was a substantial risk that the market would be overwhelmed and be pulled in many directions, resulting in the slow deployment of mobile phones. In June 1997, the three big companies, joined by Motorola, began the creation of a standard for advanced services within the wireless domain. In December 1997, the WAP Forum was officially created.

Table 5–2
WLAN Standards

Standard	Bandwidth	Data rate	Modulation	Vendors' support	Pros/cons
802.11b	2,400–2,484	1–11 MBps	DSSSS FHSS CSMA	3	Pros: cheap Cons: not robust to interference in 2.4 GHz band
HomeRF	2,400–2,484	1–2 MBps	FHSS CSMA	6	Pros: cheap, support QoS Cons: low rate may lose to 802.11b
Wi-LAN	2,400–2,484	30 MBps	DSSS OFDM CSMA	3	Pros: 25 channels at 30 MBps Cons: proprietary
Home Free	2,400–2,484	1 MBps	FHSS CSMA	81	Pros: popular Cons: low data rate
802.11a	5.15–5.87, 5.15–5.87	6–64 MBps	OFDM FDMA CSMA	23	Pros: high data rate Cons: security issues, behind 802.11b
HiperLAN 1	5.15–5.87	23.5 MBps	GMSK FDMA HLAN	9	Pros: popular in Europe Cons: lost battle to 802.11b
HiperLAN2	5.15–5.87	6–54 MBps	OFDM FDMA TDMA	8	Pros: identical to 802.11a, optimized for real-time applications Cons: need time to market

The WAP Consortium

The WAP Forum is an industry association comprising over 500 members that is developing a world standard for wireless information and telephone services on digital mobile phones and other wireless terminals. The primary goal of the WAP Forum is to bring together companies from all areas of the wireless industry chain to ensure product compatibility and the growth of the wireless market.

The members of the WAP Forum represent over 90% of the global handset market, carriers with more than 100 million subscribers, leading infrastructure providers, software developers, and other organizations providing solutions to the wireless industry. A complete list of members is available at *www.wapforum.org/who/members.htm*. WAP technology was created to enable fast easy delivery of relevant information and services to mobile users. WAP is designed to work with most wireless networks. It is a communications protocol and application environment. It can be built on any operating system including PalmOS, EPOC, Windows CE, FLEXOS, OS/9, and JavaOS. It provides service interoperability even among different device families.

Handheld digital wireless devices include mobile phones, pagers, two-way radios, Smartphones, and communicators. WAP technology extends this to include the network itself, by enabling access to the Internet but also redesigning almost every protocol needed to move data across the wireless part of the network. Some WAP critics oppose WAP because it does not offer direct access to the Internet but links the phone to a WAP gateway that negotiates connections between the phone and the rest of the Internet. The data that passes between the phone and this WAP gateway is translated from standard Internet protocols to the W* protocol, in which HTML becomes Wireless Markup Language (WML), TCP becomes Wireless Transfer Protocol (WTP), and so on (see Figure 5–1). The names imply that the W* world is simply a wireless Internet, but in fact the WAP Forum has not only renamed but also redesigned the core of these protocols. WML, for example, is not in fact a markup language but a programming language and therefore much more difficult for the average content creator to use. These redesigns enable WAP to do error checking and to be compatible with different kinds of voice and data networks. The very same concept was used in the founding principles of the Internet itself, principles that have proven to be extremely flexible for more than 30 years. Critics want the principles of the Internet to apply to the wireless world. They claim that the redesign of the protocols allows the WAP consortium to change the functions of delivery and display so that the choice of the browser is locked in by the phone manufacturer, forcing the consumer to adopt a new phone every time a functional upgrade is released. Does this sounds familiar? How many times have you replaced your old phone in the past three years?

No matter what the technical arguments for WAP are, its effect is to give the phone companies control over the tools and means for access-

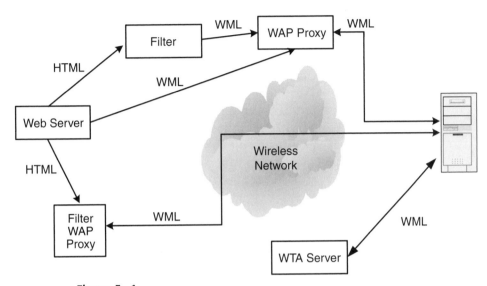

Figure 5–1
How WAP technology works

ing voice and data. The WAP consortium has developed its technology in such a way that no third party is able to reach the users of a wireless device without going through an interface that one of its member companies controls and generates revenue from. As the Internet evolves and expands to other devices beyond the computer, we will see more examples of this approach. Technology is driven by business models; although controversial, the pure existence of the Internet depends on users paying for service. Critics of the WAP consortium and of the monetization of the Internet agree that users should pay for service. The costs of making Internet resources available to the public are huge and I agree that the costs should be paid by those who use the service. However, the WAP consortium and many other similar groups are attempting to redefine Internet-related services that are now accessible for free, and I oppose these groups in their attempts to put a price tag on such services. A well-known example of this kind of controversy is the debate among ISPs in 1997, when the question of how to bill for Internet connectivity (home or office dial-up) arose. Some ISPs wanted to charge for use (a per hour or per data-transfer fee), whereas others wanted to charge a flat fee. Because demand for service defines market standards, ISPs widely adopted only one of these—today, at least in the United States, you pay a flat fee for unlimited access to the Internet (via dial-up, DSL, or cable modem). Any additional service, such as Web connectivity when you are out of the country or dialing a toll-free number, is charged separately. Such business models make sense. Phone companies are slowly adapting to market demand and today offer free WAP service and one-way email. For an additional fee, users can expand their browsing capabilities to additional sites and send email from their phone. As competition grows, consumers will benefit. In the near future, Web browsing and phone email will become free commodities, the very same way caller ID and call forwarding have become an integrated part of digital wireless calling plans.

What Is iMode?

During 1997–2000, WAP became the standard for wireless communications all over the world. Providing information through mobile devices became the latest hype. Based on this idea, in February 1999 NTT DoCoMo, Japan's leading cellular phone operator, launched a service called iMode, which enabled users to use their mobile phones to access the Web and send email. Before this, the number of Internet users in Japan had been one of the smallest in the world. A few months after iMode services began, there were only approximately 1 million users who had subscribed to iMode. But a year after that, the number of iMode subscribers had increased to approximately 4 million users and had increased to over 20 million users by the end of 2000. Since then, the number has climbed rapidly. Today, Japan has become one of the leading countries in wireless data service, and DoCoMo has become the leading company by market value and a world-class wireless giant.

Unlike WAP, which uses proprietary technology and protocols to reach the Web, iMode uses a traditional packet-switched network, allowing users continuous access to the Internet via HTML. iMode has attracted global attention because of its simplicity and quality of service.

iMode mobile phones have become an essential accessory in Japan, offering a way for people to communicate via email, do transactions over the Internet, or play games. iMode devices have connected users to the Web at a speed of 9.6 kbps, which no other technology has done.

Table 5–3 compares the iMode and WAP services. Both services tend to transmit at a low rate; at such low-speed rates it is not possible to

Table 5-3
Comparison of WAP and iMode

Function	iMode	WAP
User experience	Always on	Request sent to server and user needs to wait for response
Network	Packet switched network	Circuit switched network
Language	C-HTML	WML (proprietary)
Users charge by	Bandwidth	Monthly plan, time spent online
Content	Responsibility of content providers, not operator	Responsibility of operator (Telco offering WAP services)
Target markets	Japan, Asia, North America (agreements with AT&T and Verizon Wireless)	Asia, Europe, Americas
Applications used with	Consumer (shopping, travel, lodging, games)	Business (banking, news, shopping)

download a full-motion video, but it is possible to download small images at a speed of 2 fps. For sending and receiving email, messages are limited to 250 characters per message. Because it uses a packet-switched network, iMode allows continuous access to the Internet, eliminating the need to establish a new connection and wait for information to download. iMode users are always connected as long as they can receive a signal. At this time, users are charged according to the amount of data being transferred and not by the amount of time they spent connected to the Internet. In the future, the model might change as demand grows and competing services are offered.

Most iMode sites are text with few graphics. They can be accessed using the navigator button on the mobile phone. iMode sites can be divided into two major groups: the official iMode sites and the unofficial sites. Official iMode sites are listed by DoCoMo and appear automatically on the menu of iMode handsets. The unofficial sites are created by other content providers without being listed on DoCoMo, but can be reached by typing the URL into the device. Because iMode is available only in Japan, most sites are in the Japanese language. iMode facilitates both entertainment and business functions. With iMode-enabled devices, users can do business over a mobile phone using secure wireless transactions, as well as:

- Send and receive email
- Access information on the Internet directly
- Check train or airline schedules and reserve tickets
- Purchase or make reservations through secure sites
- Administer personal bank accounts

iMode's sites are created using a markup language called compact HTML (C-HTML). C-HTML is based on HTML 2.0, 3.2, and 4.0 speci-

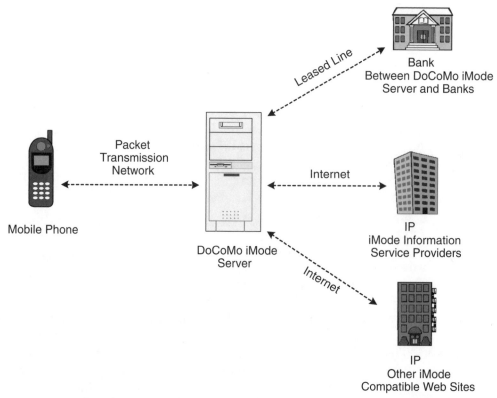

Figure 5–2
How iMode technology works

fications. However, some traditional HTML features are not available in C-HTML. These include Joint Photographic Experts Group (JPEG) images, tables and image maps, frames, and background images. Because C-HTML is a version of HTML, content providers with basic experience in HTML can create their own iMode-compatible sites.

iMode architecture uses a gateway server that is used to transfer information from iMode content providers to iMode-enabled handsets. To access information, users generate a request through the iMode server gateway (see Figure 5–2). After processing the incoming signal, the server passes the request to the appropriate content provider through the Internet. A replay from the site is then forwarded back to the end-user via the iMode server gateway.

WAP versus iMode

WAP and iMode architectures differ in their concepts and approaches. WAP has become the standard for wireless protocol in the world, but at the same time many of its users and developers criticize its functionality. There is a risk that WAP technology will not be used in future portable devices. Why are the expectations from WAP so high, and why at the same time are many developers stepping away from it?

- With all the excitement surrounding the release of WAP, people expect WAP to be as sophisticated as the Internet. They want their phones to provide them with an experience similar to that provided by their desktop computers. But, as mentioned early on, WAP and iMode devices at this stage are capable of processing text and limited images only.

- People who are on the move expect the device to provide fast and reliable information. They want to see stock quotes in real time, read weather reports, and conduct bank transactions. None of these services can perform well on a tiny display device that requires about 15–20 seconds to switch from one text page to the next. However, iMode-related services solve these problems by providing real-time connections to iMode-supported Web sites through the mobile device's built-in browser.

These are the major reasons why WAP has been criticized. In the beginning, when it was first released, WAP services targeted mostly the business community. Since then, the cost of WAP phones and services has dropped significantly, making the service available to the average consumer.

We can further compare the two similar new mobile Web phone applications now available to the consumer (and not only to the business executives), iMode devices in Japan and WAP-enabled devices in North America. iMode has become a standard for wireless communications in Japan because:

- Traditional Telco infrastructure did not exist there. There was a strong need to provide consumers with a device to connect to the Internet (which the rest of the world already had by 1999). Japan had had one of the lowest percentages of users accessing the Internet because the high cost of connectivity drove consumers away. Combining cellular phone connectivity with Internet access was a smart idea that supported a strong need at the right time.

- iMode handsets are easy to use. Each handset is equipped a with navigator button to browse the Internet. Just by clicking the menu button, the user can see the requested site on the screen. iMode sites can be accessed by clicking a few buttons on the handsets rather than by typing out the Web address.

- iMode is cheap. A monthly access fee only costs approximately $3.00 per subscriber. Receiving or sending a 128-bit data package costs only approximately 4 cents. Checking a bank balance, weather forecast, or train schedule costs only approximately 10 cents per transaction.

- iMode has more content available, although at a slower speed. One of iMode's competitors, EZ, uses WAP with a transfer rate of 64 bps, but the number of information providers for WAP is limited to only approximately 500 sites; iMode, with a 9.6-kbps transfer rate, has more than 30,000 information providers available to browse.

The biggest difference between WAP and iMode is the business model behind the technology. WAP enables providers (vendors using WAP technology) to facilitate a fee-based Web-access services. Users need to purchase plans that categorize their privileges to access email and the Internet. Service providers using WAP technology can restrict what users can see. iMode is a service users get for free (it is built into mobile devices), but they pay for its use and for bandwidth (iMode devices can access any Web site supporting C-HTML). Other technical differences between the two are listed in Table 5–3:

NTT DoCoMo is using iMode to introduce their vision of how future 3G mobile services will look. 3G technology is capable of providing higher speed communication and videoconferencing, online gaming through mobile phones, and other activities that need these higher speeds. One of the reasons why the company is trying to transform the current network into a 3G network is because of the rapid growth of iMode subscribers.

Over the past decade, mobile communications technology has made giant steps, moving rapidly from 1G analog voice-only communications to 2G digital voice and data communications. Now, with the arrival of NTT DoCoMo's Freedom of Multimedia Access (FOMA) service in Japan, the world has a glimpse of a revolutionary 3G mobile communications platform. This advanced new service provides voice transmission quality over fixed-line communications, has minimal interference or noise, and supports diverse multimedia content.

Based on the Code Division Multiple Access (CDMA) system, which complies with wideband CDMA (W-CDMA; an international standard for 3G mobile communications), FOMA is fueling the dramatic evolution of iMode and other Web-connection services. It supports full-motion video image transmission, music and game distribution, and other high-speed large-capacity data communications. FOMA brings unprecedented convenience and limitless possibilities to business and to personal lives. The question is only how soon the product will spread from Japan to the rest of the world.

Readers who are interested in more information about wireless protocols and networks should read *The Essential Guide to Wireless Communication Applications* by Andy Dornan. Dornan covers the latest developments, from the wireless Web Bluetooth to WAP to 3G, and beyond.

Streaming over Wireless Networks

Streaming video over 3G networks in North America is far from a reality. According to an FCC report released in summer 2001, it could take many years and cost billions of dollars to build a network for 3G mobile wireless data in the United States. Much of the frequency spectrum that is needed for commercial 3G operators is currently held by the Department of Defense, which, according to the report, cannot fully release these frequencies before the year 2017 and in a few cases 2030. Other parts of the spectrum are held by operators of instructional television stations and multipoint-distribution services, who may have to spend as much as $19 billion over 10 years to move to other frequencies. Another $10 to $30 billion would have to be spent to relocate other services from the bands that would be taken over by companies leaving the 3G spectrum, according to the FCC report.

According to the FCC report, it might be possible for 3G operators to share the same frequencies, from 2,500 to 2,690 MHz, as the instructional television and multipoint operators in some areas. But a nationwide plan may be nearly impossible because of significant problems of extensive interference in many geographical areas, especially where the frequencies are already in extensive use.

In the near future, fast wireless connections will become as standard as dial tones, and people will use high-speed wireless connections wherever they go. The dotcom collapse validated the way Web companies do business today and made them focus more on the financial side than the creative side of business. Dotcom companies that have consolidated or changed business focus will rise and shine with their new product offerings. The Internet cannot die—it is an essential commodity in our lives. So are wireless connections. They are efficient and essential to the way we live and work. Although they are not yet a part of our lives, in the end they will be.

What does this entire overview means to you, the IT professional? It means that you can safely ignore 3G technologies for the next three years and focus on other important initiatives, for example, the deployment of 802.11b-enabled networks to deliver high-speed wireless connectivity to portable devices. In this way, you will be able to stream video content to handheld devices that support the 802.11b protocol. Such devices are powered by Windows operating systems that are well known and deployed in enterprises. The latest addition to the family is the PocketPC 2002. This operating system was released by Microsoft at the end of 2002, and it includes full support for WLAN connectivity over data-distribution devices supported by the 802.11b protocol. PocketPC 2002 includes the Windows Media 8.0 player, which can now receive live streaming feed with the help of a wired or wireless connection. In March 2002, RealNetworks released RealOne Player for PocketPC devices and Nokia mobile phones. The player uses Real Time Streaming Protocol (RTSP) to deliver live video on wireless networks. Real Media files can be also downloaded for playback as media-on-demand.

In the public sector, consumers will need to wait for networks to mature the way they have in Europe and Asia. With NTT DoCoMo's plans to deploy an AT&T 3G wireless network in approximately three years, consumers can rest assured that they will be offered the service once it becomes available.

Wireless Service Providers

For a realistic look at 3G, recall Metricom's Ricochet and OmniSky wireless service for mobile devices. Both companies had a great vision, but they failed to attract enough subscribers. Metricom had a decade of wireless connectivity experience, a system that worked and that already had millions of potential subscribers with enough bandwidth to be extremely useful, a patented network system, and no visible competitors in the field. However, Metricom lost hundreds of millions of dollars and counted merely 45,000 subscribers by August 2001. With no cash in the bank, the company filed for bankruptcy, shut down its $1 billion high-speed wireless network, and sold it to Aerie Networks (a Denver-based broadband provider) for $8.25 million.

At the time of writing this book, I can count on one hand the number of wireless service providers that support WLAN services to portable devices. Wall Street experienced a major shake-up between summer 1999 and spring 2000 when the technology sector struggled against a weak economy and a loss of consumer confidence. Companies' layoffs reached rates of 5–20%. Large and small corporations consolidated their businesses or changed direction to stay afloat. Many ISPs filed bankruptcy, among them companies providing wireless connectivity. Ricochet was the leading wireless ISP. Ricochet closed its doors in summer 2001, and OmniSky faced financial trouble with its falling stock prices. Both companies offered wireless connection services to customers who wanted to be always connected. Connectivity to the network was established by Personal Computer Memory Card International Association (PCMCIA) cards inserted in laptops or handheld devices. It was hard to name a reliable service provider that we could count on for the next 12 months. Our best bet was to use AT&T or Verizon Wireless services with limited coverage, as the two companies started expanding their wireless business to fill the market void left behind by Ricochet.

The story of Ricochet will be told for many years in business and technology classrooms. Metricom (which owned Ricochet) was founded in 1985 and had built a network that provided wireless Internet access in major North American cities at speeds of 128 kbps. Ricochet had a small but loyal number of followers, with many raving about its wireless technology. The service, which cost approximately $75 per month, was a technological marvel but too expensive to attract anyone other than early adopters and tech-savvy business people. Ricochet launched an expensive marketing campaign to try to attract more customers. The campaign lasted a few months and was followed by Metricom's filing for bankruptcy after failing to secure enough subscribers or cash to keep it going through summer 2001. Court records outline that it left a debt of nearly $1 billion and that WorldCom, Metricom's largest creditor, claimed a debt of over $355 million.

A few months later, Metricom (which had been valued in its peak times at $1 billion) was sold to Aerie Networks for $8.25 million, a Denver-based broadband provider. Aerie indicated at the time of purchase that it intended to restore some portions of the Ricochet network, perhaps in its home state of Colorado and in California. Under the deal, Aerie received Metricom's assets, except for approximately $134 million that the company has in the bank, which was dedicated to creditors.

Another service provider that failed to survive was MobileStar, which had provided wireless service for Starbucks coffee and dozens of hotels. It shut down before it could receive a fresh cash infusion from VoiceStream Wireless and OmniSky.

OmniSky itself reported financial troubles and announced it was laying off 100 people as part of an effort to cut $20 million from its budget. The cutback came a month after the company had reported second-quarter revenues of $5.4 million, or a loss of 38 cents per share. In September 2001, the company paired with AOL to offer OmniSky for AOL, which gave AOL members access to their email and instant messages. But analysts from various firms, including Lehman Brothers, have said the deal failed to attract enough subscribers to lift OmniSky's fortunes. At the time of writing this book, OmniSky's future was unclear and reflected the ongoing shakeout in the wireless provider market.

The industry has recognized the opportunities presented by the next generation of networks and has already invested heavily in licenses and infrastructure for wireless data services. Carriers are faced with the task of marketing these services and encouraging users to migrate to high-speed data networks. If they succeed, a surge in subscribers is expected as users recognize the benefits of faster data speeds, new applications, and lower use costs, opening up further opportunities in the wireless arena. Subscribers to mobile Internet services will vary significantly, specifically in their choice of access device–Smartphone, PDA, or laptop–which will largely influence their patterns of use; consumers and corporate users will use different devices because they will have different needs.

Summary

- Desktop computers are being replaced by mobile devices that can store essential information on the move.

- WLANs help users access information without the need to connect actual cables to their devices.

- WLANs provide value-added services to traditionally voice-only devices. This includes email capabilities, instant messaging, and video.

- Once deployed, 3G wireless networks will introduce new multimedia capabilities to mobile devices.

- Streaming over a WLAN is possible by adopting 802.11b standards. WLAN infrastructures support Ethernet-based (wired or wireless) connectivity between portable devices and other computers on the network thus enabling transmission of streaming media using TCP/IP.

Part II

ENCODING AND STREAMING VIDEO

6

Video Capture

The Art of Compression

When video is converted from analog to digital, each frame is broken up into hundreds of pixels. Each pixel is represented by one or more bytes that represent the color of that small area of the image. Each video conversion requires computer memory and computation time. The higher the quality of video, the greater the number of frames per second; and the larger the image size, the greater the number of pixels that must be converted in a given period of time. For example, when you are capturing video at 30 fps, the computer must not only be capable of handling many pixel conversions, it must also perform many conversions very quickly in order to keep up with the continuous stream of video. The computer must also be able to handle the audio conversion simultaneously and to synchronize this audio signal with the video signal as it captures and stores it on the hard drive.

Compression techniques are either lossy or lossless. Lossless compression methods keep all the information from the original source and cannot be reversed. Lossy compression methods change the original data, so it can be reversed. Lossless compression techniques reproduce the highest compressed samples of media, but only lossy methods are capable of compressing audio and video enough so it has the low bit rate necessary to stream media files on the Internet. Neither one is better than the other; each has its uses. In fact, lossless and lossy techniques are often used together to obtain the highest compression ratios. Table 6–1 lists how much compression is necessary in order to transmit NTSC, HDTV, and film-quality video over lines ranging from a 28-kbps dial-up modem all the way to a fiber optic connection.

Table 6–1
Required Compression Ratio for Broadcast Quality Video

Channel	Bit rate	NTSC TV 168 Mb/s	HDTV 933 Mb/s	Film quality 2300 Mb/s
28K modem	28 kbps	5,600:1	31,000:1	76,000:1
56K modem	56 kbps	3,000:1	17,000:1	41,000:1
ISDN, LAN	64–144 kbps	1,166:1	6,400:1	16,000:1
T-1, DSL	1.5 Mbps	112:1	622:1	1,500:1
Ethernet	10 Mbps	17:1	93:1	230:1
T-3	42 Mbps	4:1	22:1	54:1
Fiber optic	200 Mbps	1:1	5:1	11:1

To start compressing media after reading this book, you do not need to become an expert in compression techniques. All you have to do is learn how to make good choices about hardware and software to maximize the production of high-quality compressed videos. The art of compression is a combination of knowledge and experience. The secret is to experiment all the time; rules are made to be broken. It is also important to know the technical limitations of hardware and software on your encoding workstation.

Compression Tools—Hardware

To select a system to compress video from analog or digital to streaming format, first determine the video source, the required capture format, and the end target for your compressed media. There are different types of media sources, varying by video or audio quality. Capturing media for broadcast or industrial playback is different from capturing media for DVD or television playback or from capturing video for webcast. There are many types of capture cards available. To simplify, we concentrate here on hardware supporting streaming video as the end application. When choosing a capture card, consider the following questions:

- Are you going to use the media for live encoding or for video on demand?
- What type of input source will you use (VCR, camera, or audio-visual source)?

- Do you plan to use the card as an output device? If the answer is yes, find a capture card that supports both a video-audio output format that fits your needs and one or more of the capture formats as listed in Table 6–3 (later in the chapter).

Media compression converts analog or digital video to a desktop format that can be used later as source media for encoding streaming video. The first step in capturing media is to digitize the source content–that is, to convert it from analog to digital. The source content can be in the form of live broadcast or it can be on tape. Before capturing video, determine the resolution of your target media. Uncompressed higher resolution video equals higher image quality, but results in larger files and in additional system resources that are required to render files. The formulas for finding the data rate for uncompressed content are:

Video resolution $\times$ Video frame rate $=$ Total number of pixels per second

Total number of pixels per second $\times$ Number of bytes per pixel $=$ Number of bytes per second

The frame resolution and the number of frames per second are the factors that determine the bit rate. There are two ways to reduce the bit rate (file size). One is to reduce the resolution (size and frames per second); the other is to use codecs that provide compression during the capture process. Some capture cards provide a list of codecs such as RGB, YUV2, or YUV-9. The industry commonly uses two implementations in digital video: Common Interchange Format (CIF) and Quarter Common Interchange Format (QCIF). CIF provides the video signal at half of the available screen, whereas QCIF uses a quarter of the screen. Table 6–2 provides an overview of video resolution versus bit size.

Table 6–2
Video Resolution versus Quality

Resolution (pixels)	Frame Rate	Name	Quality	Bit rate (Mbps)
720 × 480	30	Digital Original	DVD	160
640 × 480	30	Full Screen	Broadcast	128
320 × 240	30	CIF	VHS	32
160 × 120	15	QCIF	Web Video	4

It is very clear that even the small window size of the QCIF uncompressed video format requires 4 Mbps of bandwidth that most Internet users do not have. If you are going to provide video from a Web site, you will need to compress your media.

For readers who need to compress audio, the very same rules apply. Audio often starts out in an analog format, and like video must be converted to digital format before being encoded to a streaming audio format. To digitize audio, or sample audio, the rate must be equal to or greater than twice the highest frequency component of the analog signal. The human ear can hear sound up to a frequency of 20 kHz. To accurately capture digital audio, the sampling rate must be at least 40,000 times per second (40 kHz). Most capture cards support a 44,100 (CD quality) or 48,000 frequency at 16-bit stereo. If you have enough hard-disk space on your workstation, it is recommended that you capture audio at the highest rate possible. Later on, while encoding, you will decrease the audio sample rate to match the appropriate streaming file size and modem speed.

When capturing audio, make sure the input level is as high as possible without distortion. If you use an external mixer such as the Mackie 1202-VLZ, you have more flexibility in controlling the audio levels before outputting to the encoder workstation. If you import the audio source using your system sound card or your capture card input sound jacks, use the workstation or the capturing program to adjust the line or microphone input sliders so that the level remains in the green area (it can sometimes touch the yellow area, but it should rarely go into the red).

Capture Card Comparison

The Macintosh operating systems were designed to provide tools for two groups of users: the "I do not care how it works, but I want to see results now" people, who want to use computers but are discouraged by the PC graphic interface, and the creative community of graphic designers and nonlinear video editors who need faster processing and higher resolution displays. Macintosh computers were widely adopted by the U.S. educational system. These systems were cheaper and much simpler to operate. For a long time, PCs were considered to be business tools. The market changed a few years ago when Microsoft launched its new campaign calling for the use of PCs to "live, work, and play." The rest is history. The term "telecommuter" was born, PCs became faster and easier to operate, and the world saw the birth of the Internet and all types of paper transactions became electronic. How does all this relate to capture cards? The answer is that technology shapes social events, which in turn shape technology. Before the digital revolution, traditional vendors such as AVID, Sony, and C-Cube designed high-end capture and editing systems for the broadcast community. With the beginning of the PC revolution, a handful of startup companies such as Nogatech, Winnov, and Viewcast introduced a low-cost solution for capturing non-broadcast-quality video to computers. Their target customers did not have $100,000 high-end workstations but low-budget home PCs. In the mid-1990s, Pentium 200-MHz computers with 64 MB of RAM and a Windows 95 operating system were capable of capturing QCIF video in 15 fps. The manufacture cost was low and, therefore, the cost of the product decreased. A redefinition of who would be using digital media products in the next 10 years created a shift in the development of hardware and software for video processing, a noticeable change that created a new industry—prosumer digital video. Now, not only do wedding videographers use the technology, but multimedia production houses use it as well to lower the cost of equipment. A massive migration from high-end production hardware to low-end but just-as-effective production tools started. Prosumer digital video was successful thanks to new software compression tools that replaced the more expensive hardware solutions.

With the development of faster CPUs and a significant drop in the cost of RAM, PC users can, like their fellow Macintosh users, experience new multimedia applications. Software developers for the PC environment made good use of ActiveX and DirectX controls, resulting in powerful games and applications that were able finally to compete with the legacy of the well-respected Macintosh operating system. Microsoft's and Apple's new operating systems, Windows XP and Macintosh O/S X, are getting closer. These powerful systems now perform better than ever, and the real beneficiaries of the computer wars are the end consumers.

To select a proper capture card for your needs, review Table 6–3. Capture cards are described by their operating system. Note that Windows 95, 98, ME, 2000, and XP are compatible with peripheral-component-interconnect- (PCI-) and USB-based capture devices. These operating systems can operate FireWire capture cards with an appropriate FireWire card to be installed in a PCI slot. Windows NT cannot

Table 6–3
Capture Card Comparison[a]

Name	Osprey	Winnov	Pinnacle	Matrox	ATI	Canopus
Model	100; 210; 500	1000	DV200; DV500; Pro One; DVD 1000	RT2500	Radeon 8500 DV	DV Storm SE Plus
PCI/USB	PCI	PCI	PCI	PCI	PCI	PCI
Operating System NT/2000/XP	Yes	Yes	Yes	Yes	Yes	Yes
Editing tool	No	No	Premiere 6	Premiere 6	No	Premiere 6
Compression format	AVI/Wave	AVI/Wave	DV[b]	MPEG[b]	AVI/Wave	DV[b]
Real time editing	No	No	Yes[c]	Yes[c]	No	Yes[c]
DVD Authoring	No	No	Yes	Yes	No	Yes
Real Time Edit	No	No	Yes	Yes	No	Yes
Input	Analog composite/ S-Video/ RGB	Analog composite/ S-Video	Analog composite/ S-Video/ Firewire	Analog composite/ S-Video	Analog composite/ S-Video/ Firewire	Analog composite/ S-Video/ Firewire
Output	No	No	Yes	Yes	Yes	Yes
Can create AVI/ Wave files directly	Yes	Yes	Yes	Yes	Yes	Yes
Support for DV/ Firewire	No	No	Yes	No	Yes	Yes
Price range	$249.00– 999.00	$249.00	$249.00– 1499.00	$799.00	$399.00	$1299.00

[a]Compatibility with all three streaming formats and their encoders (Sorenson broadcaster for QuickTime, Real Producer 8.5, and Windows Media Encoder 7.1) installed on a workstation with Windows NT 4.0 or Windows 2000 Professional operating system.
[b]Requires conversion of DV or MPEG format to AVI or WAV file.
[c]Pinnacle Pro One, DVD 1000 and 2000, Canopus DV Storm, and Matrox RT2500.

Table 6-4
Capture Cards and Encoding Software Compatibility

Capture Card		Encoding Software		
Video Format	**Ext.**	**QuickTime Streaming**[a]	**Real Video**[b]	**Windows Media**[c]
AVI	AVI	Yes	Yes	Yes
MJPEG	MPG, MPEG	No	Yes	Yes
MPEG1	MPG, MPA, MPEG	Yes	Yes	Yes
MPEG2	MPG, MP2, MPEG	No	No	Yes
Audio File	AU, AIFF	No	Yes	No
WAV File	WAV	Yes	Yes	Yes
MPEG3 (MP3)	MP3	Yes	Yes	Yes
DV Source	DV	No	No	No

[a]Sorenson Video 3 and Sorenson Broadcaster 1.5.
[b]RealSystem Producer Plus 8.5.
[c]Windows Media Encoder 7.1.

operate USB-based capture cards. However, as listed in Table 6–3, not all media encoders recognize a DV source. If you use a FireWire card, make sure you are capturing an AVI or a WAVE file with the proper codecs that can be recognized later by your media encoder.

Because your intention is to prepare media and stream them, remember that QuickTime, RealPlayer, and Windows Media encoding software do not support all types of media input. When selecting your capture card, verify that it is compatible with the required media format inputs of the encoding software. Table 6–4 lists which types of media format are accepted by which types of encoding software.

▶ **Important note:**

Currently you cannot convert MPEG-2 files with RealSystem Producer. Only Windows Media and Sorenson Broadcaster accept MPEG-2 as a video source. MPEG-1 is recognized by all three encoders, but it requires DirectX 6.0 to be on the system.

Table 6-5
Osprey and Winnov Comparison

Item	Osprey Cards	Winnov Cards
Video Formats		
YUV–YUV 4:1:1	Yes	No
YUY2–YUV 4:2:2	Yes	Yes
YVU9–YUV 4:2:0 (Intel Indeo® Raw)	Yes	Yes
YV12–YUV 4:2:0	Yes	Yes
RGB8–8-bit RGB (256 colors)	Yes	Yes
RGBH–16-bit RGB (64K colors)	Yes	Yes
RGBT–24-bit RGB (16.8M colors)	Yes	Yes
RGB–32-bit RGB (24M colors)	Yes	No
Hardware compression proprietary format	No	Yes
Software compression proprietary format	No	Yes
Video Input		
NTSC-M	Yes	Yes
NTSC-J	Yes	Yes
PAL–BDGHI	Yes	No
PAL-M	Yes	Yes
PAL-N	Yes	Yes
SECAM	Yes	No
MXC–Winnov camera	No	Yes
Audio Formats		
WAV–8-bit and 16-bit mono or stereo	Yes	Yes
Sampling 11, 22, and 44 kHz	Yes	Yes
Audio Input		
Stereo AUX In (3.5mm Stereo mini jack)	No	Yes
Stereo Line In (3.5mm Stereo mini jack)	No	Yes
Mono Camera MIC	No	Yes
CD-ROM internal	No	Yes
RCA Stereo Line In	Yes	No
3.5-mm Stereo mini jack	No	Yes
XLR Line In Unbalanced	Yes	No

Most production houses make smart decisions by using their hardware for other purposes. It saves money and space. If you select a capture card for capturing media in DV or MPEG formats, verify that it supports output formats listed in Table 6–5. Based on my experience, I recommend using Osprey and Winnov cards for your encoding workstation. All the technical instructions in this book assume the use of these two capture cards. Which one is better? That is up to you, the user, to decide. Each one provides different functions than the other, but in general both are pretty much standard among producers who stream video. Review Table 6–3 and decide which capture card you wish to use.

Compression Tools — Software

The quality, frame rate, and frame size of your digital media content are largely determined by the codec you select when creating content. Codecs are drivers that convert from one format type to another. A codec can convert between one compression or uncompression format to another compression or uncompression format. By using codecs for compressing audio and video data into smaller packages that do not consume as much hard disk space or network bandwidth, multimedia applications can provide richer and fuller content.

The average end-user does not have to know what a codec is to play media-based content. However, if you are creating the content, there are some things that you should know. The best way to make sure that the codec you use to encode your content will be available to all end-users is to use only those codecs that are part of official player applications from Apple's QuickTime, RealPlayer, and Windows Media. That way you know the codec is either already installed or will be installed automatically when the codec is needed. Streaming media players have a feature called Automatic Upgrades, which checks for the required codec whenever an end-user starts to play audio or video content. If a user with an older version of a codec attempts to play back content encoded with a newer version of the codec, the player will automatically connect to the vendor Web site and download and install the necessary upgrades.

Most software developers include in their new releases support for the leading proprietary encoding software from Microsoft Windows Media, RealNetworks RealPlayer, and some of the QuickTime encoding solutions. For exporting streaming video files from most nonlinear systems, there are two software solutions: that of the original software manufacturer or compression technology owner, such as Microsoft corporation or RealNetworks, and that of third-party vendors such as the Discreet Cleaner tool or Adobe Premiere export plug patch, which creates Windows Media and RealPlayer files. Both Microsoft and RealNetworks have developed a line of tools that allow the creation of media for on-demand use or live webcasting. Apple's QuickTime format has adopted the very same approach, and there are off-the-shelf compatible export plug-ins available for Cleaner as a QuickTime player export function. Some of the software manufacturer's original coding solutions provide better quality than the original software. Some third-party solutions provide a faster and more reliable compression. It is up to the individual to test each tool and decide which one to use.

Encoding Software Comparison

Apple distributes a free QuickTime Player that can view QuickTime streaming files. If you pay an additional $29.99, you can purchase Quick-Time Pro, which exports a long list of formats including QuickTime streaming files. RealNetworks offers a free version of their encoder, Real-System Producer, with limited functionality, and a version for $199.95 that is fully functional, RealSystem Producer Plus. Microsoft offers a free fully functional version of Windows Media Encoder that encodes stream-ing video for live broadcasts for on-demand presentation. RealSystem and Windows Media Encoder accept video and audio sources for live broadcast and can encode and convert, in real time, analog or digital content to streaming format. Apple's QuickTime Pro cannot encode a live feed. To produce a live webcast with the QuickTime format, you need to use Sorenson Broadcaster. For acceptable source formats from disk see Table 6–4. QuickTime and RealPlayer use RTSP for streaming. Micro-soft uses its proprietary MMS protocol and now supports streaming over HTTP, which resolves firewall issues (recall that RTSP and MMS default first to UDP and TCP ports to enter a network). Another advantage of the Microsoft encoder is its ability to integrate synchronized multimedia presentations in real time during a webcast. QuickTime and RealPlayer use SMIL language to create interactive applications for display on-demand. Windows Media Encoder 7.0 and later support event insertion to live streams; that is, you can flip pages, insert images to pages, and ro-tate advertising banners during a live webcast. And last, if your encod-ing workstation is equipped with sufficient power (CPU and RAM), and your network card supports enough bandwidth, you can webcast your live stream to a small audience without having to connect a media dis-tribution server. At the moment, only Windows Media Encoder 7.0 sup-ports this function. For a more detailed explanation of how to use encod-ing software, see Chapter 8.

Creating streaming files can be a painful process if it is not done properly. Readers range from users who need to encode a single file to put on their company Web site to the IT department of a large enterprise. It is possible that you will be faced with the need to encode hundreds of hours of content. The advantage of using proprietary QuickTime, Real-Video, and Windows Media encoding software is in webcasting live presentations or being able to customize an encoding profile (see Chapter 8) to fit the needs of your media. These encoding solutions provide, for example, the ability to name files, to slice them, or to enter meta tag information so that files can be linked to online search solutions. One large disadvantage these encoding solutions have is the lack of batch processing. Microsoft has addressed this issue by releasing a batch Encoder as part of the Windows Media 7.0 Resource Kit. To create batch jobs for Quick-Time and RealVideo formats, you need to rely on third-party vendors.

All the big three companies have released their software to third-party vendors, who developed applications to encode streaming files. Adobe adopted RealVideo and Windows Media streaming formats and includes an export plug-in on its Adobe Premiere version 5.0 and higher. Terran Interactive was the first vendor to release one product, Media Cleaner, that can take multiple audio and video formats as source, exporting them to multiple audio and video formats. In summer 2001, Discreet acquired Media Cleaner and renamed it Cleaner. Cleaner accepts input from the following formats: DV, QuickTime, Video for Windows (AVI), MPEG1, MPEG2, OpenDML, Macromedia Flash, MPEG Layer I audio, MPEG Layer II audio, Audio Interchange File Format (AIFF), audio (AU), Sound Designer II, WAVE, and other video, audio, animation, and still-image formats. It exports to the following formats: RealSystem, QuickTime, Windows Media, MP3, DV, AVI, MPEG1, MPEG2, MPEG Layer I audio, MPEG Layer II audio, AIFF/AIFC, WAVE, and other video, audio, animation, and still-image formats. Cleaner is a great solution for converting files. However, these software solutions are intended to create media on-demand files and do not support live encoding.

Choosing What Best Fits Your Needs

Some users prefer one technology over another; some need to encode streaming files in one format rather than another. I recommend that you acquire all three formats, configure your system to support all three formats, and become familiar with the software of all three formats. Until a universal streaming format is adopted by all major streaming vendors in the market, we will continue to use all three formats. You should also consider purchasing a video-editing program and a file-format-conversion program. Adobe Premiere is a standard software bundle sold with most capture cards. The program has an easy-to-use project timeline supporting multiple layers of audio and video, real-time effects, titles, animation, and more. Discreet Cleaner has become a standard software conversion solution among postproduction houses. Its only drawback is its slow media processing. Set your goals and do market research before purchasing any capture devices. Prices change often and new technologies are introduced regularly. Remember to define clearly what your objectives are and to use your research and judgment to select the best tools for your needs.

Summary

- When choosing a capture card, consider the type of production needs you will have. Capturing from a live source is different than encoding from a file on your hard drive.
- The frame resolution, number of frames, window size, and audio quality determine the size of your captured media file.
- Capture cards come in all colors, shapes, and prices. Make sure you select the card that will support the applications you want to use. Live webcasting of streaming media is supported by only a limited number of capture cards.
- Use the Sorenson Webcaster (to webcast in QuickTime format), RealSystem Producer, or Windows Media Encoder to webcast live events.
- Third-party encoding software provides supplementary support to create batch encoding jobs or interactive synchronized multimedia presentations.

7

Encoding Workstation

Building Your Own Encoding Workstation

After you have chosen a good capture card (Chapter 6) and determined the software you will be using to encode your live streams or the format you want to serve video on-demand files, the next step is to build your own encoding workstation. The following step-by-step process will make it easy for you to prepare a budget and then to assemble the components before you start building the station itself. Many people have the perception that encoding stations must be powerful machines with four CPUs, hundreds of gigabytes of hard-drive space aligned in a RAID configuration, and the latest hardware and software available on the market. But I have built encoding stations using very basic components. These stations compressed digital files and encoded streaming video for various modem speeds. When a computer cannot keep up with the conversion workload, a good capture program can compensate for the overloaded CPU and lack of sufficient RAM by dropping frames and other data. Rather than compromise the computer system, a good capture program senses that the system has reached its limits and it will not force the computer to continue converting data. When this happens, you will experience dropping of frames. The secret to capturing high-quality, high-bandwidth video is to use a computer system that can handle the bandwidth. To capture a good source of media, you need a fast CPU with a large amount of RAM, a fast PCI bus, a fast hard-disk drive with proper storage capacity, and a network connection that can handle the high bandwidth if you plan to stream to other computers. Your capture cards and external hardware should also be capable of producing high-quality images and sound. Keeping in mind that some readers will require a full screen

Table 7-1
Options for Building Your Own Encoding Workstation

	Minimum Components	Recommended Components
Processor	Pentium II 266 MHz or later	Dual Pentium III 700 MHz or later
Memory	128 MB RAM	512 MB RAM
Network card	10/100 MB TCP/IP Ethernet card	100 MB TCP/IP Fast Ethernet card
Hard disk	IDE hard drive 5,400 rpm or higher, with 25 MB for encoding software and 500 MB for content creation	Ultra160 SCSI hard drive 10,000 rpm or higher, with 75 MB for encoding software 36 GB for content creation
Audio card	Sound card compatible with Creative Labs Sound Blaster 16, and 2 good speakers	Sound card compatible with Creative Labs Sound Blaster 16, and 2 good speakers
Video card	Video card that supports video for Windows and at least 8 MB memory	Video card that supports video for Windows and at least 16 MB memory
Capture card	Osprey 200 or Winnov Videum PCI AV Board video capture cards	Osprey 500 or 1000, Winnov Videum 1000 video capture cards
Software	Windows 95/98/ME, Windows 2000 SP2, Windows NT SP 5 or Internet Explorer 5 or higher	Windows 2000 Professional SP2, Windows NT 4.0 SP 6a or Internet Explorer 5 or higher
Video Quality	320×240, 15 fps	640×480, 30 fps

displayed in NTSC 30 fps, whereas others will be happy with a 320 × 240 pixels screen at 15 fps, I consider two options for a good encoding workstation. Table 7–1 contrasts the two: a lower-end, minimum encoding workstation and a high-end encoding workstation. These recommendations are not meant to endorse one vendor over another. The table lists hardware and software components that work best when combined together to encode streaming media files. Notice the similarity in the lists of components needed to make the workstations. The differences are mostly in the CPU and amount of RAM.

The first step in building your first encoding workstation is to select a good computer that will allow flexibility in the installation process. If you plan to designate a used computer to be your workstation for capturing video, make sure it complies with the specifications listed in Table 7–1. If you are taking this opportunity to purchase a new computer, select one of the leading computer manufacturers such as Dell (*www.dell.com*), Compaq (*www.compaq.com*), or IBM (*www.ibm.com*). All three have industrial-strength workstations designed to handle heavy loads, such as capturing and compressing video files. A good encoding workstation maximizes its workload by having an even distribution of work on the CPU, built-in memory, and cooling fans to keep it from overheating (extensive heat slows down overall performance, resulting in poor capture or compression results). If you decide to use existing clones (computers that have been assembled by your staff or by a vendor), keep in mind that these systems normally are not performance tested in the same ways that official workstations are tested by the vendors listed in Table 7–1. Be prepared for possible hardware or software failure during installation and afterward when you start working on your multimedia projects. If you decide to choose a computer workstation vendor, list the alternatives and compare their pros and cons in detail, including:

- Have you used this vendor's technical support before? How well did they troubleshoot your calls?
- How long have you had to wait on the phone to reach their technical support?
- What type of technical support will you receive and for how long?
- How quickly can you receive spare parts?
- Can you disassemble the computer alone or will you need to wait for the vendor's technician to perform the maintenance? (Having to wait for the vendor's technician can slow down emergency repairs.)
- What does your replacement warranty include? (Some warranties cover labor and parts for the first year and parts for 1–2 years after that.)

Most IT personnel have experience in handling technical support issues related to hardware or software. Troubleshooting equipment or software has become an integral part of modern technology. Never underestimate the power of new technology—it can perform miracles for your project timeline or damage it badly. Vendors with inefficient or poor technical support can be a very frustrating experience. These incidents can put you over budget in addition to your system's being down for troubleshooting and a potential loss of business and customers. If you are a newcomer to the world of the new media, here is an opportunity to learn that customer service and technical support are not less important than the equipment or software you buy. Sometimes they are more important than the product itself. In short, take my advice and cover yourself and your equipment with the proper warranties.

▸ **Important note:**

A fast CPU enables a computer to keep up with the demand to process a stream of bits, whereas a fast PCI bus moves those bits easily between the capture device and the processor. A large amount of RAM eases the load on the CPU by enabling bits to be cached as they are converted. A large hard disk with a fast access time helps in balancing the load on the computer as it writes data quickly and efficiently. As you capture data, you can use the System Monitor included in Microsoft Windows 2000 and Microsoft Windows NT to view the CPU and memory use. If the CPU percentage constantly hits 100%, there is a very good chance of degradation in capture quality. I recommend that you use a computer with dual PCI buses. Even a very fast single PCI bus may not be able to handle both the bit stream produced by the capture card and the stream going to the hard disk drive.

Recommended Components

Your workstation will require special configuration to support the capture of real-time video and the compression of streaming media files. Based on the specifications listed in Table 7–1, the following is a list of components that you will need for assembling your encoding workstation. After reading these sections, proceed to the installation section.

Computer

Based on the suggested configurations listed in Table 7–1, select a computer with enough CPU power and built-in memory to handle the job of capturing and encoding your media. Your choice should have an appropriate fan system to keep your CPU and hard drive within the appropriate range of temperature. When setting up the workstation, allow an adequate distance between the back of your workstation and the wall. Store it in a cool room and keep it away from direct sunlight. Direct sunlight can heat up your workstation. Keep any unnecessary cables and objects away from your workstation. When you operate your system, it should produce a steady and low engine background noise. If you hear clicking or loud noises, consult your vendor's technical support before attempting to install additional components to your system.

Monitor

When video is captured, a video source is moving from one point to another, passing through a pipe that may change its size and resolution. The compression effect changes the shape and quality of the video and audio signal and creates a duplicate digital file that consists of the new parameters that were specified during its creation. Moving images generate many artifacts that are not always visible to the naked eye. Most postproduction facilities use high-end image-control devices that improve the quality of the image, color, and balance. These devices are very expensive and may be suitable to the type of work you want to perform. Therefore, it is recommended that you use a good monitor that will allow you to see when you are processing bad video. Use a 17-in. or wider monitor in your workstation. Set the screen resolution to $1,024 \times 768$ pixels or higher. Set your monitor to high color (16-bit) or more to produce a resolution of at least 65 million colors. To change your screen settings, click your right mouse button and choose Properties. Click on the Settings tab, enlarge your screen area properly, and then change your colors. Click on Apply and on OK.

Power Supply

Protect your computer from power outages or, more important, from sudden power spikes and ongoing line noise. A small investment today will save a larger investment tomorrow. Buy an uninterruptible power supply system that has both surge protection and a battery backup. Make sure the unit has a battery backup that can power your workstation and monitor for at least 15 minutes. This will allow you to shut the system down properly in case of a power outage.

Backup System

Always be prepared for a disaster. Computer workstations tend to crash due to work overloads. Make it a rule to always back up important data. An encoding workstation should only compress streaming files, not become a stand-alone computer or network storage place. Back up all your media regularly. If you are not under pressure to free your hard drives quickly, use a digital linear tape (DLT) solution. DLT storage tapes can save up to 70 GB of compressed data (2 : 1) on a single cartridge. The only drawback is its slow data-transfer rate of 5 MBps. Faster solutions are SCSI, USB, or 1394 FireWire devices, which save your media at rates between 20 and 400 MBps. Remember that only Windows 98, ME, and 2000 support USB technology and 1394 FireWire PCI cards. If your station operates on Windows NT, use a SCSI backup device. Check with your equipment vendor to be sure that the backup system uses SCSI II with a data-transfer rate of at least 80 MBps or higher between your workstation and the backup device. Another cost-effective solution for backup is to burn CD-ROMs. This solution is limited to 640 MB of space per CD. The size of media files depends on the ratio you use to capture your raw video files; most uncompressed media files are large and will not fit on a single CD. Using a DVD burner is an alternative; a DVD stores up to 5.3 GB of media on a single disc. Use standard backup software such as Veritas Backup Execute. If your operating system is Windows 2000 or NT, it comes with Microsoft backup software.

Capture Card

A handful of vendors today offer a variety of video capture cards that cost less, use computer resources better, and produce cleaner and crisper video quality. Some capture cards support audio input as well, some use the built-in audio card of your computer system, and some offer video capture only and you will need to connect your audio source directly to your line input on your system's built-in audio card. I recommend using a card from the first group. An independent capture card that takes care of your video and audio source provides better synchronization between the video and audio feeds, and it operates faster, using less system CPU and RAM resources. Which capture card you select depends on two factors: what plans you have for your media (where you want to display the captured media, i.e., window sizes and quality) and your budget (the unavoidable question). Capture cards come in all prices, ranging from $69.00 to $5,000.00.

Sound

Most computer systems come with a standard sound system; some even provide a subwoofer or a surround-sound system with four speakers and a subwoofer. To get a good idea of the quality of the sound you will be processing, buy a good pair of professional dynamic stereo headphones. These headphones normally cost less then $200.00. With your new headphones, you can monitor sound without interference from noises in the room or outside the office.

Another good investment is a Mackie MIC/Line Mixer. This low-cost audio mixer provides analog and digital professional processing to input sound from multiple sources and output it to one or more devices. When you connect your audio source to your mixer, you can monitor levels, add effects, and listen to the sound before it is processed out to your capture workstation. More savvy users can add audio limiters and compressor chains to their audio mixer device. The proper treatment of an audio signal before it is captured creates a crisper and healthier sound. Every Windows operating system includes built-in software to monitor and mix microphone and line inputs and outputs, but there is nothing like a good old traditional mixer to handle your audio levels before you digitize them.

You can now connect your sound speakers to the monitor or line-out jack of your capture card or audio card. Osprey cards let you use your system's built-in audio card as an output for your speakers. Winnov cards take ownership of the system's built-in audio card. It is necessary to route the line-out or speaker-out jack from the system's built-in audio card and connect it to the AUX input of your Winnov card. This loop will pass all the audio that you want to monitor out from your system through the Winnov card. Now connect your speakers to the headphone-output jack of the Winnov card, as described in the manufacturer's installation session. This will provide real-time room monitoring of the captured audio signal or more enhanced playback options. By using your dynamic stereo headphones connected to the appropriate speaker output of your system, you will be able to identify any unwanted artifacts in the sound.

Software

To capture a live feed with your capture card and to encode it for a live webcast, you can use only the original encoding software that Sorenson Broadcaster, Microsoft, and RealNetworks supply. If you capture to a local disc (to a file), you can use third-party software such as Adobe Premiere or the software that comes with most capture devices. If you are sending a live streaming signal to your media distributor server, use encoding software provided by Apple, RealNetworks, and Microsoft. The encoder must talk to the media distribution server. It creates a communications tunnel to transfer the encoded signal between the workstation and the distributor server. These software components are not released as part of QuickTime, RealVideo, or Windows Media open software development kit (SDK) available to the public. It is true that some third-party products such as Cleaner encode streaming files for on-demand use. However, I recommend that you use the original software tools provided by the three leading streaming video vendors.

Hardware Installation

After you have verified your components checklist, you can assemble your encoding workstation. I will assume that you are using the Recommended Components specifications for your workstation, as described in Table 7–1. The hardware and software under Minimum Components will work fine; however, the encoding results in terms of window size, frames per second, and processing power will not satisfy most users. In addition, the price difference between the two systems is not significant. An additional initial investment for the Recommended Components specifications will prolong the working life of your system and produce better output results.

▸ **Important note:**

These instructions for installation describe how to assemble an encoding workstation on a computer using the Windows operating system. Macintosh and Linux operating systems are well-respected systems, but I am not able to describe the installation process on machines using these operating systems due to the lack of compatible hardware and software for capturing and encoding streaming video files. Each one of these operating systems supports a degree of capturing video, but only the Windows operating system is fully compatible with the necessary hardware and software tools needed to capture and create streaming video files for all three leading formats (QuickTime, RealVideo, and Windows Media).

Prepare your working area. The room should be dust free and properly cooled. Make sure you have enough white light in the room; fluorescent lights are the best and most IT departments use them. Wear an antistatic strap when installing any hardware on your board. Electrostatic discharge can cause damage to your computer circuitry, followed by complete or intermittent failures. At least, touch a piece of grounded metal (such as your computer chassis) to discharge any static electricity before starting the installation. Use a flashlight to illuminate the interior of your workstation. A set of tools is handy for opening and closing the casing. Use standard computer kits that come with Philips or flat-head screw drivers. A compressed-air container will help you clean the dust from your old computer in case you decide to recondition it into a working station. Gather all your new software and hardware (if you are upgrading an existing system). Make sure you have all the components listed in Table 7–1. Place your workstation on a table and point the light on it. Use your computer manufacturer's handbook and follow the steps to properly open your workstation. If you do not have a handbook, log on to the vendor's Web site and follow the links to the technical support area. Most companies list detailed instructions for their products.

Remember the rules for a healthy installation. Most operating systems need to first detect a hardware device before they can assign a software program to it. I first describe the hardware installation, followed by the operating system software configuration, and wrap up with the installation of the software programs that will make the hardware work. If you need to install additional RAM or a second hard drive, start with the first part of the directions. If your system is ready and you need only to add a capture card and software, proceed to the capture card installation part.

System Preparation

1. **Turn off the computer and all peripheral devices.** Unplug the computer and peripherals from the wall outlet.
2. **Follow your vendor's instructions to remove the cover of your computer.** Make sure you have full access to the motherboard. If you have to move any interior cables, move them carefully. In case you need to disconnect the power, integrated drive electronics (IDE), or SCSI chain cables, label them first with small stickers and draw a diagram describing where they belong. When your installation is complete, you will then be able to reconnect these cables.

3. **Use compressed air to clean the interior dust from your system.**
4. **Go to additional RAM installation.**

Additional RAM Installation

1. **Carefully read the vendor's instructions before attempting to upgrade your system's RAM.** Make sure you are in compliance with your vendor's conditions for uninterrupted technical support for your system. Some computer vendors define an uninterrupted support contract as allowing only their staff to perform maintenance on your system.
2. **Locate an available RAM slot on your motherboard.** Wear an antistatic wrist strap or touch a metal object connected to the ground. Open the clips at both sides of the RAM slot. Unpack your additional RAM. Use two fingers on each side to snap in the memory card. You will hear a click when the card has been inserted properly in the slot. Make sure the card is seated firm.
3. **It is recommended at this stage that you boot up your computer.** Reconnect all loose cables and reboot your system. Watch carefully to see whether the computer senses the additional RAM. If your system fails to locate the additional RAM, disconnect all the cables, open the lid, and repeat the insertion process again. Then reboot again and see if your operating system can recognize the additional RAM. If the system fails to recognize the new RAM again, contact your hardware manufacturer for technical support.
4. **If your system recognizes the additional RAM, go to hard drive installation.**

Hard Drive Installation

1. **When you add additional hard drives to your system you must be in compliance with your vendor's conditions for uninterrupted technical support for your system.** Some computer vendors define an uninterrupted support contract as allowing only their staff to perform maintenance on your system.

2. **Before you purchase additional hard drives for your system, speak with your vendor's technical team and get their technical advice about the type to purchase.** Adding additional hard drives can have a negative effect on RAID settings, may require a completely new RAID configuration, may require the installation of additional fans, or may interrupt the power balance of your system. In short, an additional drive can have a negative effect on the general performance of your system.

3. **When you have the proper hard drive, unplug the computer and peripherals from the wall outlet.**

4. **Follow your vendor's instructions to remove the cover of your computer.** Make sure you have full access to the motherboard. If you have to move any interior cables, move them carefully. In case you need to disconnect the power, IDE, or SCSI chain cables, label them first with small stickers and draw a diagram describing where they belong. When your installation is complete, you will then be able to reconnect these cables.

5. **Use compressed air to clean the interior dust from your system.**

6. **Locate the place where you can mount an additional hard drive.** Follow your vendor's instructions to mount the new hard drive in place. Make sure the drive is seated firmly.

7. **Connect the drive to the proper IDE or SCSI chain, or connect it directly to the motherboard.** Plug in the power cable. Reconnect all loose cables.

8. **It is recommended at this stage that you boot up your computer.** Watch carefully to see if the computer senses the additional hard drive.

▌ **Important note:**

Follow your vendor's instructions to configure the presence of a new hard drive in the BIOS of your system. After you have made changes to the BIOS of your system (if necessary), continue with the boot process.

9. **If your system fails to recognize the additional hard drive, shut down the system and disconnect all cables.** Open the lid and make sure all the cables are aligned properly.

Check to see that there is a green light on your hard drive; this means the device is getting power properly from the motherboard. You may have a conflict in your chain or in the BIOS configuration. Contact your hardware manufacturer for technical support.

10. **If your system recognizes the additional hard drive, go to capture card installation.**

Capture Card Installation

1. **Find an available PCI slot on your motherboard.**
2. **Remove the protective slot cover from the back of the computer using a screwdriver.** Save the screws; you will use them later to secure the capture board to the chassis.
3. **Install the capture board in the available slot.** Hold the card at the edges and align the pins on the board with the pins in the connector. Press firmly until you hear a click and the board is seated evenly.
4. **Secure the capture card with the screws that were holding the protective slot cover.**
5. **Connect your video and audio source to the back of the card.** Use Table 7–2 and Figures 7–1 through 7–3 as references.

Table 7–2
Audio and Video Connectors

Connector	Type	Connect to
S-Video	4-pin mini-DIN	Only S-Video devices such as VCRs, camcorders, or videocameras
MXC	8-pin mini-DIN	Winnov videocamera
Composite	RCA or BNC jack	VCRs, camcorders
AUX audio in	3.5-mm stereo mini jack RCA stereo jack	Audio output from VCR or another sound card
Line/MIC in	3.5-mm stereo mini jack RCA stereo jack	Microphone, VCRs, or audio from other sources
Stereo audio out	3.5-mm stereo mini jack	Input audio to VCRs, speakers, headphones, or sound systems

Figure 7–1
S-Video plug

Figure 7–2
RCA connector

Figure 7–3
Mini jack connector

System Audio Configuration

To provide a single point of control on your computer audio, use the following method. Winnov cards take ownership of your audio card; Osprey cards work in parallel with the system's built-in audio card. If you are using an Osprey card, go to step 4. If you are using a Winnov card, start with step 1 to make some changes to reroute your audio out and CD-ROM drive through the card to play back sound.

1. **External connection:** Connect the external audio out of your system's built-in audio card to the AUX Audio In connector at the back of the Winnov card. Use a 3.5-mm stereo mini jack.

2. **Internal connection:** Locate your CD-ROM drive inside the open workstation. Some capture cards provide a four-pin connector to connect your system's CD-ROM drive directly to the capture card. Refer to your vendor's documentation. If the board supports this function, locate the audio cable attached to your CD-ROM audio out port. Follow the cable until you find its other end, normally connected to your system's motherboard. Pull slowly the cable out and reconnect it to the appropriate place on your capture card.

▶ **Important note:**

Make sure the pins match. Do not try to force the connection. Doing so will result in damage to your system and, in most cases, hardware manufacturers will not provide technical support for device malfunctions caused by wrong handling.

3. **Return all cables and connections to their places.** Close the lid of your computer and plug all the cables into the back.
4. **Boot up your computer.** If you are using an operating system that supports Plug and Play, your system should detect the new hardware you have just installed.
5. **Install the capture card software, and then continue configuring your sound.** A window will pop up and prompt you to provide software for the installation.
6. **Use the software provided by your capture card vendor.** Point to the folder containing the proper version for your operating system. Use the vendor-recommended configuration for installation.
7. **The installation wizard will guide you through the installation.** If your system has partitions, it is recommended that you install the application in the C partition, where your operating system is installed.
8. **After a successful installation, close all applications and reboot your computer.** In the event of a partial or wrong installation, repeat the process by locating the setup file on the vendor's software CD and double-clicking on it. Refer to your vendor's installation guide for more information.

9. **Configure the sound settings.** After your system reboots, click on Start, Control Panel, Sound & Multimedia. A window labeled Sounds and Multimedia Properties will pop up. Click on the Audio tab. Select from Sound Playback which device you will use to play back sound. Click on the Preferred Device and choose your capture card or built-in audio card. Click on the Volume tab to adjust the levels. Next, click on Preferred Device in the Sound Recording section and select which device you will use to record sound. Click on the Volume tab to adjust levels. Click on Apply and OK.

▶ **Important note:**

If you are using a Winnov card, select the Winnov card option for both playback and recording. If you are using an Osprey card, select your computer's built-in audio card for playback and the Osprey card for recording.

Summary

- The power of an encoding station is determined by a combination of the CPU power, available RAM, read-write speed of its hard drives, and ability of the operating system to process heavy workloads.
- Verify in advance that you have all the necessary components to build an encoding workstation. Proceed with the installation as described.
- Hardware installation comes before software installation. Software will always look for hardware devices to provide it with source media.
- Use original (Sorenson Broadcaster for QuickTime, RealSystem Producer, or Windows Media Encoder) encoding tools to broadcast live media to your media distribution servers.

8

The Encoding Process

Testing Your Encoding Workstation

Once your encoding workstation is fully assembled, it is time to perform a few tests to verify the proper installation of hardware and software described in Chapter 7. Follow the instructions in this chapter to guarantee the proper operation of your workstation. If programs fail to run on your workstation, it indicates a serious problem. When troubleshooting a computer, you must first identify whether the problem is due to a hardware or software malfunction.

Testing Capture Cards

First connect your media source to the capture card you have installed in your computer. Shut down your workstation and disconnect the power cord. Use professional audio and video cables. Monster Cable offers a variety of manufactured cables and connectors that are available at retail stores such as Radio Shack, CompUSA, and video stores that sell audio and video cables. Inspect the video and audio output of your future media source and order audio-video cables that are long enough to connect between the media source and your encoding workstation. Always purchase a longer cable than you need. You might need to change the position and distance between the video or audio sources and your capture workstation. Roll the cable properly to avoid damage to the cable or disturbance to the media signal. I recommend that you purchase cables that provide shielding for maximum protection against radio frequency interference (RFI) and electromagnetic interference (EMI). Monster Cable manufactures audio-video cables that are recommended by video professionals. For more information log on to *www.monstercable.com*.

When you have the proper cables, proceed to connect your source media. Audio cables are often separated to left and right sources (stereo left and right channels). Capture cards support single or dual inputs. If necessary, get an audio coupler that will convert your incoming double audio source to a single-jack output. Plug the audio source to your audio input jacks. Some capture cards support XLR-jack input. Most require two separate RCA jacks or a single Mini stereo plug. The video source can originate from a composite source (using BNC or RCA jacks) or an S-Video source. Use S-Video cables for better video quality. Most capture cards for streaming applications do not support RGB input. Cards with RGB component video input are more costly because they deliver higher video resolution. Because streaming video applications currently deliver video at a rate of 56–300 kbps, using a high-end capture card will not make much of a difference in the output video quality. Connect all the cables and boot up your workstation.

Next configure the workstation properly to help the capture software recognize the system hardware. First, open the computer control panel. Launch Sounds and Multimedia and click on the Audio tab. Select your capture card as the preferred recording device. Unless you are using a Winnov capture card, select the computer built-in audio card or software as the default playback device. Click on Apply and then OK.

Winnov Cards

Winnov cards come with a built-in full duplex audio card. They take ownership of the computer's original audio card. Workstations with Winnov capture cards must route the system-internal audio card through the Winnov card. This can be done internally during the capture-card installation or externally afterward. To establish an external connection, take a short stereo Mini plug cable and connect it between the system speaker's line out jack to the Winnov AUX input. Next, start your playback and open the Winnov application by clicking Start/Programs/Winnov Videum/Utilities/Videum Configure. You will see the administration interface. Click on the Information tab. If your workstation has more than one card, select the card that was connected to your source playback. Workstations with only one capture card do not require this setting. Click on the Video Input tab and select the source that applies to your playback settings. Click on the Audio Input and select the source to your audio playback. These settings reflect the way you have already connected the playback source and the workstation capture card. Make sure you see activity in the audio meter area. Click on the Audio Output tab and select the proper audio output. Click on OK. Open the Winnov capture interface and verify that you can receive video and audio. Technically the workstation is ready to start capturing media.

Osprey Cards

Osprey cards do not take ownership of the workstation built-in audio card. They instead rely on the existing built-in audio card or use their own audio card (for version 200 and higher). Viewcast Corporation (the maker of Osprey cards) offers a series of audio-video capture cards. Viewcast supports a range of capture tasks from simple capture tasks with the Osprey version 100 to MPEG2 hardware encoding with the latest Osprey 2000DV Pro. It is just a question of what you can afford. If you install two or more Osprey cards on one workstation, the first card will use your workstation audio card and the second card will display an error because it will not recognize an available card to handle its audio stream. For multicard support, use the Osprey 200 or higher. If you are planning to encode streaming content with Microsoft's Windows Media Encoder version 7.0 or higher, install the Osprey versions 200 or 500; lower-numbered versions are not supported by Windows Media Encoder 7.0. Osprey version 200 and higher will ask you if you want the card to be the primary audio card. You can accept and repeat the process of routing audio from the previous default audio card to the Osprey card, or you can decline and keep Osprey as a secondary card. If you choose the second option, make sure to tune the default recording selection in your control panel properly before recording a session. An Osprey card cannot be installed on the same workstation as a Winnov capture card. Both cards will attempt to use the same computer resources, creating a software conflict. If you are planning to work with multiple cards on one workstation, install cards that are the same brand. Once the card is installed, proceed to configure the incoming audio and video sources. Technically the workstation is ready to start capturing media.

Testing Video and Lip Sync

Perform one last test to verify the integrity and quality of the captured video and proper lip sync (to see that the audio matches the mouth movements of characters in the video feed). Record a short clip to disk. First, adjust audio levels. To access your computer audio management software, click on Start/Settings/Control Panel. Select Sounds and Multimedia. Click on the Audio tab. Pull down the menu of your Sound Recording Preferred Device and select the audio card that is connected to your audio source. Click on the Volume button. A new window will display input selections (see Figure 8–1). Select your input source (CD, Microphone, or Line In) and adjust the level. Keep this window open when you capture media for fast adjustments to incoming audio levels. Repeat these steps to adjust the playback levels of your computer sound speakers.

To adjust video levels use your capture card software tools. Both Winnov and Osprey cards provide full control of video brightness, contrast, saturation, and hue. To adjust levels open the video capture card application. If you have more than one capture card on your workstation, select the one you will be using for this test. Start source playback. Verify that the video signal appears in the capture card window. Now open the

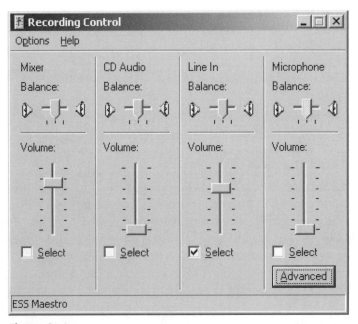

Figure 8–1
Computer audio device control

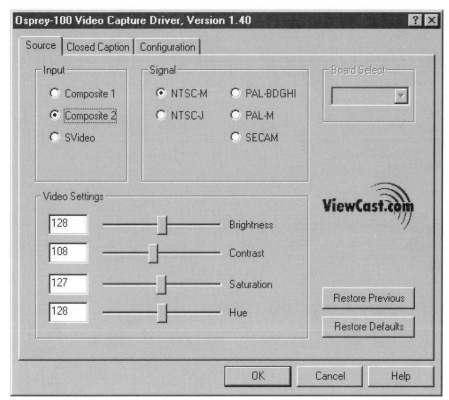

Figure 8–2
Sample of Osprey video levels control

video levels window and adjust levels of Brightness, Contrast, Saturation, and Hue (see Figure 8–2). Video signal inputs over composite connections will produce different levels than video signals over S-Video or RGB inputs. To properly adjust both audio and video levels, use a bar and tone source. Create a color bar and audio tone tape in advance to test your equipment. Color-bar signals can be obtained from most professional cameras. The tone signal is generated by audio mixers or professional audio devices. Consult your video vendor for more information.

Use the compression codecs supplied with your capture card and test that all of them generate a clear video clip with proper audio. Refer to the capture card codecs table in Chapter 6 for more information. View your captured AVI file for errors.

Live Webcast or Media On-Demand

Once the capture card is capable of capturing AVI and WAVE files, it is time to test the encoding software that creates streaming files. Recall the difference between encoding media for a live webcast and encoding media for on-demand viewing. Live broadcasting of streaming content, or webcasting, is the transmission of live video over IP networks. Live webcasting has many forms. It is used to stream broadcast content in real time using Unicast or Multicast methods of distribution, or it is used to retransmit prerecorded content in real time. The term "live" refers to sending a video or audio signal in real time over the network. Examples of live webcasts are concerts, games, and news that are transmitted over the Internet as they happen in real time. Corporations use live webcasts to broadcast announcements to employees as the event takes place. Examples of prerecorded webcasts are games and concert replays that are available on the Internet after the event takes place. This method is often used to replay content to audiences living in different regions or countries in different time zones.

Video on-demand was first associated with cable television. In the early 1990s, cable operators and television networks experimented with the possibility of giving the audience the option to select media for playback. Rather than subscribers sitting on their couches watching the evening news and sitcoms in the order the network broadcast them, a video on-demand solution would have given subscribers the power to select their preferred programs from a large database of digital media. The concept failed due to network-congestion issues, but was revisited as soon as digital television and broadband became realities. The Internet and broadband channels have introduced a second stage of this long-awaited technology. The delivery has changed; instead of sending the media to subscriber's home television sets, delivering movies over IP is being tested by major Hollywood studios. The industry is committed to bringing video on-demand to every home in America.

Media on-demand is a powerful concept that will provide us with unlimited access to information over computer networks. In years to come, we will use the Internet to watch media related to our work, media that inform us about world events, and media that entertain us in our free time.

To illustrate the significant development and deployment of video on-demand, here is an example of how video rental companies plan to distribute entertainment content in the future. Blockbuster, a subsidiary of Viacom, has over 7,800 stores and more than 90,000 employees worldwide; it is the largest chain of video rentals in the United States. Since it was first introduced to the market back in 1985, the company has grown into the world's number one video chain with more than 51 million U.S. and Canadian member accounts active during 2000, plus several million additional member accounts worldwide. In 2000 alone, an estimated average of more than 3 million customers walked into U.S. Blockbuster stores every day. At first, only VHS movies were available for daily or weekly rental. With the introduction of computer games (Saga, Nintendo, Sony Playstation, and Microsoft XBox), Blockbuster stores offered daily or weekly rentals of games and game platforms. When the first DVDs were introduced, Blockbuster offered daily and weekly rentals of DVDs. In summer 2000, the company announced a partnership with Enron Broadband Services to deliver the ultimate video on-demand experience to broadband subscribers. In March 2001, Blockbuster and Enron said that they had broken off their exclusive partnership to deliver movies over the Web, signaling new static over the highly anticipated creation of video on-demand services. The split came as Hollywood studios were rushing to create video on-demand services in response to a growing threat from Napster-like online video piracy companies. Blockbuster won the right to distribute content from a variety of movie producers, including a deal with Vivendi Universal's Universal Pictures, its biggest content partner to date. The company also had broadband-distribution agreements with Metro-Goldwyn-Mayer, Artisan Entertainment, Trimark Pictures, and Lions Gate Entertainment. The initiative taken a year earlier turned out to be wrong; Blockbuster had to play by the rules of its content partners, aborting the launch of an independent online distribution system. The company made a strategic decision to wait for the right moment and for the blessing of its content licensors before it launched an online distribution system.

This example shows how delicate the situation is. With all the excitement involving streaming media on broadband networks, there are still numerous issues to be addressed before such services will become available to the public. Two of these issues are a limited audience and security concerns related to the protection of content distributed over the Internet.

RealSystem Encoding Tools

To encode streaming media in RealVideo format, use RealNetworks Real-System Producer Plus. The software costs $199.00 and is available for download at *www.real.com*. A free version called RealSystem Producer Basic is available too, but the software is limited and lacks many functions available in the purchased version, such as the ability to crop images, customize bandwidth, and select multiple bit-rate settings. Real-System Producer Plus comes with eight preconfigured profiles that target audiences with connectivity ranging from 56 to 512 kbps. The software provides full codec control—users have the option to optimize a particular codec, to optimize the bandwidth assigned to each audience, or to configure how the system responds under severe conditions.

RealSystem Producer provides filters to improve media quality:

- Inverse telecine—This prefilter is added to clean up specific types of source content for broadband RealVideo. Movie film is generally photographed at 24 fps. When a film is converted to digital video at 30 fps, extra frames are added by merging frames together or copying entire frames. The film-to-video conversion process is called telecine. The inverse-telecine filter looks for the frames added during the telecine process and removes them, thus eliminating redundant encoding and improving the quality of the frames that are encoded. The result is significantly improved encoded video quality.

- De-interlace filter—This removes artifacts that can be introduced when encoding NTSC-PAL-formatted video (PAL stands for Phase Alternation Line). These artifacts are usually seen as a jaggedness surrounding a moving object.

In addition RealSystem Producer Plus offers three codecs that can be used to improve image quality:

- RealVideo G2—This is a basic RealVideo codec that works with all RealPlayer versions from G2 and higher.

- RealVideo G2 with Scalable Video Technology (SVT)—This is a codec that is compatible with RealPlayer versions 6.0.6 and above; it requires additional CPU power and memory on the client side. This codec improves the ability to play back to users with multiple connection speeds. It adjusts the frame rate and the window size according to the end-user capability to connect to the Internet, and it corrects playback performance by resending more packets to reconstruct lost data.

- RealVideo 8.0–This is the codec that provides the best quality output for all bit rates, but uses more processing power than the other codecs. It is compatible with RealPlayer 8.0 and above. Your audience's RealPlayers must be updated before they can view clips created with this codec.

Additional codec performance is achieved by the new two-pass encoding option that increases the quality of the output video by analyzing video data before encoding the input video. The first pass analyzes the entire clip, looking for transitions and overall complexity. The second pass encodes the clip using the analysis from the first pass.

Combining two-pass encoding with variable bit rate (VBR) delivers a generational improvement in broadband video quality over the Internet. RealSystem Producer version 8.0 introduced VBR video compression. This feature enables the video codec to vary the bit rate throughout the clip, depending on the type of content being encoded. More bits are spent on high-action scenes, taking away bits from low-action scenes. This greatly improves the quality of narrowband and broadband video.

RealSystem Producer supports SureStream, a feature that allows RealServer to dynamically adjust the stream for each listener, depending on the dynamic network conditions of the user's connection. During encoding you specify which modem speeds you are streaming for. If the network path becomes congested, RealSystem senses how much bandwidth it has and delivers the proper stream. Once the congestion is gone, the connection scales up again. See Table 8–1 to estimate the storage requirements of your streaming files. The table assumes 60 minutes of source content encoded to 60 minutes of streaming media.

Table 8–1
RealSystem Producer Storage Requirements for Streaming Files
(60 minutes of content)

Aggregate Bit Rate	Approximate File Size
22 kbps	9.6 MB
37 kbps	16.4 MB
50 kbps	22 MB
100 kbps	44 MB
300 kbps	134 MB
1 Mbps	440 MB

Here is an exercise using RealSystem Producer. This tests the ability of RealSystem Producer to see an audio-video source originating in your capture card and webcast it to a RealSystem Server, with the option to capture the video to your hard drive.

1. Open the capture card software interface and configure it to see video and hear audio. When you see video and hear audio, minimize the interface.

2. Launch RealSystem Producer. Start a new session. RealSystem Producer cannot broadcast to RealServer if the source is not a live feed. Prerecorded files can only be recorded back to disk.

3. To broadcast a live feed to RealSystem Server:

   • Choose your media device by selecting source video and audio card settings. There are two options for output: recording your live feed to disk or broadcasting in real time to RealSystem Server.

   • To record to disk, click on Output/RealMedia File and point to the place where the file will be stored.

   • To webcast the signal to a RealSystem Server type the RealServer IP, which port to use for the outbound stream, the file name, the user name, and the password to connect to the RealSystem Server (Username and Password are assigned in RealSystem Server live encoder settings; see Chapter 9). For example:

RealServer:	192.168.1.3
Port:	4040 (default)
Filename:	live.rm
Username:	your_user_name
Password:	your_password

   • If you webcast the signal to RealSystem Server, it is also possible to record the file locally. This setting requires additional RAM memory and a dual CPU board. Check Archive Broadcast to File to record to disk the same feed you are sending to RealSystem Server.

4. The wizard will memorize your settings. Now choose your output selection. First select SureStream for multiple bit rates or a single-rate option.

5. For a scalable stream, select SureStream and check the desired speeds, from a 28-kbps modem to a 512-kbps DSL or modem. I recommend that you create two files of SureStream video: one for

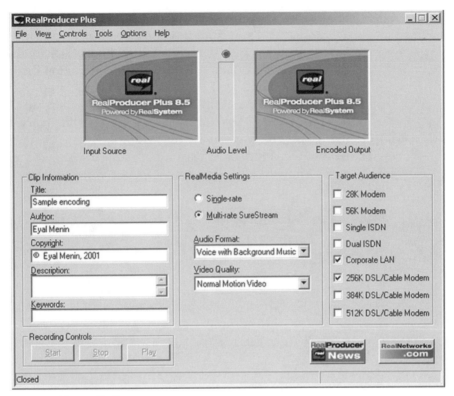

Figure 8–3
RealSystem Producer interface

users ranging from 28 kbps to 128 kbps with window size 240 × 180 pixels and one for users ranging from 150 kbps to 512 kbps with window size 320 × 240 pixels.

6. For the single-rate option, check only one speed.

7. Enter the clip information (e.g., title, author, and copyright; see Figure 8–3).

8. The choices among various audio formats and video qualities apply only to single-rate bits. Settings for SureStream and multiple-bit rates are controlled by the Options/Target Audience Settings tab on the encoder main interface. RealSystem Producer comes with default settings. To change these settings, open Target Audience Settings from the Options tab. Scroll the video or audio settings to see the default settings. The Audio tab will show defaults for Voice Only, Voice with Background Music, Music, and Ste-

reo Music. To change these settings, scroll the rates up or down. To change the video frames-per-second settings, click on the Video tab. To change the bandwidth settings, click on the Target Bit Rate tab. Remember that bandwidth limitation dictates how much audio and video you can stream. For example, if you set the bandwidth to 100 kbps and attempt to stream audio at 64 kbps, you will have only 34 kbps for video delivery. For best results, use the encoder default settings.

9. RealSystem Producer Plus supports the resizing and cropping of the source video. To change output video settings, click on

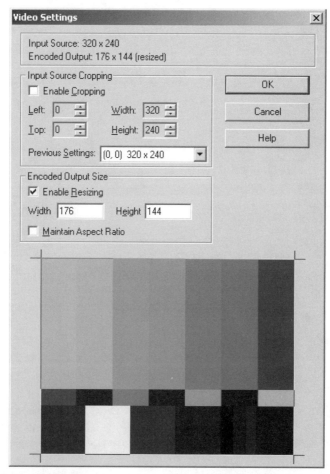

Figure 8–4
RealSystem Producer Plus video settings window

Options/Video Settings (see Figure 8–4). Choose to either crop the image or resize it. For the default video window size over the Internet, refer to Table 8–3 (later in this chapter).

10. Start encoding a session. Monitor the incoming video feed in the two video windows in the encoder. Use the audio meter to monitor the incoming audio. Record a short clip to file. Stop the encoder and watch the clip to check the sync between the recorded audio and video. To close the audio-video monitor screen in the encoder, click on View/Show Input Source. Select Input Source, or Show Encoded Output, or Show Audio Meter.

This concludes the test of RealSystem Producer's ability to encode a captured audio and video feed through your workstation capture card. To establish a connection between the encoder and the server during a live webcast, refer to the instructions in Chapter 10.

QuickTime Encoding Tools

QuickTime uses three separate tools to stream video. Sorenson Broadcaster encodes live video for webcasting in real time using QuickTime Server (for Macintosh) or Darwin Streaming Server (for Windows) as a distribution server. QuickTime streaming files for media on-demand can be created by using QuickTime Player Pro or Cleaner software. Sorenson Broadcaster can save a capture session to disk, but the quality is poor compared to the files converted by QuickTime Pro or by Cleaner. Sorenson Broadcaster is really designed to process video for real-time streaming, not for media on-demand. To purchase QuickTime Player Pro go to *www .apple.com/quicktime/buy*. Cleaner can be purchased online at *www.discreet .com/products/cleaner/*. Follow the instructions on the Web site to install the software properly on your workstation. There is a difference between QuickTime files that are designed for streaming, called hinted files, and QuickTime files that are designed for download, called progressive download files. The main difference is in the way they are produced. Progressive download files are large files that require a long wait time to download over dial-up connections and that are downloaded to disk. Progressive download files are played back locally from the user's computer. Hinted files are QuickTime files that reside on a QuickTime or Darwin Streaming Server. Hinted files stream over IP networks the same way that RealSystem and Windows Media files stream. To create a QuickTime hinted or a progressive download file, use QuickTime Player Pro, Cleaner, or Sorenson Broadcaster.

QuickTime Player Pro

Open QuickTime Pro. Click File/Open Movie and browse to find your prerecorded source media. Import your media into QuickTime player. Play the media and verify that it has audio and video. Click on File/Export. An export window will appear. First, select Movie to QuickTime Movie from the drop menu. Then use the Options tab to adjust the video and audio settings (see Figure 8–5). Under Video Settings, change the compression codecs, playback quality, frames per second, key frames, and data limit. Use Table 8–2 for the proper settings. Use the Video Fil-

Figure 8–5
QuickTime Pro movie export settings

Table 8–2
Streaming Media Window Size Versus Quality

Size (pixels)	Modem Type	Total Bandwidth (kbps)	Audio Rates (kbps)	Frame Rate (fps)	Quality
320 × 240	LAN, DSL, Cable	150–750	32 normal 64 music	30	Near broadcast
240 × 180	ISDN or LAN	64–150	16 normal 20 music	15	Good
176 × 144	56 kbps or ISDN	56–64	8 normal 10 music	8–15	Poor
160 × 120	56 kbps	28–56	5 normal 8 music	5–8	Jerky

ter option to change video settings, adding color or sharpening the image. Under the Video Size option, adjust the output image size. The Sound Settings allow you to specify the desired audio compression codecs. Use QDesign Music 2 to adjust the rate-per-target-audience output. Remember to check the Prepare for Internet Streaming box, and select Hinted Streaming. Click on OK and save the file.

Cleaner

Follow the instructions to install Cleaner on your computer. Cleaner is the best conversion software on the market. However, it requires many computer resources to operate and relies heavily on CPU power and RAM. I recommend that you install Cleaner on workstations with dual CPUs and 256 MB of RAM or more. If you experience a slow conversion of media, do not be alarmed. The defaults on the software are designed to maximize the media output. It uses the best combination of filters to avoid bad images and sound. The results normally are very good compared to other media conversion software packages.

To create QuickTime streaming files with Cleaner, launch the application. Click on File/Open and search for the media you want to use as a source for the conversion process. The software will recognize AVI, QuickTime, and MPEG extensions. You cannot initiate the process if you use streaming files or a video signal originating in a capture card; the media must be digitized and saved to one of the three formats. Click on OK and import the media to Media Cleaner. A window will pop up with the source media. Note that a record has been created in the Cleaner Batch window. Next, you need to specify your choices for conversion and destination (of the output media). Using the right mouse button (in PCs), select either the wizard to assist you in determining your compression settings or preexisting profiles. To select a profile, click on Settings/ Apply Settings and scroll down. From the drop menu, select QuickTime –Streaming and choose your audience bandwidth. This selection will help you use the default settings in the software to encode your media. Refer to Table 8–2 for the proper settings for various target audiences. Using your right mouse button (in PCs), select the target destination. This location can be on your own workstation or on any other computer on your network. Click the Play icon in the lower right part of the batch window. Cleaner will start the conversion process.

Use Cleaner to convert multiple files to QuickTime format or to any other streaming format. The default settings use frame size, codecs, and other filters based on the standard for streaming files, as described in Table 8–2. To modify the default settings, follow the user instructions in the software Help section.

Sorenson Broadcaster

With Sorenson Broadcaster you can start streaming audio and/or video without any knowledge of compression, networks, or protocols. Purchase the software online at *www.sorenson.com*. Follow the instructions on the Web site to install the software properly on your workstation. The software comes with several predefined streaming configurations that let you create a basic broadcast, announce your broadcast, and start streaming within minutes. Before you start your broadcast, make sure Quick-Time 4.1 or later is installed on your encoding machine and that your audio and video capture devices are functioning properly.

Creating a Live Stream with Sorenson Broadcaster

1. Start the application. The encoder interface will launch along with a monitor window (see Figure 8–6). Select the Broadcast Properties button.
2. Click on the Source tab. You can use the predefined settings to encode audio or video, or you can choose User Defined to specify settings.

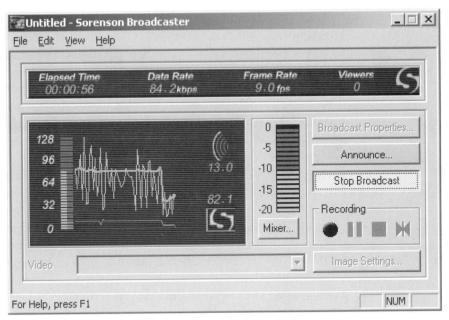

Figure 8 – 6
Sorenson Broadcaster interface

3. If you use User Defined settings, select your audio device from the drop menu. Configure the device by specifying the input method. Next configure the compression to be used. I recommend that you use QDesign Music 2 and adjust the sample rate according to your bandwidth. From the Video menu, select the proper capture card. Configure the device and specify the source and format of the video feed (see Figure 8–7). This part is an interface to your capture card settings.

4. Click on the Publishing tab. Enter the clip information (e.g., title, author, and copyright). If you are using a poster frame, browse your hard drive to locate it.

5. Click on Network. Define your webcast as a Unicast or Multicast, or Relay it to a distribution server. (See Chapter 10 for a comparison of the two webcasting methods.) Like Windows Media Encoder 7.0 and RealSystem Producer Plus, Sorenson Broadcaster can host up to 25 requests for playback as it webcasts a live video or audio feed.

6. If you choose Multicast, you will be assigned an IP address. If you choose Unicast, specify your workstation IP address. If you choose Relay, you will need to do additional configuration.

7. If you select the Relay option, you need to provide additional information to the encoder and to your distribution server (see Figure 8–8). Leave the assigned Multicast IP address as is. At the Program Area, select your environment. If you stream to your local LAN, use 1–Local. If you stream to your company WAN, use 15–Company. If you stream to the Internet, use 64–Country. Enter your distribution server IP number (where your DSS resides). Next, note the relay input audio and video port numbers. If your media distribution server is located behind a firewall, you need to open these ports for incoming traffic. The Destination Audio and Video Ports indicate the ports used to transmit audio and video from Sorenson Broadcaster. If your encoder is located behind a firewall, you need to open these port numbers for outbound audio and video traffic.

8. Create a reference link for the audience to see your webcast. On the Sorenson Broadcaster main window, click on the Announce

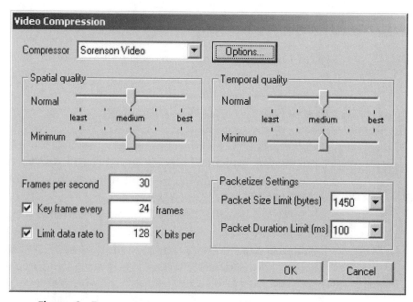

Figure 8–7
Sorenson Broadcast video compression settings

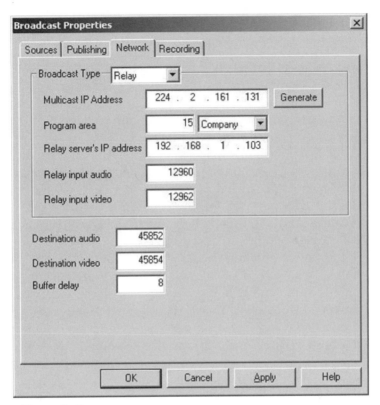

Figure 8–8
Sorenson Broadcast network settings

button. A window will pop up prompting you to save the reference file. Name the file and from the drop menu select Reference Movie as the Save as Type. Click on Save.

9. Transfer the reference movie file to your Web server. Point in your HTML page to this reference file.

10. Start Sorenson Broadcaster. Test the video feed by logging on to the Web page listing the link to the reference movie file. Click on the link and see if your QuickTime player will pop up to stream the live webcast.

Windows Media Encoding Tools

Since the introduction of Netshow Encoder version 3.0 in 1998, Microsoft has invested heavily in the development of a software encoder to create streaming files for both corporate and entertainment users. Today, Windows Media technologies provide high-quality audio and video to consumers, content providers, solution providers, software developers, and corporations. Windows Media offers the industry's only integrated rights-management solution and the most scalable and reliable streaming technology, according to tests by independent labs. Windows Media Technologies includes Windows Media Player for consumers, Windows Media Services for servers, Windows Media Tools for content creation, and Windows Media Software Development Kit (SDK) for software developers. Windows Media Player, available in 26 languages, is the fastest growing media player, challenging the market domination of RealNetworks RealPlayer. Its unique architecture permits the display of Web content in the player, making the player a fully functional multimedia engine. Unlike SMIL (the technology RealNetworks uses to display interactive presentations inside RealPlayer), Windows Media has full browser support for the very same components a browser supports (e.g., Java; Perl; or Dynamic Hyper Text Markup Language, DHTML). Like RealSystem Producer, the Windows Media encoder can webcast live video or audio feeds and can record to disk. The encoder provides an open platform for the user to modify encoding profiles or to rely on the default profiles that come with the software. To encode streaming files in the Windows format, download the latest encoder from *www.microsoft .com/windows/windowsmedia/*. Follow the installation instructions. The software will prompt you to reboot your system; close all applications and reboot. When you are back in Windows, open your workstation capture card software interface and configure it to see video and hear audio. When you can see video and hear audio, minimize the interface.

Webcasting Live Video

1. Launch the encoder and select Broadcast, Capture, or Convert a File Using the New Session Wizard. Click on OK.
2. Select Broadcast a Live Event from Attached Devices or Computer Screen. Click on Next.

3. Select the audio and video devices you are planning to use. Adjust the video settings or input method of your audio device (see Figure 8–9). Click on Next.

4. Select your outbound port. The default setting is port 8080. If your workstation is located behind a firewall, consult your network administrator to find out which ports are available for outbound traffic. Click on Next.

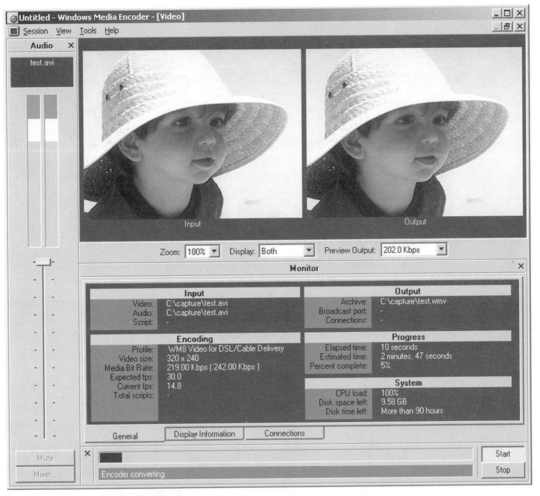

Figure 8–9
Windows Media Encoder 7

5. Select from the preset profiles. You can either edit these profiles or create new profiles. Follow the recommendations listed in Table 8–2 to create or modify your profiles. Click on Next.
6. To archive a copy of your webcast, choose a location on your hard drive. Click on Next.
7. Choose between the options of webcasting just your live feed or making use of the prerecorded content in your live webcast. Such files can serve as a welcome, an intermission, or a goodbye clip. To use this option, prepare short clips with proper information. These must be streaming files encoded in the same format and specifications as your planned webcast. Click on Next.
8. Enter the clip information (e.g., title, author, and copyright). Click on Next.
9. Review your settings and click on Finish. Return to the previous part of the wizard by clicking on the Back button.

You can now webcast live video. If you have decided to include additional prerecorded files, they will appear at the left side of the console. Click on the live or on-demand source of video to switch between the live feed and recorded files and generate an output signal. Refer to Chapter 9 to configure the Windows Media Server to distribute your webcast signal in a Unicast or Multicast mode.

Creating a Windows Media File

1. Launch the encoder and select Broadcast, Capture, or Convert a File Using the New Session Wizard. Click on OK.
2. Depending on your media source (e.g., tape device or camera connected to the workstation capture card or a precaptured AVI), select between Capture Audio or Video from Attached Device or Convert an Audio or Video File into Windows Media File. Click on Next.
3. If you selected Capture Audio or Video from Attached Device follow steps 3–9 from the Webcasting Live Video section, specifying where you want to save the streaming file and if you are planning to play it back from a Web server or media server.
4. If you selected Convert an Audio or Video File into Windows Media File, locate your source file on your hard drive and specify where you want to output the streaming file. Click on Next.

Table 8–3
Recommended Encoding Settings[a]

Aspect Ratio	Target Audience	Window Size	Bit Rate	Audio (voice)	Audio (music)	Frame Rate (fps)
Single bit stream						
4:3 Standard	Download or broadband	640 × 480	500–1000 kbps	64–96 kbps	64–96 kbps	30
	Broadband	320 × 240	400–650 kbps	44–64 kbps	64–96 kbps	30
	Mid-broadband	240 × 180	100–300 kbps	32–64 kbps	44–64 kbps	15
	Low band	176 × 144	Below 100 kbps	12–16 kbps	20 kbps	8–15
16:9 Letterbox	Download or broadband	640 × H[a]	500–1000 kbps	64–96 kbps	64–96 kbps	30
	Broadband	320 × H[a]	400–650 kbps	44–64 kbps	64–96 kbps	30
	Mid-broadband	320 × H[a]	100–300 kbps	32–64 kbps	44–64 kbps	15
	Low band	192 × H[a]	Below 100 kbps	12–16 kbps	20 kbps	8–15
Multibit streams						
4:3 Standard	Download or broadband	640 × 480	750 kbps + up 500 kbps + up	44–64 kbps	64–96 kbps	30
	Mid-broadband	320 × 240	300 kbps	32–64 kbps	44–64 kbps	15
	Low band	176 × 144	100 kbps 34 kbps 28 kbps	16 kbps 8 kbps 6.5 kbps	20 kbps 10 kbps 8 kbps	8–15
16:9 Letterbox	Download or broadband	640 × H[b]	750 kbps + up 500 kbps + up	44–64 kbps	64–96 kbps	30
	Mid-broadband	320 × H[b]	300 kbps	32–64 kbps	44–64 kbps	15
	Low band	192 × H[b]	100 kbps 34 kbps 28 kbps	16 kbps 8 kbps 6.5 kbps	20 kbps 10 kbps 8 kbps	8–15
Audio only						
	96–128 kbps	n/a	n/a	96 kbps	96 kbps	n/a
Audio-only multibit stream						
	64 kbps	n/a	n/a	64 kbps	64 kbps	n/a
	32 kbps	n/a	n/a	32 kbps	32 kbps	n/a
	20 kbps	n/a	n/a	20 kbps	20 kbps	n/a

[a] n/a, not applicable.
[b] Aspect ratio height varies per letterbox width size.

5. Specify whether the streaming file will play back from a Web server or a media server. Click on Next.
6. Select one of the preset profiles. You can either edit these profiles or create new profiles. Follow the recommendations listed in Table 8–2 to create or modify your profiles. Click on Next.
7. Enter the clip information (e.g., title, author, and copyright). Click on Next.
8. Review your settings and click on Finish. Return to the previous part of the wizard by clicking on the Back button.

Table 8–3 lists the recommended settings for QuickTime (both QuickTime Pro and Sorenson Broadcaster), RealSystem Producer, Windows Media Encoder, and any other third-party encoding tool such as Cleaner. Use the information as a reference. Different media clips require different settings depending on the way the media were recorded. Content with "talking heads" requires a different setting from content showing a car race.

Summary

- The proper operation of your workstation relies on the step-by-step configuration of both hardware and software. Become familiar with your capture software before proceeding to encode streaming files.
- Live webcast is totally different than the creation of streaming files for video on-demand. The production of a live webcast is much more complicated because it requires connectivity between the encoding workstation and the distribution server.
- Both RealSystem and Windows Media encoders can produce live webcasts and video on-demand files. The Windows Media encoder is free software. RealSystem Producer Plus is bundled with a few purchased webcast tools or it comes as a purchased stand-alone encoder.
- To webcast in QuickTime format, purchase Sorenson Broadcaster. To create QuickTime files for video on-demand, use Cleaner or QuickTime Pro. QuickTime files are available as progressive download files or as hinted streaming files.

9

Media Servers

Building Your Own Media Server

Compared to encoding workstations, which capture and encode a limited number of streams, media servers require greater speed and wider memory. Encoding workstations compress media (using an intensive CPU load), but recently designed PCI-based capture cards process the video, freeing computer resources to do other tasks. The purpose of media servers is to support data requests from multiple users at the same time. No other tasks should be assigned to your media server. If you want to run other applications, such as word processing, email, Internet Information Services (IIS) Web server, or Structured Query Language (SQL) database, I recommend assigning a different computer to handle them. A good media server should be capable of making the best use of its hardware and software to provide a stable and scalable delivery of content to the largest audience possible. To achieve this, a media server must be built with careful consideration.

Virtually all mid-range computers today use either Intel-based Pentium 4 or higher processors for Windows or RISC (Reduced Instruction Set Computing) processors for UNIX. The features of RISC systems make them faster than Intel architectures when operating in a multiprocessor environment, but streaming-technology servers are mostly limited to Windows operating systems (with the exceptions of RealSystem Server, which supports UNIX, and QuickTime Streaming Server, which was designed for Macintosh). Streaming software requires a faster CPU and more RAM to delivery good quality video at rates of 300–1,000 kbps.

The large computer manufacturers do not build media servers. You must acquire a server with the proper hardware and software specification and designate it to act as a media server. In general, media servers require at least dual processors and at least 256 MB of RAM. Selected computer manufacturers offer servers that can be customized to serve as media servers–the tower or rack-mount options offered by Dell PowerEdge Series or the Compaq Proliant Series, for example.

In the past, I provided consulting services to companies or enterprises that were interested in deploying streaming media on their internal networks or for presenting their content to the public. Group discussions took place and plans were drawn up to prepare budgets for equipment purchases. When I drafted the list of components needed to build encoding workstations and media servers and the estimated cost, the topic of saving money by assembling these computers inhouse always came up. In every case, my position was the same. I oppose the assembly of computer parts to build stand-alone workstations or servers when these computers are expected to compress and deliver streaming video. IT people are a group of talented individuals, struggling everyday to catch up with the race for new technologies that are changing at the speed of light. In the Internet age, technologies that were popular six months ago must be upgraded or they will become obsolete. Building an encoding workstation or a media server, which is in all respects a critical component of a new emerging medium, is a risk. In the very near future, production companies and enterprises will rely on stable redundant systems to deliver their media over IP networks. There is a significant difference between assembling a desktop clone that can be replaced in a few days (in the event of failure) and assembling an encoding workstation or a media server that is expected to be up 24/7. An employee without a desktop PC for a few days (until it can be replaced by the IT department) will cause a minimal loss of productivity to the company. However, a non-operating encoding workstation that cannot encode an urgent piece of media or, worse, a media server that cannot serve streaming files to company employees or to visitors on the company's Web site will result in a much larger loss of productivity. In some cases, it may even result in loss of business.

The solution is to rely on well-shaped vendor systems that provide support for equipment that needs repair or a fast replacement. Most computer vendors offer technical support and hardware replacement plans with response times ranging from 4 to 24 hours. These plans are reliable and I have used them many times. You call the toll-free number of the vendor, a technician identifies the problem and either (based on your support plan) dispatches a live technician to your site or ships you a replacement part overnight. Another, not less important consideration tilting the scale toward external purchase rather than the internal assembly of parts is the fact that computers and servers built by computer vendors have been tested for reliability, stability, and redundancy before they are added to a production line. These vendors' technical support personnel have experience solving malfunctions of parts and software. Their cumulative knowledge is based on hundreds if not thousands of similar cases. The bottom line is that I strongly recommend contacting a computer vendor such as Dell or Compaq when you purchase your next encoding workstation or media server. First, buy an off-the-shelf server that runs under an operating system such as Windows NT 4.0 or Windows 2000 and then add to it the necessary components to make it a media server.

However, there are exceptions. In the event that the encoding workstation or the media server you are planning is not mission critical, meaning that you are working under no pressure; the encoding workstation or media server is one of many (and therefore easily replaceable); you are conducting an experiment trial; or you expect no damage from a server being down, then proceed with the assembly of parts and build your own media server. This chapter covers preferred components for media servers and helps you prepare a wish list before contacting a vendor.

Recommended Components

Table 9–1 shows the minimum and suggested hardware and software requirements for an average media server that hosts QuickTime Darwin Streaming Server, RealSystem Server, or Windows Media Services Server. These recommendations are not meant as an endorsement of one vendor over another. It is a list of hardware and software components that work best when combined to host streaming media files on an IP-based network. To install additional parts on your old or new system, refer to the vendor's instructions. Be aware that some vendors will void your warranty if you replace or install parts on their equipment.

Table 9–1
Building Your Own Media Server

	Minimum Components	Recommended Components
Processor	Pentium II 266 MHz or later	Dual processor Pentium III 1 GB or later
Memory	128 MB RAM	1 GB RAM
Network card	10/100 MB TCP/IP Ethernet card	Dual 100 MB TCP/IP Fast Ethernet card
Hard disk	IDE hard drive 5,400 rpm or higher; 50 MB for media server software and 500 MB for content hosting	Multiple Ultra 160 SCSI hard drives 10,000 rpm or higher in RAID 0, 3, or 5 configuration; 50 MB for media server software and 20 GB for content hosting
Audio card	Not applicable	Not applicable
Video card	Video card that supports video for Windows and at least 8 MB memory	Video card that supports video for Windows and at least 16 MB memory
Software	Windows 2000 SP2; Windows NT 4.0 SP 6a; Internet Explorer 5 or higher; Microsoft terminal Service (Win2000); or remote connection software (WinNT); Software firewall	Windows 2000 Server SP2; Windows NT 4.0 SP 6a; Internet Explorer 5 or higher; Microsoft terminal Service; SSH connection software; Hardware firewall
Backup	CD burner with SCSI connection	DLT tape system; DVD Burner with SCSI connection

CPU

Media servers are not like other computers. They experience a large number of requests from many users at the same time. For example, the president of a company with 2,000 employees recorded a message and asked his IT team to encode the video and post it on the company intranet site. If all the employees were encouraged to watch the video, in a matter of hours the media server would be hit by hundreds of requests. A normal desktop PC will crash under such an overwhelming use of resources; a media server that is properly configured can handle this capacity. I recommend a dual CPU machine. Using fewer media servers that are load balanced, as opposed to one media server, is the best solution; this distributes users over multiple media servers for the best performance.

Hard Disks

Other components that you must consider are hard disks. Most hard disks today operate using either the Advanced Technology Attachment/Integrated Drive Electronics (ATA/IDE) with an average data throughput of approximately 2–9 MBps. An important feature of a multimedia hard drive is its capability to read and write quickly. Video files are normally larger than image or text files. A hard drive that has slow read and write capabilities will perform poorly when multiple requests to read a video file are sent to the media server. I recommend using fast or wide Small Computer System Interface (SCSI) hard drives with 80 MBps or greater throughput and 10,000 revolutions per minute (rpm). The current generation of high-capacity SCSI hard drives includes 36–72 GB drives made by Seagate, Hewlett-Packard, IBM, and Compaq. Order either Wide Ultra 2 drives (80-MBps output) or the new Wide Ultra 3 (160-MBps output).

Due to hard-drive wear and tear, your stored media may become corrupted. Because digital data is stored bits, some of the bits may lose their ability to be recognized by a computer and therefore will not play back properly. To avoid damage to your stored data, install a RAID solution. This requires multiple hard drives (all similar in model and capacity) and uses either a hardware or software controller to bind all the hard disks together. The RAID solution takes a part of the total space available and creates a backup of the stored media. This backup constantly monitors for loss of data in the normal storage section and replaces corrupt media when necessary. The installation of a hardware- or software-based RAID system is complicated and requires extensive knowledge in computer technology. Unless you are familiar with the process, ask your computer vendor to include this option when you purchase your new media server. RAID solutions are expensive because they use additional components, but in the long term they are efficient and may save the cost of reproducing lost media or lost business revenues.

Memory

A media server supporting a large number of users requesting streaming files at the same time requires a lot of memory. A server's reliability depends on its ability to perform designated tasks with available resources. Every application running on a server uses a certain amount of existing memory. Media servers should run with a minimum of 256 MB of RAM. Windows Media Services can be monitored using the Windows NT or 2000 server performance monitor tools. QuickTime and RealSystem Server do not provide this function, but it is known that they require additional memory as the number of users accessing the media grows. For best performance, calculate approximately 256 MB of RAM for every 50 MB of throughput you plan to serve. For example, with a dual CPU Pentium III server with 256 MB of RAM, you can serve approximately 175 requests for 256-kbps streams, 500 requests for 100-kbps streams, or 1,250 requests for 56-kbps streams. The calculation is done based on 50 Mb divided by the actual bandwidth used by a single user. For example, 50 Mb divided by 0.256 Mb equals approximately 175. This applies to a media server hosting any of the three streaming technologies discussed in this book.

Network Cards

Network cards are crucial components of your media server. They provide Ethernet connectivity between the media server, other media servers, and your audience. Most computer manufacturers provide a built-in NIC with new systems. Check your server order to verify that the NIC is a fast Ethernet card and not a $^{10}/_{100}$ Ethernet card. The throughput of $^{10}/_{100}$ Ethernet cards ranges between 40 and 50 MBps instead of the 100 MBps that fast Ethernet offers. I recommend that you have more than one NIC in your media servers. Additional cards will provide fault tolerance and more bandwidth. Assign to each NIC a separate IP number. A common way to balance traffic (and increase capacity) during a live webcast is to include in the reference file links to more than one IP number. When the first NIC maximizes its throughput capacity, users will roll over to the next card.

Here is an example of how to create a rollover process. The action is hidden inside the reference file that is called by the user. When the user initiates this call, the reference file calls the media server. If more than one media server is listed in the reference file, the reference file will attempt to reach the first server on the list. If that attempt fails, it will try the second media server, and so on. Try some rollover techniques using the following instructions.

QuickTime Streaming

This solution is provided in the SMIL file reference. Here is an example of a SMIL file. Copy and paste the syntax, replacing the media server's settings with your own.

```
<smil>
    <head>
    <meta name=TITLE content =Show Name/>
    <meta name=AUTHOR content =Who Produce the Clip/>
    <meta name=COPYRIGHT content =© Company, Year/>
    </head>
    <body>
    <seq>
    <video src=rtsp://dss_serverIP_1/alias.sdp />
    <video src=rtsp://dss_serverIP_2/alias.sdp />
    </seq>
</body>
</smil>
```

Use this SMIL file as reference to the live stream. More instructions on how to create a Unicast or Multicast stream are available in Chapter 10.

RealSystem Server

This solution is provided in the RAM or SMIL reference. Here is an example of a SMIL file. Copy and paste the syntax, replacing the media server's settings with your own.

```
<smil>
    <head>
    <meta name=TITLE content =Show Name/>
    <meta name=AUTHOR content =Who Produce the Clip/>
    <meta name=COPYRIGHT content =© Company, Year/>
    </head>
    <body>
    <video
    src=rtsp://RealServer_serverIP_1:port/ramgen/encoder/alias.rm />
    <video
    src=rtsp://RealServer_serverIP_2:port/ramgen/encoder/alias.rm />
    </body>
</smil>
```

Use this SMIL file as reference to the live stream. More instructions on how to create a Unicast or Multicast stream are available in Chapter 10.

Windows Media

This solution is provided in the ASX file. Copy and paste the syntax, replacing the media server's settings with your own.

```
<ASX Version=3.0>
<TITLE>Show Name</TITLE>
<AUTHOR>Who Produce the Clip</AUTHOR>
<COPYRIGHT>© Company, Year</COPYRIGHT>
    <entry>
    <ref href = mms://windowsmedia_serverIP_1/stream_alias />
    </entry>
    <entry>
    <ref href = mms://windowsmedia_serverIP_2/stream_alias />
    </entry>
</ASX>
```

Use this ASX file as reference to the live stream. More instructions on how to create a Unicast or Multicast stream are in Chapter 10.

Software

A stable operating system can deliver reliable service. Whether or not you choose to install an operating system such as Windows NT or Windows 2000 on the server that you have designated as a streaming media server, make sure you comply with all the necessary steps during the installation. If you install the operating system yourself or if it has already been installed on the computer when you buy it, there is still more work you need to do before you can proceed with the installation of streaming services. As we all know, Microsoft is constantly updating its software with numerous patches that improve software reliability and security. First, launch Internet Explorer and let Windows search for the latest updates on the Microsoft Web site, *windowsupdate.microsoft.com*. Refer to the recommended software requirements listed in Table 9–1 and install the proper service pack for your operating system. Next, install security patches or critical updates, as recommended by the software installation wizard on the Microsoft Web site. After you have installed the proper service pack, upgrade Internet Explorer to the version listed in the table.

Next, install a firewall to protect your media server from unauthorized intruders. Consult your IT department and ask them to assist you in allocating the server a location on the network where it will be accessible to employees logging on from both the local network and the public Internet. A low-cost and easy-to-install software firewall solution such as Check Point (*www.checkpoint.com*) or Internet Security Systems (*www.iis.net*) is your best option. Firewalls completely block UDP or TCP ports, making it almost impossible to stream video on the server. Refer to Chapter 2 for the ports used by streaming software. Calculate the risks of opening these ports on your firewall. What you are concerned with is the necessary ports that an encoder, player, or server needs to communicate when a request for a stream comes in and how the requested media will stream out. Review Table 2–3 in Chapter 2 and make a list that covers all three technologies. Then configure the firewall and open these ports. If you are not an IT administrator, ask your IT department to be part of your streaming-solution deployment team. I strongly recommend consulting an experienced network administrator before configuring a firewall.

After installing a firewall, plan how you would like to facilitate the remote control of the server. Windows Terminal Service provides a reliable solution to accessing the media server from everywhere over an IP network. Add, if possible, additional security by enabling Secure Shell (SSH) connectivity on the media server. SSH is a UNIX-based command interface and protocol for securely gaining access to a remote computer. It is widely used by network administrators to control Web and other kinds of servers remotely. SSH commands are encrypted and secure in several ways. Both ends of the client-server connection are authenticated using digital certificates and passwords are protected by being encrypted. Consult your IT department to install SSH on your system. For more information about SSH encryption technology and its advantages for creating safe communication between two computers log on to this book's companion Web site, *www.streaminghandbook.com*.

Last but not least, monitor your server performance using Microsoft System Performance Monitor. Select from the monitoring options the items that describe the best memory loads, processor use, network interface use, and overall system performance. The numbers showing performance during peak time will give you a good idea of whether your system can handle heavy loads and, if not, how to reconfigure it for optimization.

Load-Balancing Solutions

Media servers are limited in capacity. Their ability to serve streaming files to multiple users depends on a combination of resources that includes CPU power, RAM, and, most important, network cards. Network cards have multiple IP numbers that are used to identify a server on computer networks. A load-balancing solution will distribute the processing across an array of media servers so that no single server is overwhelmed by the load. There are two ways to implement load balancing: by using Domain Name Service (DNS) round robin or by using Windows Load Balancing Service (WLBS). Both solutions increase the throughput of media and provide redundant fault-tolerance performance. DNS can be configured by the network administrators who control the network segment where your servers are located; the configuration is done on a DNS server. WLBS has to be configured in every computer and server that is assigned as a member of the load-balancing scheme.

DNS Round Robin Solution

The DNS round robin method works by answering DNS queries with an entire list of IP addresses rather than a single IP address. For example, if Web page links call streaming media files residing on a media server, this generates a DNS query. The media player that performs the query usually chooses the first IP address and then references that server during the connection. To ensure that the same IP address is not chosen over and over, the list is rotated so that a different IP address appears at the top of the list each time. To illustrate, let us assume that we have three media servers using the following names and IP addresses:

mediaserver1.domain.com   at IP 192.168.1.3
mediaserver2.domain.com   at IP 192.168.1.4
mediaserver3.domain.com   at IP 192.168.1.5

To set up the servers so that media-player (client) requests rotate via round robin, use multiple A records. An A record is a DNS record that maps a host to IP addresses. In this example we want all clients that access our media server to use the name *mediaserver.domain.com*. To share all requests among the three servers, set up the A records as follows:

```
mediaserver.domain.com. 60 IN A 192.168.1.3
mediaserver.domain.com. 60 IN A 192.168.1.4
mediaserver.domain.com. 60 IN A 192.168.1.5
```

The period at the end of the name *mediaserver.domain.com* in each A record is mandatory because names without ending dots are sometimes interpreted as relative to some domain other than the root. If the dot is missing, the requests will loop in an endless cycle without recognizing the proper IP number of the server.

There are advantages and disadvantages to using round robin DNS for media servers. The main advantages of DNS round robin are that it is simple to configure and it is free. Adding a few records to your DNS entry table allows lists of servers to appear and act as a single server. The first disadvantage of round robin is that it is not a true sharing or load-balancing technique. Load-balancing solutions measure the load on the servers and forward client requests to other servers in order to distribute the work load evenly. A round robin solution does not measure the server load; rather it splits client requests among multiple servers, regardless of their actual ability to provide service. For example, say that 100 clients attempt to access content; 20 clients have 56-kBps connectivity and the remaining 80 have 300-kBps. They are all directed to the first IP. If an additional 50 clients with 56 kBps join the webcast five minutes later, they also will be directed to the first IP. Only when the first IP exceeds its network card capacity will the next client be directed to the second IP on the round robin list and only because there was no response from the first IP (because its output capacity was exceeded). The second disadvantage is that, if one of the servers is not operating well or is down, client requests will still be forwarded to this IP address, resulting in no response.

WLBS Solution

WLBS allows incoming IP traffic to be dynamically distributed across multiple servers. It transparently distributes the client requests among the hosts and lets the clients access the list of servers using one or more virtual IP addresses. This solution provides clients with access to a pool of IPs that appear to be a single server. WLBS servers communicate among themselves to provide the following:

- **Failure detection**—The WLBS servers constantly monitor one another to make sure all the servers are healthy. If a server fails, the others adjust and take over the workload. Similar technology is used in a primary- and backup-domain controller scheme.
- **Load balancing**—WLBS servers use a distributed algorithm to statistically map the workload. The hosts communicate with one

another to determine the status of the pool and which hosts are available for load balancing.

- **Scalability**—WLBS can be scaled to meet the demands of the service. As traffic increases, just add another server to the pool, with up to 32 servers possible in any one pool. Now your capacity is limited to 32 servers multiplied by the number of megabytes per card—if there are 100 MB per card on each server, this equals 3,200 MB throughput.

To learn more about WLBS and to download an instructional white paper, log on to *www.microsoft.com/ntserver/techresources/deployment/NTserver/WlbsDeploy.asp*.

Hardware Installation

Media servers operate as command centers. Their job is to host streaming media files by maintaining maximum performance. To provide reliable service to your customers (both internal corporate customers and external clients), keep in mind the dual rule, or the rule of redundancy. Redundancy means that you need dual processors to balance CPU loads, dual fans in case of a breakdown, dual power houses in case one burns out, dual NICs in case one fails, RAID storage in case of bad clusters, and a 24/7 monitoring system that will alert you or the administrator of the server to potential failures. Do not compromise—this basic configuration of hot swappable drives, multiple fans, and power houses is preferable.

In a perfect world, you would be able to order a server that already has all these components. Then you would just need to install software to make the server run. However, you might already have a server and want to configure it as a media server. Budget considerations can mean that you are using existing hardware for a new purpose, which means that it will have to be converted.

To make things simple, take a blank paper and split it into two columns. In the left column, write the specifications of your existing hardware. In the right column, write the minimum or recommended components, as listed in Table 9–1. Price whatever items are missing and check their compatibility with both the old-hardware vendor and new-parts vendor. Assemble the missing parts and proceed with the installation according to the manufacturer's instructions. Normally, you will need to add more RAM and additional hard drives. If your system requires an additional CPU or adding RAID configuration (hardware or software), consider purchasing a brand-new system instead. With the cost of entire systems dropping, it might not be such a bad idea to buy a completely new server.

Software Installation

For maximum performance, I recommend that each media server be installed on a separate computer. Media servers use extensive CPU power, RAM, and bandwidth to facilitate multiple-user connections to live webcasts. Media on-demand requires fewer resources. The exception is a server with a high volume of concurrent requests. All three servers are ready to stream content when you first install them and will stream on-demand presentations and files that you place in the content directory. However, each media server has to be configured differently to stream live webcasts or to multicast live webcasts.

The following instructions are for the installation of each of the three media servers on a Windows NT 4.0 or Windows 2000 Server. You must have administrator privileges on your domain network or on your computer to perform the installation. After the installation, test the performance by simulating multiple requests for both live and on-demand media. A careful observation of performance will provide you with a good diagnostic of how your server will perform under severe conditions.

QuickTime Server
(Darwin Streaming Server for Windows NT or 2000)

Darwin Streaming Server operates on a Windows operating system only if it is installed on Windows NT 4.0 with service pack 5 or higher or on Windows Server 2000 with service pack 2. Look at the server hardware requirements listed in Table 9–1 for the correct hardware and software settings necessary to operate Darwin Streaming Servers.

QuickTime Streaming Server Public Preview requires the Mac X operating system. It is designed to run on Macintosh computers. Apple includes a QuickTime Server with every Mac X operating system. For other operating systems, the Darwin Streaming Server is available for Linux

(Red Hat 5.2 and later; 6.2 highly recommended), Solaris 7, FreeBSD UNIX 3.4, and Windows NT Server 4.0 or Windows 2000 Server. Apple provides technical support only for QuickTime Streaming Server running on the Mac X operating system. The DSS is equivalent to QuickTime Streaming Server. It includes powerful streaming enhancements and a Web-based administration interface. Documentation for the installation of DSS on a Windows operating system is currently very limited. To install the server on a Windows platform, follow the instructions listed here. If you run into difficulties consult the online companion Web site for this book at *www.streaminghandbook.com*.

Here is the installation process:

1. Download the latest version of DSS from *www.publicsource.apple.com/projects/streaming/*.

2. Download ActivePerl version 5.6.1 or higher from *www.activestate.com/Products/ActivePerl/download.plex*. Select the MSI option.

3. Remember that the minimum requirements for software installation on a Windows NT 4.0 server are service pack 5 or higher and Microsoft Windows Installer 1.1, available from http://download.microsoft.com/download/platformsdk/wininst/1.1/NT4/EN-US/InstMsi.exe. There are no further requirements for a Windows 2000 server. To access the administrator area you need Internet Explorer 5.0.

4. Install the ActivePerl application. Accept the terms in the license agreement and follow the instructions to install Perl on the C drive. Do not install it on another drive because DSS will look for it using this path: *C:\Perl\perl.exe*. If the installation goes smoothly skip steps 5–7 and go to step 8.

5. If the MSI version does not install properly and you get an error message, download the as-packaged version. This 12-MB file is a compressed file with a .zip extension. Unzip it and open the package in your *Temp* directory.

6. You now need to use the command prompt to install ActivePerl. Open the *Temp* directory, and double-click on the *Installer.bat* file. This opens the command prompt (in MS-DOS) application and you will be asked to designate where you want the application to install. Type *C:\Perl*. Follow the instructions on the screen with Y (for yes) to all questions.

7. When ActivePerl finishes installation, verify that a Perl directory has been created on your C drive. Open the *Bin* folder

and double-click on *perl.exe*. This opens the command prompt again.

8. Now proceed with the installation of DSS. Put the compressed file inside your *Temp* folder and unzip it. Extract the folder contents to *C:\Darwin Streaming Server*. Make sure DSS has been extracted and is installed on your C drive. Open the directory, locate the *Install.bat* file, and double-click on it. This launches the command prompt program and you will see the installation proceeding in the window. When you are prompted, hit any key to finish and exit.

9. When both ActivePerl and DSS are successfully installed, test your DSS server. To configure the server, first launch the administration Web interface. For DSS administration to operate via a browser, Perl must be active. Open *C:\Program Files\Darwin Streaming Server* and double-click on the *streamingadminserver.pl* file. If the file launches a command prompt window, proceed to the following steps. If it asks what application it should use to open the file, use the browse function to locate *C:\Perl\bin\perl.exe* and assign it as the default application. Minimize the command prompt window and launch a browser. Then follow these steps:

Step 1. Type in the address *http://your_computer_name:1220/*. The setup assistant will prompt you to assign a new user name and password. Write down this information for future reference.

Step 2. Specify if you want the communication between your browser and the media server to be encrypted. If you are planning to manage your server from a remote location (connecting with a browser over the Internet), I recommend that you enable this option.

Step 3. Assign one or more folders for live media reference or on-demand files. The default will be *C:\Program Files\Darwin Streaming Server\Movies*.

Step 4. Streaming on port 80 allows you to stream through firewalls. Check the box only if you do not have a Web server on the same computer as the DSS. A Web server operating on the same computer as the DSS will create a conflict in transmission because Web servers use port 80 for the delivery of Web pages and more.

Click on Enter and the DSS administrator interface will launch.

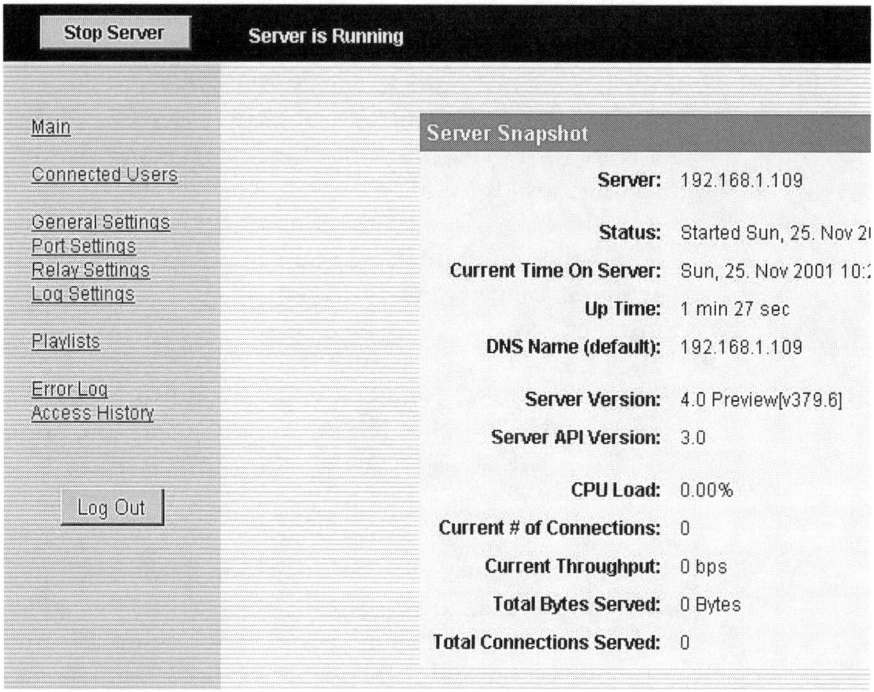

Figure 9-1
Apple Darwin Streaming Server settings

Figure 9-1 shows the administrator main window. Verify the information listed, and then use the left menu navigation bar to review the server settings or to make changes. Note at the upper right corner of the screen the name that DSS uses as identification when communicating with QuickTime players or with other Darwin Streaming Servers. If you are using a domain network with DNS support, use this name to reference the DSS server. You can use the computer IP number if your network is using assigned static IP numbers. In a network with dynamic assigned IP numbers, I recommend that you use the computer name.

RealSystem Server 8 (for Windows NT or 2000 Server)

To install RealServer you have two options. You can download a free evaluation package that will support up to 25 concurrent streams, or you can purchase a RealSystem Server of 100 seats or more from Real-Networks. To install RealSystem Server you need the installation file and a license file that is generated when you order either of the servers online. Follow these steps to install RealSystem Server on your media server:

1. Copy and paste the installation file (10-MB file) and the license file onto your hard drive.
2. Create a new folder on your C drive, *C:\Program Files\Real\RealServer\License,* and put the license file inside.
3. Double-click on the installation file.
4. The install wizard will ask you to close all applications. Click on Next.
5. Browse to locate the license key. Use the path to the folder you created in step 2, *C:\Program Files\Real\RealServer\License\file_name.lic.* Click on Next.
6. Accept the terms and conditions. Click on Next.
7. For better performance, choose to install RealSystem Server on the C drive. Click on Next.
8. Enter a user name and password. Remember to write them down. You will need them later to log on to the server administrator interface. Click on Next.
9. You will be asked to verify the port numbers that RealSystem Server will use to stream RTSP, PNM, and HTTP streams. Click on Next each time.
10. If you want to install RealSystem Server as a NT service, leave the box checked (recommended). Click on Next.
11. Verify your selection and click on Continue.
12. RealSystem Server will install. This may take a few minutes. A window will pop up when the installation is complete. Select Launch the RealSystem Administrator and click on OK.
13. Your default browser will pop up. Enter the user name and password you selected in step 8. Click on Enter.
14. Use the left menu bar to configure the server. Click on Configure/General Setup and do the following (see Figure 9–2):
    - **Ports**–Verify that all ports you selected before are entered.
    - **Logging On**–Enable logging on with a rolling frequency of one month. Apply the same to error logs. Click on Apply and confirm the change. The change will place after the server restarts.

- **HTTP Delivery**–Not applicable.
- **IP Binding**–If you have more than one NIC (and IP), assign an individual IP to RealServer.
- **MIME Types**–Not applicable.
- **Mount Points**–Current settings point all media requests to be pulled from: *C:\Program Files\Real\RealServer\Media*. If you wish to change this, use the Edit Mount Point and point to *E:\RealRoot*, for example. Click on Apply and restart Real-Server (not your media server).
- **Connection Control**–Assign RealSystem Server the amount of allocated streams. For example, if you licensed 100 seats, enter that number here.
- **ISP Hosting**–Not applicable.

Figure 9–2
RealSystem Administrator Port setup page

15. You are now ready to stream media on-demand from your Real-System Server. Put a few streaming files in your *Content* directory and test the stream.

16. Open RealPlayer and type in the File/Open Location option *rtsp://realserver_ip:port/file_name.rm*.

Windows Media Services 4.1 (for Windows NT or 2000 Server)

Windows Media Server is integrated into the Windows NT and 2000 Server operating systems. Original equipment manufacturer (OEM) versions of the Windows NT and 2000 Server may not have the media services active. To install new Windows Media Server components, download the software from Microsoft's Web site, *www.microsoft.com/windows/windowsmedia/download/default.asp*. Refer to Table 9–1 for the minimum requirements before installation, then follow these steps:

1. Copy and paste the server application file to your hard drive. Close all applications and then double-click on the file.

2. Confirm the installation. You must agree to the license agreement. Click on OK.

3. The Windows Media Server wizard will list all the components it plans to install. Click on Next.

4. Verify that your computer has all the required Windows-related software. Click on Next.

5. Choose a complete installation. Windows Media Server can only install if the computer has the Windows NT or 2000 Server operating system. Click on Next.

6. Choose the path for installation. To avoid future conflicts, select the C partition as the location. Click on Next.

7. Agree that your system can create the Windows Media folder.

8. Select the location to store your streaming media. This should be a partition with at least 500 MB of space. Click on Next.

9. Select Do Not Enable HTTP Streaming. Click on Next. (Before you can enable HTTP streaming, you must first eliminate a potential conflict between the built-in IIS that is the default on the Windows NT and 2000 Server operating systems and the Windows Media Server—they will both try to use port 80 to stream content over HTTP.)

10. Let the system create a new account. Click on Finish.

11. Wait until the installation is complete. This may take few minutes. When the installation is complete, you will be asked to launch the Windows Media Server Administrator interface. Click on OK.

12. The administrator interface will launch as a Web page in your browser (see Figure 9–3). Use the menu on the left side to access Configure Server/Server Properties. Configure your server as follows:

- **General**–Use this area to limit the server throughput by setting maximum clients, bandwidth, or file bit rate. For better performance, limit the server by bandwidth. In Maximum Bandwidth, calculate and enter 80% of the maximum bandwidth capacity of your server's combined network cards. For example, if you have one Fast Ethernet 100-MBps network card, enter 80,000 for 80 MB.

- **Publishing Point Security**–This provides secure access to content. At this stage, leave the settings as is.

- **Distribution Authentication**–This area is used to secure streams between two media servers. At this stage, leave the settings as is.

- **Publishing Point Logging**–Check daily, weekly, or monthly log generation. Note the path to where the server saves the logs. Use these logs later to monitor media use and server performance.

- **HTTP Streaming and Distribution**–Specify here if you want to enable the media server to stream over HTTP ports. HTTP outbound streaming is enabled by default through port 80 on the host computer. If you have a Web server on the same computer, you must either disable the IIS or configure the computer registry to route the Windows Media Server outbound stream over port 8080. Windows NT Server requires that you modify the registry manually. Windows 2000 Server is configured in advance (OEM versions only). Changes in this section will require you to completely reboot the system.

13. When you installed the Windows Media Server, the system created a storage bin for your streaming media files. To modify an existing directory or add a new one, use the left menu and open

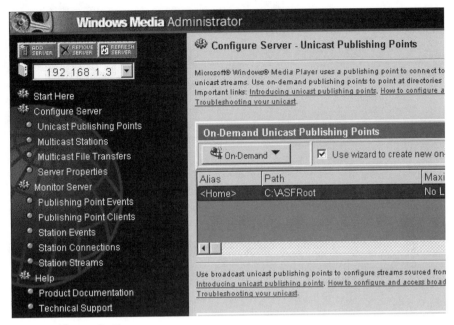

Figure 9–3
Windows Media Services Unicast Publishing Points setup page

Configure Server/Unicast Publishing Points. The upper section lists this directory.

14. Open Windows Explorer. Find the path to this directory, and then copy and paste a streaming media file into it.

15. Launch your media player. Select File/Open and type *mms:// your_windowsmediaserver_IP/file_name.asf* to test the media server.

If your computer runs an IIS and you wish to stream media using HTTP, you need to make changes in your system registry. To edit the registry and enable the Windows Media Unicast service on a Windows computer with a IIS 4.0 or higher do the following:

1. Start Registry Editor—click on Start, click on Run, and then type *Regedit.*

2. In Registry Editor, use the tree view to navigate through the following path: *HKEY_LOCAL_MACHINE\System\Current ControlSet\Services\nsunicast.*

3. Double-click on DependOnService.

4. Open the Multi-String Editor.

5. Type *W3SVC* at the end of the list of services. W3SVC is the setting that makes Windows Media server components dependent on Microsoft IIS.

6. Reboot the computer.

Summary

- Media servers are required to serve multiple user requests at the same time. Plan the deployment of a reliable media server by carefully considering its components. Always prepare for a failure. Build your server with dual hot swappable components that can be replaced when necessary.

- Use RAID storage to protect your content media. In addition, carefully design your media server by placing it behind a firewall and enabling users to access it both on a secure network and through the Internet.

- Deploy multiple media servers to guarantee smooth performance. Use a WLBS solution to distribute client requests among multiple servers.

- All three streaming technologies can operate on a Windows NT or Windows 2000 server. It is necessary to preconfigure the server to support its proper operation. This includes upgrading and updating your software to ensure secure, reliable, and stable performance.

10

Streaming Content

Unicast versus Multicast

Unicast and Multicast are two methods used to deliver streaming content across networks to end-users. Each has advantages and disadvantages; it is up to you to decide which method is best for your needs. The best way to understand the differences between the two methods is by observing the relationship between the player-client and the host media server.

A Unicast stream has a one-to-one client-server relationship. This is similar to the experience of operating your VCR. When a user makes a request to stream media, the server acts on the request and sends a unique individual stream to that client, one stream for each request. No other client has access to this stream. Each client has its own connection that can be terminated by the client or the server operator.

The main advantage of a one-to-one connection is that the communication channel between the client and the server stays open as packets travel from the server to the client, meaning that a communication channel exists between the two, which maximizes the ability to compensate for lost data and to deliver a better experience to end-users. Based on this special communication channel between the player-client and the host server, users can pause, fast forward, and rewind the incoming stream, but only in media on-demand streams. During live Unicast webcasts, users cannot control the real-time stream. Figure 10–1 illustrates a Unicast data flow.

A Multicast stream is more like the experience of watching television. The media server generates one single stream that allows multiple player-clients to connect to it. Users watch the content from the time

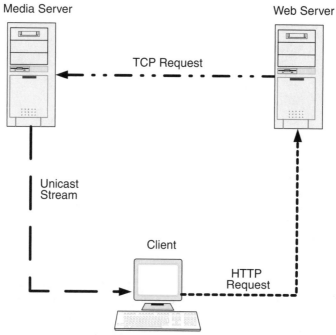

Figure 10–1
Sample of a Unicast schema

they join the broadcast. The client connects to the stream, but not to the server. During a Multicast stream, clients cannot send feedback data to the server, which means that the player-client cannot request the replacement of lost packets. This method saves network bandwidth and is mostly used for live broadcasts. Unlike a Unicast stream, clients cannot experience the video stream from its beginning (unless they logged on when the webcast started). To distribute Multicast streams, a network must be equipped with routers and switches supporting Multicast protocols. Figure 10–2 illustrates a Multicast data flow.

Multicast streams provide efficiency and cost savings at many levels. The distribution of one single stream is less expensive than the distribution of 1,000 streams. The question is, why is everyone not using Multicast? The main reason that they are not is that most ISPs do not have hardware to support packet delivery via Multicast protocols. When the Internet became public, ISPs designed their networks with hardware and software to deliver images, text, and all kinds of applications, but not video. Only in the past few years, with growing public demand for broadband connectivity, have ISPs started upgrading their networks to increase bandwidth capacities and support media delivery over streaming protocols. A major revamping of the Internet backbone is on its way. The upgrade of services is being done by the leading ISPs, such as Qwest, AT&T, MCI, and Sprint, who are struggling to maintain a presence in a changing environment. Lack of resources and market fluctuations are slowing the process; however, investors and legislators are working together, and many analysts predict that in 5–10 years broadband connectivity will become a commodity like telephone lines and television transmission.

Traditional streaming media companies on the Internet distribute streams to their users via Unicast delivery. This is because, with the exception of users connected to their corporate Multicast-enabled networks, the majority of users connected to the public Internet cannot participate in Multicasts. As the number of Unicast connections grows, so does the load

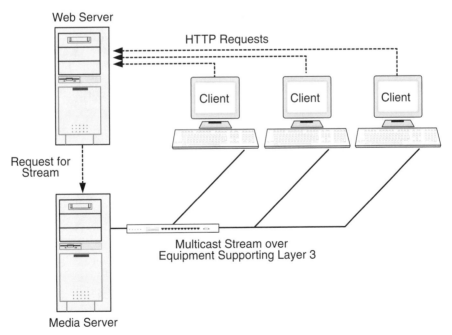

Figure 10–2
Sample of a Multicast Scheme

on the servers and the network bandwidth at the host's position. Unicast, therefore, does not scale well in high-volume implementations. In a controlled environment, such as an enterprise network, a well-planned Multicast infrastructure can greatly increase the scalability of streaming media events. Because in a Multicast stream one copy of the data is sent out on the network, one, one thousand, or even ten thousand connected users can watch the very same stream replicated on compatible public or enterprise networks. That stream can be a 100-kbps or a 1,500-kbps stream.

Although Multicast may seem like an ideal solution for bandwidth conservation, like a live television broadcast it does not give the end-user controls to rewind, fast forward, pause, or stop the stream. Therefore, Multicast events are most appropriate for live broadcasts or scheduled rebroadcasts (in which content is prerecorded and played back at predefined intervals).

A well-formulated streaming media strategy using Multicast should consider the following:

- Hardware and network requirements for enabling Multicast
- A method for allocating and deallocating Class D Multicast addresses for summing (participants in a Multicast webcast are assigned dynamic class D IPs; for more on IP classes see Chapter 2)
- A method for reaching non-Multicast-enabled users such as remote sites or people who log on to the corporate network over dial-up modems or secure VPNs
- Network impact when Multicast is enabled
- Multicast security
- Proper tuning for optimal performance

How Media On-Demand Works

A media on-demand session is initiated when a user visits a Web page and makes a request to see video. The Web page is hosted on a Web server, visible to the network by using a routable IP (an IP that is visible on the Internet). The Web page lists information about the media, such as topic, content description, clip length, and so on. The Web page normally provides links to media playback accommodating several modem speeds. Users with dial-up modems select a low-bandwidth link; users with broadband select high-bandwidth links. For samples and illustrations of media on-demand schemes, see Chapter 2. The user's request generates an HTML call to the reference file. This reference file contains information about the clip, such as copyright owner name, title information, type of protocol it should use to stream back the media files (e.g., RTSP, HTTP, or MMS), and the host server it should search for the media. For example, a call to a RealSystem Server looks like this: *rtsp://server_name_or IP:port_number/media_file.extension.* To allocate the host server reference files, use the server name (associated with the proper DNS settings) or the server IP number. These actions are performed in milliseconds. The host media servers receive a request to play back a media file located on its root directory and to stream it back to the origin of the request. Media on-demand can be called from within interactive Web interface platforms using active databases and fancy graphics, but for the purpose of this book, we illustrate the action of pulling a streaming media file in a simple way. The process works like this:

1. The reference file is called from an HTML page, for example, *http://www.webserver.com/reference_folder/file_name.extension.* The reference file can reside on the same Web server as the page calling it.
2. The reference file calls the source media file. The reference file contains:

- Clip title
- Copyright (who owns the clip)
- Author (who made the clip)
- Media host source (where the actual media resides)
- Streaming protocol to use for playback
- Optional meta tags (events that create interactivity)

Here is an example of a media host source and streaming protocol to use for playback in a reference file:

```
rtsp://www.quicktime_server_name.com/media_folder/file_name
.mov
rtsp://www.realvideo_server_name.com:port_number/media_
folder/file_name.rm
mms://www.windowsmedia_server_name.com/media_folder/file_
name.wmv
{protocol}{server name and port}{folder name}{clip
name and extension}
```

3. The host server receives a request from a player (or a browser acting like a player if the player is a plug-in to stream back the media file, using the requested protocol, from the host server to the initiator of the request (the streaming media player).

4. The user receives a streaming playback of its request. The media are not cached on the user desktop–the user must make a second request and initiate this process again to watch the clip again.

▸ About Extensions:

QuickTime uses the extension .mov (movie file) to name both the reference file and the actual media file. RealSystem uses the extension .ram (real audio media) to name the reference file and .rm (real media) to name the actual media. RealSystem has a variety of other extensions that indicate text and images. Windows Media uses the extensions .asx (ASF stream redirector) and .wax (Windows Media audio redirector) to name the reference file and has a variety of extensions for its actual media files, .asf (active stream format), .wmv (Windows Media video), and .wma (Windows Media audio). These are listed in Table 10–1.

Table 10–1
Streaming Media File Extension List

Extension	File Type	Remarks
QuickTime Streaming Clip Extensions		
.mov	Movie file	Actual QuickTime file. There are two types of movie files: progressive download file, and a streaming file; streaming file must be "hinted" to stream
QuickTime Reference Extensions		
.sdp	Session Description Protocol (SDP) file	Contains information about the format, timing, and authorship of the live broadcast

Table 10–1
Streaming Media File Extension List (*continued*)

Extension	File Type	Remarks
.mov	QuickTime movie reference file	Reference file pointing to the actual media server where the media is hosted
RealSystem Streaming Clip Extensions		
.rm or .ra	RealAudio	Actual streaming file
.rm	RealVideo	Actual streaming file
.rp	RealPix streaming image markup	Image file converted to Real format
.rpa	RealPix Ad rotation	Banner that is converted to Real format
.rt	RealText streaming text	Static or scrolling text converted to Real format
.swf	Flash player file	Flash that can be streamed through QuickTime and Real Video player
RealSystem Reference Extensions		
.ram	RAM file to launch RealPlayer	Reference files pointing to the actual media server where the media is hosted
.rpm	RAM file for embedded presentation	Reference file used to embed Real Player in Web pages
.smil, .smi	SMIL file for layout and synchronizing presentations	Reference file used to add additional objects to presentation or to create interactivity
Windows Media Streaming Clip Extensions		
.asf	Advance Streaming Format	Data structure that defines Windows Media content
.wmv	Windows Media Video format	Video files
.wma	Windows Media Audio format	Audio files
Windows Media Reference Extensions		
.asd	ASF Stream Descriptor	Configuration file containing encoder settings describing characteristics of a stream
.asx	ASF Stream Redirector	Reference files pointing to the actual media server where the media is hosted

Whereas television sets scan images horizontally, streaming video players receive the streaming video signal as a flow of data packets. These packets are sent by the server responsible for distributing the streams in Unicast or Multicast. These packets travel together or separately over computer network, and are reassembled by the player before playback. The player does not perform horizontal scanning; rather, it verifies that all the packets are there. If some packets are missing, the player sends a request to the server to resend missing packets. The server then memorizes which packets are missing and it resends them immediately.

The player uses a technique called buffering–it stores the packets of video in RAM in their order of display for three to five seconds (default setting) and then plays them. In this way, the viewer gets a constant replay. This technology allows sufficient time for the player to request missing packets and receive them before they are due to be played back. If the client player is successful in retrieving the missing packets, it will display them in the correct order. If too many packets are missing, the software player will continue to attempt to retrieve them, resulting in constant buffering and poor playback; if the packets cannot be retrieved, the player will run out of content for display and the stream will stop. If you notice on your streaming player that the message "buffering" or "network congestion" appears, this is an indication that the player has not succeeded in retrieving the missing packets in time and, therefore, cannot play back additional video. Extensive buffering indicates congestion on the network.

Another source of delay in the playback of streaming video is bottlenecking–that is, too many packets trying to move across a network with a limited amount of bandwidth. This happens when a user attempts to stream a media clip that is not suited for the bandwidth of his or her Internet connection. When the media player makes a request to a Web page to play back a streaming file, it travels across several networks; the user resides on his ISP's network and the request to stream a file is to a host computer that resides on another network. If a user attempts to stream a file encoded for playback at 300 kbps over a network limited to 100 kbps, for example, the player will try unsuccessfully to retrieve the file from the host server. The file encoded at 300 kbps will travel across the Internet, but the packets will stop at the user's ISP at the point where its individual network connection begins, resulting in constant buffering without the ability to display media.

How to Set up an On-Demand Unicast Stream

All three media servers use almost the same concept to configure media on-demand or to enable the distribution of live webcasting. Once you have learned how to configure one media server, the same rules will apply to the other formats. To simplify the process of configuring these three media servers, the following instructions are divided by streaming formats and are for Windows NT and 2000 operating systems only. When applicable, the differences between the media servers are noted.

QuickTime Darwin Streaming Server (for Windows NT or 2000 server)

1. Open a browser and type the name of your DSS server and 1220 (the port number). For example, to access the DSS used in this example, I typed *http://192.168.1.3:1220*.
2. Enter your user name and password.
3. During the installation of DSS, you were prompted to create a path for the directory in which the streaming files will be stored (see Chapter 9). The path to this folder can be found by clicking on General Settings in the DSS menu.
4. To change these settings, create a new directory and then enter its path. For example, *E:\QTRoot\Media*.
5. Place all streaming media files in the designated directory. Reference files to live Unicast or Multicast webcasts (files ending with the .sdp extension) should be placed in the same directory so they can be recognized by DSS.
6. There are two ways to point to your streaming media files:

   - Create a reference file with QuickTime Player Pro or with the MovieRef utility (this utility can be downloaded from *www.apple.com*). The reference file contains a link to the actual streaming file. Post the reference file on your Web server. Create a link from your Web page to the reference file, for example:

     ```
     <a href=clips/clip_name-56.mov target=_blank> clip
     name </a>
     ```

     When a user clicks on the Web page link, the request goes to the reference file on the Web server, and the reference file redirects the request to the media server.

- Point directly to the media server. This method is not secure because you will be exposing the actual link to the media file. Any visitor to your Web site can use this link for their own purposes. To point directly to the media server, copy and paste this link onto your Web page, replacing the server and file names with your own:

```
rtsp://dss_server_name:544/folder/file_name.mov
```

7. Open a browser and test the links to the streams.

RealSystem Server 8.0 (for Windows NT or 2000 server)

1. Launch the RealSystem 8.0 Administrator. During server installation, a shortcut to this page was placed on your desktop. If the shortcut is missing, go in your desktop interface to *Star/Programs/ RealServer/RealSystem 8 Administrator*. You can remotely access the server from another computer by pointing to *http://you_ realmedia_server_IP:remote_admin_port/admin/index.html*. For example, to access the RealSystem used in this example, I typed *http://192.168.1.3:19237/admin/index.html*.

2. Enter RealSystem Administrator user name and password. These are the name and password that you assigned during installation. If you have forgotten your password, open Notepad and drag the server configuration file, *Program Files/Real/RealServer/rmserver .cfg*. Look for the password in there. Remember not to save this file again or all changes you have made to it will take effect.

3. Click on General Setup on the left navigation bar. A menu will drop down. Click on Mount Points. Mount points are an equivalent to Windows Media on-demand publishing points; they are folders that store streaming content. You can create one centralized folder for all your content or create multiple folders, for example, one folder for each client. During installation, the server selected a default mount point, *C:\Program Files\Real\RealServer\ Content*. Media files located in this folder or its subdirectories will stream properly.

4. Test your settings. First copy and paste a media file into *C:\ Program FilesRealRealServer\Content*. Then, open your RealPlayer. Click on File/Open Location and type *rtsp://you_realmedia_*

server_IP:port/my_folder/file_name.extension (e.g., *rtsp://192.168.1.3: 554/folder/test.rm*). Port 554 is the default outbound port used by RTSP protocols.

RealSystem can serve streaming media files from other drives on your computer or from other computers on your network. The media files stream the same way as do media files hosted on the C drive of your local computer. The process is identical to streaming files stored locally. When the user makes a request for a stream, using the reference file, the HTTP call initiates a stream. The RealSystem server searches internally, finds the appropriate mount points, and streams back the file. This method accommodates large numbers of media files stored across multiple locations. However, the use of additional mount points, especially if not stored on the same machine as the RealSystem server, requires fast point-to-point connections between the RealSystem server and the storage device. Network cards are limited to the delivery of 10, 100, or 1000 MB. Factor this consideration into your network architecture as you plan to deploy a streaming media infrastructure.

To create additional mount points on other drives on your system or on another computer on your network, follow these steps:

1. Add a new line to the mount point list.
2. Replace the default Mount Point Name in the Edit Mount Point box with a name of your choice.
3. Type a description for this new point in the Description box.
4. In the Base Path box, type a path to the folder hosting your media (e.g., *D:\RealRoot\Folder\Content*). Click on Apply. A window will pop up confirming the creation of the additional mount point.
5. You must restart the server for the change to take effect. Close the window and restart the RealSystem server by using the button at the top of your administration interface.
6. Test your settings. First copy and paste a RealMedia file to your new folder (here *D:\RealRoot\Folder\Content*). Then, open your RealPlayer. Click on File/Open Location, and type *rtsp://you_ realmedia_server_IP:port/folder_name/file_name.extension* (e.g., *rtsp: //192.168.1.3:554/music/test_mountpoint2.rm*).
7. RealPlayer will stream the media. The player might buffer constantly. If the stream does not appear, check your settings. If the stream playback is constantly buffering, this is an indication of a

poor network connection between your RealSystem server and the storage device for your media.

▶ **Important note:**

Do not attempt to store your media files on another computer unless it is running a Windows operating system. Media servers operating on a Windows computer will not identify other operating systems unless your network has been configured as a domain network that recognizes computers with other operating systems and unless proper protocols and services have been installed to support other operating systems.

Windows Media Services 4.1 (for Windows NT or 2000 server)

1. Launch Windows Media Administrator. A shortcut to this page is located at *Start/Programs/Windows Media/Windows Media Administrator*. At the left navigation bar, click the Configure Server/ Unicast Publishing Points icon. Publishing points are the equivalent to RealSystem mount points. A window will appear in the right section of your browser. It has two sections: the upper is the On-Demand Unicast Publishing Points and the lower area is the Broadcast Unicast Publishing Points. Click on the On-Demand icon of the Unicast Publishing Points and add a new publishing point.

2. A window will pop up. Click on Next. Click on Create A Publishing Point. Click on Next, and give an alias name to your new publishing point. Enter a path to your media directories where you want to store Windows Media files, for example, *C:\ASFRoot\ Video_Folder*. Click on Next.

3. The next screen will list the URL for the media you are planning to create and which add-on items have to be created to play that stream (generate an ASX, generate a HREF link tag, or generate an HTML with embedded tags). Verify the way your server is listed in the URL. It is better to use IP numbers to help the packets faster identify the server (DNS resolution slows down the

process). You can make changes to the listed URL by using the Change Server icon and retyping the IP number. Click on Next.

4. The window will ask for confirmation. Review all the details and if they are correct click on Finish.

5. Now you have to save the ASX or HTML page that you requested the software to create to your hard drive. Rename it if necessary and remember where it was saved.

6. The next window offers a test of the stream. Click on the choices created and verify that the stream works.

7. Test the entire configuration setting. Launch Windows Media player. Use File/Open and type the path to your sample media file: *mms://media_server_name/root/folder/file_name.wmv*. The player should stream back the media file you have specified. If the file does not stream, restart the entire process from the beginning.

▶ **Important note:**

In the process of generating a new Unicast stream, the Windows Media server often refers to the actual name of the host computer when it creates an ASX for your live or on-demand stream. If your computer name is Myserver, the path in the ASX might look like *mms://Myserver/root/folder/file_name.wmv*. Correct the mistake by dragging your ASX to Notepad and retyping the proper name or IP number of your media server. The ASX should look like this:

```
<asx version = 3.0>
<title>clip name</title>
<entry>
<ref href = mms://correct_DNS_or_IP/root/folder/file_name.wmv/>
</entry>
/asx>
```

To modify an existing publishing point so it will pull media files from another hard drive on your computer or from another computer, follow these steps:

1. Click on Unicast Publishing Point in the navigation bar.
2. Highlight an existing publishing point and click on the On-Demand icon.

3. Choose Properties. In the Directory Path, type the path to your new publishing point or browse to identify the new location on your computer or on your network.

4. Click on OK.

To create a new publishing point with reference to media files on another computer, follow these steps:

1. First map a new network drive. Point to the folder on the other computer.

2. On your Windows Media Administrator interface click on the On-Demand icon and add a new publishing point.

3. In the Path box, browse and locate your newly mapped network drive.

4. Finish the setup and test your stream.

How to Set up a Multicast Stream

We have seen that Unicast streams are generated when users use their media players to access media on-demand. The media is encoded and located on the server for random viewing by users. Naturally they will not use too many Unicast connections to the server because they will log on at different times of the day or the week. Unicast streams are also used to webcast a live audio or video signal. A workstation encodes an incoming video or audio signal and sends it in real time to the network or the Internet. When users are notified about a live broadcast, they all log on at the same time and they each request one single Unicast stream. Now the load on the media server increases as hundreds or maybe thousands of users request Unicast streams at the same time. This scenario calls for a Multicast solution—the server sends out one stream and multiple users see it at the same time. Users can join the live broadcast in progress but will not be able to see it from the start.

At the present time, DSS and RealSystem support Multicast streams only for live webcasting. All media on-demand files are streamed using Unicast. Windows Media extend the idea of distributing one file to many users, allowing the Multicast of static files that have been encoded before. This solution allows streaming administrators to create programs using prerecorded media and to play back these programs as either Unicast or Multicast streams. To set up a Windows Media Multicast stream from prerecorded media, follow the instructions on creating a Multicast stream when the source is from a local Advanced Streaming Format (see the section How to Set up a Live Multicast Stream).

How to Set up a Live Unicast Stream

Producing a live webcast to be distributed via Unicast topology is similar to creating a media on-demand Unicast point. The difference is that the source for the webcast arrives not from a local file on the media server but from an encoder or another webcast station. Firewalls present serious difficulties when you deploy streaming media servers on a network. To learn how to configure the basic tasks of webcasting a Unicast or Multicast stream on your newly installed media servers, shut down all firewalls between the encoder and the media server and between the media server and the player-client. After you have successfully established communication between the encoder and the media server and after you are able to see the webcast through your client player, enable the original firewall settings. Now you will experience difficulties encoding and streaming with QuickTime and RealSystem; these two technologies communicate over UDP ports. The Windows Media Services attempts to communicate first over UDP or TCP ports and then rolls over to HTTP ports. (See Chapter 2 for more on firewall issues and how to configure each of the three streaming technologies to work with firewalls.)

QuickTime Server (Darwin Streaming Server for Windows NT or 2000)

1. Connect your source media (video and audio signal from a tape or from your television) to the workstation encoder capture card.
2. Open your capture card management software and verify that you get a clean audio and video signal. If you have more than one capture card in your workstation, configure the software to point to the selected card.
3. Open Sorenson Broadcaster. Use the broadcast properties Source tab to configure your audio and video source and compression

settings. For the best performance, follow the recommended settings in Table 8–3.

4. Use the Network tab to select the type of webcast. Select Unicast and type in the IP number of your media server (where the DSS is installed). Click on OK.

5. Save a reference file to your webcast configuration. Click on the Announce tab. Select a path to the media folder (on the DSS media server computer). Name the file and make sure it has an .sdp extension.

6. Click the Start Broadcast key. The left window will display statistics showing rate of audio and video transmission.

7. Next, go to the DSS computer. The DSS must be active. Open Windows NT or Windows 2000 services and verify that DSS service started.

8. To test the Unicast stream, launch your QuickTime player. Click on File/Open a URL in New Player and type *rtsp://dss_server_name:554/file_name.sdp* (the location of the SDP file you saved before from the Sorenson Broadcaster interface).

9. If the player launches your live webcast stream, you are done. If the player attempts to connect but either buffers endlessly or does not achieve connection with the server, repeat all the steps.

RealSystem Server 8.0 (for Windows NT or 2000 server)

1. Connect your source media (video and audio signal from a tape or from your television) to the workstation encoder capture card.

2. Open your capture card management software and verify that you get a clean audio and video signal. If you have more than one capture card in your workstation, configure the software to point to the selected card.

3. Launch RealSystem Producer Plus. Start a new session. Choose Media Device and verify that your input source is using the proper capture card. Select in your output options Live Broadcast. You can archive the broadcast to a local file for the faster turnaround of media on-demand. This option requires a powerful workstation with recommended components, as described in Chapter 7.

4. Configure your live broadcast options:

RealSystem Server–Enter the IP number of your RealSystem server.

Server port–Port 4040 is normally used.

Filename–Assign a name to the webcast and add .rm at the end.

Username–Type in your server access user name.

Password–Type in your server access password.

Click on OK.

5. Verify that your input window shows video and that the audio meter shows sound.

6. Make changes to the output signal. Click on Options/Video Settings and crop or resize the output video size. Click on Options/Target Audio Settings to change the bandwidth assigned to the audio or video streams. Click on Options/Video Preferences to change video codecs and filters.

7. Start broadcasting.

8. RealSystem Producer Plus will show an error message if it cannot communicate properly with RealSystem. Some reasons for an error message are:

   • The user name and password are wrong. To edit the existing user profiles, launch RealSystem Administrator. Use the menu to enter the Configure/Security/Authentication. Highlight SecureEncoder and click on the Edit a User in RealM icon. Override the old password or create a new user. Save your new settings.

   • A firewall is blocking communication between the encoder and the server. The encoder uses TCP through port 4040 to send information. The server responds via UDP port 554. Open these ports in your firewall to enable communication between the two computers.

   • RealSystem Server is not set up for live encoding. In RealSystem Administrator, use the menu to access Configure/Broadcasting/Encoder. By default, RealSystem Server creates /Encoder/ as a mount point for live webcasts. If the mount point area is blank, type */encoder/* there, use port 4040, enter a timeout of 30 seconds, and use EncoderRealm for authentication.

9. Test your live webcast stream by launching RealPlayer and, in the File/Open location, typing *http://realserver_IP:554//ramgen/encoder/file_name.rm*.

Windows Media Services 4.1
(for Windows NT or 2000 server)

1. Connect your source media (video and audio signal from a tape or from your television) to the workstation encoder capture card.

2. Open your capture card management software and verify that you get a clean audio and video signal. If you have more than one capture card in your workstation, configure the software to point to the selected card.

3. Launch Windows Media Encoder. Select Broadcast, Capture, or Convert a File. Click on OK. Select the option to broadcast a live event from an attached device. Click on Next.

4. Select and configure your video and audio capture card. Click on Next.

5. Enter an HTTP port number or let the encoder select it for you. Click on Next.

6. Choose a profile from the drop menu. Click on Next.

7. You can archive a copy of your webcast on the local hard drive. This option requires a powerful workstation with recommended components, as described in Chapter 7. Click on Next.

8. For this exercise, select No, I Want to Broadcast from My Selected Device Only. Click on Next.

9. Type in the title, copyright information, and other related information. Click on Next.

10. Review your settings. To make changes, hit the back button. Otherwise, click on Finish.

11. Start webcasting.

12. Open the Windows Media Server Administration interface. From the left menu, select Configure Server/Unicast Publishing Points. The interface shows on the screen as two parts. The upper part is for configuring media on-demand. The lower section is for configuring live Unicast events.

13. Select Broadcast/New and follow the wizard. Click on Next. Create a broadcast publishing point. Click on Next.

14. Select Windows Media Encoder as the source. Click on Next.

15. Enter an alias for the webcast. For example, *Live from NY.* Specify in the path the IP of your encoder workstation, for example, *msbd://192.168.1.3,* or use HTTP if you are behind a firewall, for

example, *http://192.168.1.3*. Look at your encoder interface and select the Connections tab (in the lower part of the encoder interface). Type in the port number you were assigned. Click on Next.

16. Change the server name to your Windows Media server IP number. Click on Next.

17. Verify all your settings and click on Finish. The media server will save an ASX file. Click on Close.

18. Double-click on the ASX file that was created in step 17. This action will open the media player and access the source of the stream. Test your Unicast stream.

How to Set Up a Live Multicast Stream

QuickTime Server
(Darwin Streaming Server for Windows NT or 2000)

1. Connect your source media (video and audio signal from a tape or from your television) to the workstation encoder capture card.

2. Open your capture card management software and verify that you get a clean audio and video signal. If you have more than one capture card in your workstation, configure the software to point to the selected card.

3. Launch Sorenson Broadcaster. Click on Broadcast Properties. Choose Media Device and verify that your input source is using the proper capture card for the audio and video feed.

4. Select the Network tab and enable Relay. Enter the following:

   • Multicast IP address–This is assigned by Sorenson Broadcaster.
   • Program area–Type in 15 for local LAN or 64 for WAN.
   • Relay server IP–Type in the IP of your DSS server.
   • Relay audio and video ports–These are preassigned. Open your firewall if needed.
   • Destination audio and video ports–These are preassigned. Open your firewall if needed.

   Click on OK.

5. Start webcasting.

6. Now it is time to configure your DSS to distribute the Multicast signal. Open a browser and type *http://DSS_name:1220/*. Enter your user name and password.

7. From the left menu, choose Relay Settings. Relays can be used to support large broadcasts and ease the load on a single server; they are used to distribute the incoming signal to multiple servers in Unicast or Multicast mode. Proper distribution is then achieved by routing users to the server closest to them. (See the description of CDN technology in the section Networks –Advanced in Chapter 2.)

8. In the relay section, enter the following:

   • Relay name–Assign a name to the event. Click on Enable.
   • Hostname or IP address–This is either the Unicast or Multicast IP of the encoder workstation.
   • Mount point–Type in the path name to the webcast stream. For example, if the path to your media folder on the DSS server IP is *rtsp://192.168.1.3:554/media/file_name.sdp*, type */media/file_name.sdp*.
   • Request incoming stream or wait for incoming stream–Choose either Request (enter the IP of the encoder workstation) or Wait (no need to enter information; the encoder will point to the DSS IP).
   • Destination settings–Using these, you can forward the incoming signal either to a second DSS or to the network as a Unicast or Multicast stream.
   • Hostname–Type in the IP of the destination DSS.
   • Relay via TCP–This creates a SDP file for the destination DSS. Enter your user name and password, if required to access the second DSS.
   • Relay via UDP–This waits for users to pull the webcast.
   • Base port–Type in the port number that the destination DSS uses to listen to streams.
   • Multicast TTL–This is the number of times a media stream can hop on network routers before the stream or packets will be stopped. Set a value between 0 and 255.

   Save the new settings.

9. Launch QuickTime player and type *rtsp://multicast_DSS_name:554/mount_point/file_name.sdp*.

▶ Important note:

DSS requires that Perl be active. Add DSS to your Windows NT or Windows 2000 services, and configure it to automatically run when Windows starts. To access the administration interface, you must first activate Perl and then open the administrator file. To open the file, first locate it in *C:\ Program Files\Darwin Streaming Server\streamingadminserver.pl,* and then launch the file by double-clicking on it. Open your browser and type *http://localhost:1220/.* This will launch the administrator interface. If you enabled the remote access of the administrator interface over the Internet, type *http://server IP:1220/.*

RealSystem Server 8.0
(for Windows NT or 2000 server)

1. Open a browser and type *http://real_server_IP:port/admin/index .html,* substituting your RealServer IP and the port you are using to monitor the administrator interface. If you have forgotten the port number, open *C:\Program Files\Real\RealServer\rmserver.cfg* in Notepad and look for the VAR Admin port.
2. Type in your user name and password. (This information was entered during the server installation; see Chapter 9.)
3. From the left-side menu bar, choose Configure/Multicasting/ Back-Channel. Enter the following:

   - Enable Multicast—Enter yes.
   - Enable SAP—Enter no.
   - PNA port—Enter 7070 (this is the same as listed in your default port value).
   - RTSP port—Enter 554 (this is the same as listed in your default port value).
   - IP address—Enter the range 225.0.0.1 to 225.0.0.100 (this will secure a range of 100 available IP numbers for 100 people to join your Multicast stream).
   - Time to live—Determine how far you need to send your webcast and enter the proper configuration (this is based on the following values: 1 for local LAN site, 32 for first-level ISP router hop, 64 for second-level ISP router hop, 128 for third-level ISP router hop).

- Resend–Enter yes.
- Multicast delivery–Enter no (this sends a Unicast stream to clients who cannot get your Multicast signal).
- Client access rule number–Enter 100 (the default).
- Client IP address–Enter any.
- Client netmask–Leave this blank.

Click on Apply and restart RealSystem Server.

4. Open RealSystem Producer Plus and configure it to send a stream to RealServer, as described in the section How to Set up a Live Unicast Stream. Name this webcast or file *multicast.rm*.

5. Go back to the RealServer Administrator interface and click on the Monitor option in the menu. Verify that the Connection tab shows the IP of your encoder and that the file name is *multicast.rm*.

6. Launch RealPlayer and type into the Open a Location: *http://RealServer_IP:554/ramgen/encoder/multicast.rm*.

7. Test the stream. Open the statistics option in the player, click on the Streams tab, and check that the Transport Protocol shows Multicast.

Windows Media Services 4.1 (for Windows NT or 2000 server)

1. Launch Windows Media Administrator. A shortcut to this page is located at *Start/Programs/Windows Media/Windows Media Administrator*. On the left navigation bar, click on the Multicast Stations link.

2. The screen is divided into Stations and Multicast ASF Programs and Streams. Click on Stations and add a new station. A station is an independent broadcasting point that can Multicast multiple programs in a specified order.

3. Create a new station. Name the station and add a description. Click on Next.

4. Name the program, for example, *program 1,* and name the stream, for example, *Corporate News April 12, 2001*. Click on Next.

5. Specify the source of your stream. If you are planning to Multicast a prerecorded file from your hard drive, choose Advanced Streaming Format. To Multicast a live video feed originating from

an encoding station, click on Windows Media Encoder. To Multicast (replicate) an existing Unicast video feed originating from another Windows Media server, choose Remote Station or Broadcast Publishing Point.

When the Source Is from a Local Advanced Streaming Format

1. Type the source URL on your local computer. The format must be *protocol://your_windowsmedia_server/folder_name/file_name,* (e.g., *mms://192.168.1.3/music/file1.wmv*). Click on Next.
2. Point to the local path where the file is located. Specifying this location will play back the file in Unicast mode to users without Multicast capabilities. Click on Next.
3. Specify a path to where you want to store the Multicast reference file and a file name (end it with .nsc), for example, *C:\InetPub\ wwwroot\folder\multicast.nsc.* Click on Next.
4. Specify the URL where Windows Media Player should look for the reference file for the NSC file, for example, *http://web_server_ name/folder/multicast.nsc.* Click on Next.
5. An ASX file will be created. You can request that an HTML code and an embedded player be created as well. Click on Next. Confirm your selection and click on Finish.
6. Save the ASX file in a folder. Double-click on the ASX file to test your stream. This will launch your media player and play back the source media. If the Windows Media Player fails to play back, restart the configuration or open the saved ASX file in Windows Notepad and verify that the path to the NSC reference file is correct.

When the Source Is from a Windows Media Encoder

1. For Windows Media Encoder 6.4 or earlier, type in the source URL of your encoder. Use the MSBD or HTTP protocol. The encoder always selects port 7007 as the default, *protocol://your_ windowsmedia_server:port_number* (e.g., *msbd://192.168.1.2:7007*). Click on Next.
2. For Windows Media Encoder 7 or higher, type in the source URL of your encoder. Encoder 7 or higher uses the HTTP protocol as

the default for outbound packets of live video. This method is a firewall-friendly solution for live feed generated on corporate intranets. Streaming out in HTTP mode does not require opening outbound UDP or TCP ports on your firewall.

3. If your encoder operates on a computer with IIS, you must prevent the encoder from accessing the machine default rollover to port 80 as the outbound HTTP port. Either disable IIS in the Administrator Services Tools or change the HTTP outbound port of the encoder to 8080 or another port, *protocol://your_windowsmedia_server:port_number* (e.g., *http://192.168.1.2:8080*). Click on Next.

4. Choose a standard configuration of the media encoder. Click on Next.

5. Specify a path where you want to store the Multicast reference file and file name (end it with .nsc), for example, *C:\InetPub\wwwroot\folder\Multicast.nsc*. Click on Next.

6. Specify the URL where Windows Media player should look for the reference file for the NSC file, for example, *http://web_server_name/folder/Multicast.nsc*. Click on Next.

7. An ASX file will be created. You can request that an HTML code and an embedded player be created as well. Click on Next. Confirm your selection and click on Finish.

8. Save the ASX file in a folder. Test your stream. Your encoder must encode before you test this configuration. Windows Media Server will test its settings, including a direct connection to the encoder.

9. If the Windows Media player fails to play back, restart the configuration or open the saved ASX file in Windows Notepad and verify that the path to the NSC reference file is correct.

When the Source Is from a Remote Station or Broadcast Publishing Point

1. For Windows Media Encoder 6.4 or earlier, type in the source URL of your encoder. Use the MSBD or HTTP protocol. The encoder always selects port 7007 as the default, *protocol://your_windowsmedia_server:7007* (e.g., *msbd://192.168.1.2:7007*). Click on Next.

2. For Windows Media Encoder 7 or higher, type in the source URL of your encoder. Encoder 7 or higher uses the HTTP protocol as the default for outbound packets of live video. This method is a firewall-friendly solution for live feed generated on corporate intranets. Streaming out in HTTP mode does not require opening outbound UDP or TCP ports on your firewall.

3. If your encoder operates on a computer with IIS, do not use port 80 or your system will have a conflict. Use port 8080 or any other assigned HTTP port.

4. The Windows Media server needs to reference a Multicast stream to an ASD file. An ASD file is the equivalent to QuickTime and RealSystem SDP files. It is used to identify a Multicast session and includes information about both the source of the media (a live encoder or an on-demand file) and the media host server. If the encoder uses a template stream format, use the standard configuration. If the encoder uses a customized stream format (in which you define what type of audio and codec to use), select the customized configuration and find the path to the ASD file defining this configuration. The ASD file is created by saving the preset configuration of your encoder before you start webcasting. Save the ASD file to a location where you can find it when you need it.

5. To create an ASD file in Windows Media Encoder 4.1, in the encoder click on File/Save As and name the new ASD file.

6. To create an ASD file in Windows Media Encoder 7 or higher, in the encoder click on Tools/Generate Stream Format File and name the new ASD file.

7. Copy and paste the ASD file into the media server. In the Multicast profile configuration, add the ASD file to the recognized formats. Save the NSC profile.

8. The system will create a new ASX file.

9. Start the Multicast session.

10. Locate your saved ASX file from step 4. Double-click on the ASX file to test your stream. This will launch your media player and play back the source media. If the Windows Media player fails to play back, restart the configuration or open the saved ASX file in Windows Notepad and verify that the path to the NSC reference file is correct.

▶ **Important note:**

Each technology uses a different approach to streaming video. QuickTime encoder (Sorenson Broadcaster) assigns itself as a distribution point for Unicast streams, but it is limited to its network card's true output capacity. It allows Unicast or Multicast distribution via a DSS server. In this case, the encoder specifies the IP number of the distribution server and pushes the transmission to this server. RealSystem Producer pushes the encoded feed to a designated RealSystem Server acting as a distribution point for Unicast and Unicast streams. Windows Media Encoder does not push the encoded stream; instead it waits for the Windows Media server to contact it first. The media server pulls the stream and takes care of distribution. RealSystem does not require an assigned routable IP to stream live feed. Windows Media encoder and Sorenson Broadcaster both require an IP that is visible on the public Internet. In the media server, you specify what the IP number of your encoder is. The media server then identifies the encoder by its routable IP and connects to it to pull a live media feed.

Creating Broadcast Playlists

Playlists are the equivalent to a lineup of television programs and are designed to play one after the other or in random sequence. They are used for live and on-demand webcasting. In live webcasts, playlists are used for inserting commercials or other media that are added to a live audio or video broadcast. For example, radio stations use playlists to insert commercials between segments of their live broadcasts. Playlists are used in media on-demand environments to add introductory or closing clips to a main feature clip. When listed on a playlist, media can be pulled from many sources, such as multiple media servers. The playlist contains a list of resources (on-demand files located in different locations or live streaming feed originating from different encoders) and plays them in the order they are listed. Dial-up users will experience a small buffering delay while watching the clips in order. Broadband users may not notice the change between clips unless there is congestion on their network.

Playlists are divided into two groups: client side and server side. For client-side playlists, a reference file (the ASX or SMIL file) contains links to different media files residing on a distribution server. Upon a request from a player, the media are played in the order listed inside the reference file. For example, if the reference file contains links to clips 1, 2, and 3, the clips will play back in that order. A server-side playlist is a function available in both QuickTime and Windows Media servers. QuickTime implements three methods to generate playlists, and it supports both reference playlists (client side) and server configuration playlists (server side). RealSystem implements client-side playlists using SMIL to request the playback of multiple clips during one steady connection. Windows Media implements XML for client-side playlists and uses server-side playlists in multicast sessions. The use of XML broadens the delivery of add-on functions to the actual media. For example, both ASX and SMIL files (which are XML-based) can synchronize a presentation of images, text, databases, and Web pages, with the delivery of audio or video.

▶ **Important note:**

Why are some reference files multifunction and some not? It all comes down to the language they are written in and their format. ASX and SMIL files are XML-based files. RAM and MOV files are not and so cannot interact with the player or the server. They instead pass along syntax as is, generating a playback stream. Both RealSystem and QuickTime use SMIL language to add functionality and interactivity to RealVideo and QuickTime streams.

Remember to type using lowercase letters when creating a playlist. Capital letters are not recognized properly by the media player.

Creating a QuickTime Playlist

QuickTime playlists are created in the QuickTime server. In this example, we use DSS.

1. Launch DSS and log on using your user name and password. Use the left-side menu to enter the playlist section. DSS can create MP3 and regular movie (video and audio or audio only) playlists.
2. To create a new movie playlist, click on New Movie Playlist.
3. Name your playlist.
4. Select the play mode (sequential, sequential loop, or random play).
5. Create a new mount point. This is the SDP file you will point to later when launching your QuickTime Player. A virtual mount point will be created for DSS to identify the playlist.

6. Select the path to your media.

7. Drag and drop the selected media files from the left to the right table.

8. You can select how often the media will play and what importance (weight) it will have in the playlist. Use the numbers 1 to 10, where 10 is the most popular. For example, if you want a clip to play very often, assign it number 10. This function is particularly useful when selecting random play.

9. Either send the new playlist to another DSS (enter the computer IP number, user name, and password) or save settings on the local DSS. The server will generate a dynamic SDP file and store it where you specify.

10. Open QuickTime player and type *rtsp://DSS_server:554/playlist_name.sdp*.

11. Test to be sure that the streams appear in the order entered.

Creating a RealVideo Playlist

1. To create a RealVideo playlist, open Notepad. Copy one of the samples that follow these instructions to your Notepad, replacing the sample media server information with the location of your media server and files.

2. Save the file as *file_name.ram* or as *file_name.smil*, when applicable. Open your RealVideo player and drag the RAM or SMIL file in.

3. If you pointed properly to the location of your RealSystem server, the playback will start and play in the order you have specified.

Sample Playlist

To create a simple playlist, use the RAM file and list clips in the order they will play. Copy the following into the RAM file:

```
rtsp://your_media_server:port/folder/clip1.rm
rtsp://your_media_server:port/folder/clip2.rm
rtsp://your_media_server:port/folder/clip3.rm
```

Sample Playlist with Clip Information

To add more than links to the media (RAM files can do this), you must use SMIL language. In this example, clip information is forced to be displayed in the player during playback. Remember that clips with preassigned information (clips encoded with embedded title, author, and copyright information) will override the information listed in the SMIL file. To avoid this, make sure your RealVideo files are encoded with blank title, author, and copyright lines. Copy the following into your file:

```
<smil>
    <head>
    <meta name=TITLE content =Show Name/>
    <meta name=AUTHOR content =Who Producedthe Clip/>
    <meta name=COPYRIGHT content =© Company, Year/>
    </head>
    <body>
    <video src=rtsp://your_media_server:port/folder/file_name1.rm />
    <video src=rtsp://your_media_server:port/folder/file_name2.rm />
    </body>
</smil>
```

Sample Playlist Combining Live Feed with Video On-Demand

In this example, the playlist calls a video on-demand file to introduce the webcast. When the clip ends, the live broadcast starts playing. At the end of the live broadcast (when the encoder stops broadcasting the live signal), the closing clip is pulled to conclude the webcast. This method is used to ensure that the entire audience receives essential information about the event either before or after they have watched a live presentation. Copy the following into your file:

```
<smil>
    <head>
    <meta name = TITLE content =Show Name/>
    <meta name = AUTHOR content =Who Producedthe Clip/>
    <meta name = COPYRIGHT content =© Company, Year/>
    </head>
    <body>
    <video src = rtsp://your_media_server:port/folder/clip_intro.rm />
    <video src = rtsp://your_media_server:port/ramgen/encoder/alias.rm />
    <video src = rtsp://your_media_server:port/folder/clip_end.rm />
    </body>
</smil>
```

Creating a Windows Media Playlist

1. To create a Windows Media playlist, open Notepad. Copy one of the samples that follow these instructions into your Notepad, replacing the sample media server information with the location of your media server and files.

2. Save the file as *file_name.asx*. Open your Windows Media Player and drag in the ASX file.

3. If you pointed properly to the location of your Windows Media server, the playback will start and play in the order you have specified.

Sample Playlist

Copy the following into your file:

```
<ASX Version=3.0>
<ENTRY> <REF href = http://your_media_server/folder/clip1.wmv /> </ENTRY>
<ENTRY> <REF href = http://your_media_server/folder/clip2.wmv /> </ENTRY>
<ENTRY> <REF href = http://your_media_server/folder/clip3.wmv /> </ENTRY>
</ASX>
```

Sample Playlist with Clip Information

In this example each clip has its own information, which will be displayed in the player when the proper session plays. Copy the following into your file:

```
<ASX Version=3.0>
<TITLE> Show Name </TITLE>
<AUTHOR> Who Produced the Clip </AUTHOR>
<COPYRIGHT> © Company, 2002 </COPYRIGHT>
<ENTRY> <REF href = http://your_media_server/folder/clip1.wmv /> </ENTRY>
<TITLE> Show Name </TITLE>
<AUTHOR> Who Produced the Clip </AUTHOR>
<COPYRIGHT> © Company, 2002 </COPYRIGHT>
<ENTRY> <REF href = http://your_media_server/folder/clip2.wmv /> </ENTRY>
<TITLE> Show Name </TITLE>
<AUTHOR> Who Produced the Clip </AUTHOR>
<COPYRIGHT> © Company, Year </COPYRIGHT>
<ENTRY> <REF href = http://your_media_server/folder/clip3.wmv /> </ENTRY>
</ASX>
```

Sample Playlist Combining
Live Feed with Video On-Demand

In this example the playlist calls a video on-demand file to introduce the webcast. When the clip ends, the live broadcast starts playing. At the end of the live broadcast (when the encoder stops broadcasting live signal), the closing clip is pulled to conclude the webcast. This method is used to ensure that the entire audience receives essential information about the event either before or after they have watched a live presentation. Copy the following into your file:

```
<ASX Version=3.0>
<TITLE> Show Name </TITLE>
<AUTHOR> Who Produced the Clip </AUTHOR>
<COPYRIGHT> © Company, Year </COPYRIGHT>
<ENTRY> <REF href = http://your_media_server/folder/clip_intro.wmv /> </ENTRY>
<ENTRY> <REF href = mms://your_media_server/alias /> </ENTRY>
<ENTRY> <REF href = http://your_media_server/folder/clip_end.wmv /> </ENTRY>
</ASX>
```

Summary

- Unicast and Multicast are two different ways to broadcast video over IP networks. Unicast streams may cause network congestion when multiple requests attempt to pull a large amount of data over networks with limited bandwidth.

- To distribute Multicast streams, a network must be equipped with routers and switches supporting Multicast protocols.

- Streaming content as media on-demand relies on the availability of streaming media files at a central depository. Users access the media at any time, using the Internet or corporate LANs.

- You can learn to configure your media server to stream live Unicast or Multicast events.

- Multicast events can be generated only from a live video or audio feed. Windows Media Server is an exception; it can run a Multicast stream from a local pre-encoded file.

11

Streaming to Mobile Devices

Concept Planning

After reading Chapters 9 and 10, you should feel comfortable configuring media servers to webcast streaming content to desktop computers over your local network or the Internet. The next step is the deployment of a streaming solution to mobile devices. Before planning to stream content to mobile devices, consider some technical and social facts that will contribute indirectly to your effort. Mobile devices are a direct product of an emerging telecommuting society. Telecommuting is a social phenomenon that evolved when computing changed the nature of the workplace.

Workplaces have drastically changed in the past decade. Before the arrival of personal computers, information was distributed to employees on paper. Business travelers relied on faxes and messenger services to receive materials from their homes or offices. As technology progressed, society has moved away from manufacturing and industrial focus and become information driven. Information technology has decentralized the workplace due to its rapid information transfer.

Social scientists have identified telecommuting as one of the most prevalent and socially dramatic changes that have happened during the information revolution. Personal computers, the Internet, and new exciting mobile solutions promise to provide us with tools to receive, modify, and transfer information over networks in ways never seen before. These are the advantages to using mobile devices. They give us the freedom to access information from anywhere, anytime we want. Mobile devices are small, compact, and easy to operate. We no longer are tied to a bulky desktop computer connected to a network with cables, but have a compact fast solution that we can use as we roam around and that still is connected constantly to the Web.

Mobile devices such as PDAs, SmartPhones, and Internet Appliances have some disadvantages compared with desktop computers or laptop computers connected to the Internet via dial-up networks, such as:

- **Low bandwidth**—Mobile devices rely on wireless or additional wire (e.g., a PDA connected over a serial or USB connection to a desktop) connectivity. Wireless connectivity has several drawbacks because of the amount of bandwidth that it can deliver and the limitation of existing geographical coverage. In contrast, cellular phones use many networks to maintain connectivity as users travel between coverage areas. The only way to know when coverage areas have changed is to look for the roaming sign on your cellular phone. As long as our cellular phone providers keep us connected (within our calling plan), we do not care about all these technical details. The same should apply to mobile devices using wireless connectivity.

- **Connection stability**—Wired networks provide a more reliable connection than wireless networks. Due to fading, lost radio coverage, or deficient capacity, wireless networks are often inaccessible for periods of time.

- **Small display**—The size of the screen does not limit the user's experience when a desktop computer is used to access a service. Most desktop PCs arrive with a standard XGA 1024- × 768-pixel window size. Mobile devices have smaller displays. PDAs have a 320- × 240-pixel display; SmartPhones use on average a 180- × 140-pixel size display. This is a small screen that can barely be used for text messaging. Video display and navigation become extremely difficult on such tiny displays.

- **Limited input**—Mobile devices do not always have the same input facilities as desktops. These devices use small keyboards and mouseless interfaces. Typing (or key strokes) with a pen assistant (on Palm-size PDAs) is a slower process compared to typing with a keyboard.

- **Limited memory and CPU**—Mobile devices are usually not equipped with the amount of memory and computational power in the CPU found in desktop computers. The new PocketPC devices are an exception. Using 133- to 206-MHz CPUs and built-in 64 MB of RAM, they provide a new computing experience.

- **Limited battery power**–The operating time is one of the major concerns for mobile device manufacturers. Battery power restricts operations to approximately four to five hours in most PDAs.

As a result of these issues, mobile devices are positioned as supplementary tools to access information on the Internet or as a way to create and manage personal documents stored locally and waiting to be synchronized with a desktop. Mobile devices become a substitute for desktops when we are on the move, but we still rely on PCs as the primary tool for performing traditional tasks. When we are mobile, we retrieve and display our email, read the news, or draft short messages. The information we create is either transmitted over wireless networks in real time or stored for synchronization (and transmission) after we connect the device to its host computer using cradles (housing devices that help the mobile device communicate with the computer via a serial or USB connection).

If our plan is to stream media to mobile devices, first we must learn how media can be transferred to these devices. Most portable devices connect to desktop computers or to networks to recharge their batteries, to synchronize, or to transfer information. Cellular phones are an exception. All portable devices, therefore, can receive information (or media) when they connect to a network. This can be achieved via a direct connection using a modem (dial-up connection to a VPN), Ethernet card (network connection), or wireless Ethernet card (wireless connection). If we are using a cradle, the USB or serial interface to the desktop PC supports synchronization between the portable device and its host and we must verify that this connection supports the use of the 802.11 protocol. Only 802.11-compatible hardware or software connections support streaming from the network to the mobile device. A network (for this analysis) is the public Internet or a corporate LAN that connects to the Internet. Mobile devices use two types of Ethernet cards and modems, wired and wireless. All Ethernet cards and modems support TCP/IP protocols; this means that they are capable of transferring streaming media data packets.

As described in Chapter 5, telephone companies worldwide are in the process of deploying next-generation or 3G networks that will use higher bandwidth and will eventually be able to stream video. When the technology becomes available, both the consumer and the corporate market will adopt it rapidly. Pilot programs and consumer deployment of 3G networks started in Asia (Japan) and Europe and then reached North America. The future of 3G networks in North America is currently unclear despite the fact that all major wireless providers are slowly deploying CDMA networks that can support 2.5G and the proposed advanced 3G transmissions. Emerging alternatives to 3G networks are the new IEEE 802.15 Personal Area Networks (PANs), IEEE 802.11 Bluetooth technology, and IEEE 802.11b WLANs. All standards apply to enterprise and small-office networks. Table 5–2 in Chapter 5 lists the most commonly used WLAN protocols.

Mobile Devices and the Enterprise

The mobile Internet-access market is expected to reach over 130 million people by the end of 2007, thanks to the increased mobility of the workforce and the introduction of mobile-specific applications. That is an increase from the 2.9 million active subscribers in 2000. Most enterprises use Windows clients on their desktops and either Lotus Notes, Microsoft Office, or Novell GroupWise for document processing, internal email, and management of shared resources. Each solution includes support for wireless applications and devices. At this time, only Windows-based portable devices support streaming media in a corporate environment. Both ActiveSky and PacketVideo technologies can play back or stream media on Palm devices (ActiveSky) and mobile phones, but neither of these technologies supports streaming on existing LAN infrastructures the way Windows Media plays on PocketPC devices. The main advantages of PocketPC devices compared to Palm devices (for streaming media applications) are the abilities to play sound and store large files.

Developers are rushing to deliver software platforms that support mobile devices ranging from SmartPhones and handheld PCs to PocketPCs and laptop computers. As the demand for mobile solutions increases, people feel more confident using these applications that let them access information from anywhere, anytime they want. These devices have different sizes, shapes, and functionalities. Laptop computers are considered to be mobile desktops that facilitate 95% of the functionality desktops deliver.

Characteristics

Handheld units operating with Windows CE version 2.0 or 3.0 platforms enable PDAs and PocketPC devices to be an integrated part of the enterprise environment. These devices have screen sizes ranging from one-half to one-quarter of a display; they come with or without integrated keyboards. They often have no mouse and are limited in storage. All handheld PCs are wireless-enabled—users can pick the wired and wireless connectivity options that best fit their daily work patterns. Mobile devices are becoming valuable tools for employees in enterprises, complementing traditional laptop PCs. Handheld PCs fit best in scenarios in which a manual process can be made more efficient when converted to a forms-based application that enables the rapid capture of data on a screen big enough to keep the data in context. The benefits of running a forms-based line of business applications on a handheld PC to replace paper-based processes include:

- Faster and more accurate data collection in the office or in the field
- Higher productivity
- Faster processing of data, increasing production and customer support
- Faster business reporting for decision making
- Reduced operational costs (replacing the need for data entry personnel)

The Microsoft Internet Explorer (IE) version 4.0-compatible browser is standard software included with PocketPC version 3.0 and higher. Mobile IE makes possible access to the Internet as well as to intranet applications. The appliance-like behavior of handheld devices running the PocketPC operating system delivers an instant on and off every time the power button is pushed. They have a long battery life as a result of the power-frugal computer chips running these devices, keeping them functioning for an entire day of work on a single charge, even when connected wirelessly. Because there are no moving parts, handheld PCs operate well in environments where they are bumped around. Finally, the core operating system software and applications are safely stored in read-only memory so key components cannot be disabled or removed. These characteristics result in a device that matches the needs of someone who needs quick access to data and applications when working away from a typical office setting.

Handheld devices are not intended to replace the functionality of traditional PCs. Some examples of situations where a traditional PC takes the place of a handheld PC in performing tasks are:

- When users need access to full desktop application, such as preparing a PowerPoint presentation
- When the size of the display and amount of data stored require more than a 320- $\times$ 240-pixel window and a built-in 32-MB storage space

Many people do not work in a traditional office environment. Sometimes there is a temporary workplace, as in the case of traveling salespeople or executives on the move. Other workers, such as people delivering products, factory workers, or people performing certain job tasks onsite, may use handheld devices to better organize and update their information locally or on their company's mainframe. Mobile devices enable an organization to take its traditional computing infrastructure and extend it to the furthest reaches of its business. Current application areas that have improved business when handheld PCs were deployed involve workers who are directly responsible for bringing in revenues, who manage internal operations, and who are mobile professionals. Some of these are:

- **Customer relationship management (CRM)**–CRM tools enhance the ability of those involved in the sales process, field service, and customer support. Handheld PCs are a perfect fit because they provide service at remote customer facilities. Handheld devices enable the generation of invoices, access to training materials, management of schedules, and, most important, access in real time to inventory or production-flow schedules with a wireless connection. Many developers have released CRM tools that share information among a company's backend infrastructure and the sales force front end. Such off-the-shelf products can be purchased from Nortel Networks (Clarify), PeopleSoft (Vantive), and FieldCentrix.

- **Enterprise resource planning (ERP)**–ERP systems provide the information and basic services that support the internal operations of a business, such as the management of component acquisition, supervision of manufacturing process, and tracking of product deliveries. Making these services and this information available to people without their having to wait until they reach their desktops improves productivity and reduces costs. Many enterprises have deployed ERP systems from companies such as SAP AG, PeopleSoft, and J. D. Edwards.

- **Financial services**—The 21st-century mobile professional can use handheld PCs to access insurance claims, to collect on-site pictures and data, to trade on the stock market, to track his or her finances, to support all steps of a real estate transaction, or to display products in the form of video or PowerPoint presentations.

- **Health care**—Doctors were early adopters of handheld PCs. By using wireless connections, many doctors when on the move have secure access to current patient information, can write or renew drug prescriptions, can perform inventory management and patient monitoring, or can simply keep in touch with their offices.

- **Government**—Many local, state, and federal governmental agencies and departments use handheld devices to capture and store data. An example of solutions that use handheld PCs today include supporting the client contact process in welfare-to-work programs, looking up wants and warrant information quickly, managing the logistics of moving personnel and equipment around the country or around the world, ensuring that companies are following safety requirements, and capturing data associated with lands management.

- **Manufacturing and services**—United Parcel Service (UPS), the largest carrier in the world, has announced plans to enable its entire field and processing workforce with PocketPC devices. With the help of real-time data transmission over Bluetooth-supported infrastructure, drivers will feed the company mainframe with information, speeding up data processing and tracking capabilities and billing-related functions.

These examples show how companies realize reduced costs when they use handheld PCs for managing the flow of materials in their manufacturing or service facilities around the world. The expansion of handheld PC devices will increase the demand for software applications that will help automate or process information in more cost-efficient ways. Rich media will play a significant role in the future deployment of handheld PCs on enterprise networks. Media can be served as stand-alone playbacks, or they can be synchronized with PowerPoint slides or interactive databases that will be used for presentations, training, or information.

Streaming to Handheld Devices

To stream to a handheld device, deploy Windows Media technology on your network. After I had finished writing this book, RealNetworks released RealOne for PocketPC. The player can now operate on PocketPC 2002 devices and connects to the RealSystem Mobile Server to stream real media files in real time. From my first brief look at this new product, it seems that RealNetworks has done a great job of putting RealSystems's reliable performance into its mobile counterpart, but because the product is new I have not been able to test it.

So, why Windows Media and not the other options? There are three reasons: the technology is free; it is widely compatible with most hardware and software solutions; and, most important, it was tested and seems to be easily deployed by many IT departments. Every handheld device that operates with Windows CE version 2.0 and higher comes with or will accept an installation of Windows Media Player (see Figure 11–1). With the software installed, the device can play back Widows Media streaming format. I recommend that you upgrade your operating system and media player to the latest version available on the market. This will guarantee better performance. Next, determine how your device will receive streaming media. As already explained, the way a handheld PC requests and receives a streaming file depends on the way it connects to the network (or to the Internet). Microsoft PocketPC 2002, for example, can access streaming content with IE for PocketPC, and it supports the 802.11 and TCP/IP protocols. To connect to the Internet, use the cable or cradle supplied with your handheld device or purchase a standard dial-up or wireless modem. The newly released wireless modems (using the 802.11b protocols) connect to WLANs. After you have configured your handheld device, download media on-demand or stream live content. Log on to this book's companion Web site, *www.streaminghandbook.com/mobile,* to find more about sites that stream content to handheld devices.

Wireless Ethernet cards using the 802.11b high-rate protocol are very popular. These PCMCIA cards can plug to laptops, handheld PCs, and PDAs. When networks support wireless connectivity, users move

Figure 11–1
Windows Media Player for PocketPC

freely around their offices and their connection is on all the time. Before deploying a WLAN infrastructure consider the following issues:

- **Hardware and software compatibility**–Your new wireless equipment must be compatible with your old wired network.
- **Security**–Some wireless solutions on the market have holes in their security settings. If you do not perform a proper search before purchasing, you may end up with hardware that endangers your entire network.
- **Budget**–The cost of wireless solutions is dropping. Deploy your plan in stages, providing wireless access to small groups first. Evaluate the current implementation before increasing distribution to other groups.

To facilitate the distribution of streaming media to handheld devices on your corporate WLAN, use an existing Windows Media server. Place the proper streaming files on the server, and link to the file with an ASX redirector. Chapter 10 contains sample ASX files that show how to point reference files to live or on-demand webcasts originating from a Windows Media server. Your intranet Web page will point to the ASX redirector.

When mobile users access your intranet Web site, they will initiate a call to the ASX, which will then stream the proper file to their device (across your hybrid wired-wireless network). Remember that all the firewall rules mentioned in Chapter 3 apply to streaming media with mobile devices. Handheld PCs connect to the media server over your WLAN. That WLAN is part of your LAN and, therefore, is bound by the same network rules. From the IT point of view, handheld PCs are no different than desktop PCs.

When deploying a partial or complete wireless network installation, discuss with the owners of your enterprise's intranet Web site(s) the appropriate way to provide future mobile users access to the information on the network. Marketing streaming content on mobile corporate networks is similar to marketing traditional streaming content. (Marketing streaming content on your corporate network is discussed further in Chapter 12.) When promoting streaming content to handheld PCs, keep in mind the limitations of these devices. Unlike the PC, content streamed to mobile devices will be seen on a small screen, the connection can be expected to be interrupted more often, and any interactive functionality should be reconsidered because the display is so small and it is hard to embed a media player with additional interactive elements. I recommend that you use handheld devices to play back complete streaming files (video or audio only), without additional text and images. These streams can be sent out to users via Unicast or Multicast webcasts.

The reach of an organization's computing infrastructure can grow significantly with the use of handheld PCs. By placing the right information and services in the hands of those making critical business decisions and serving customers, your business will grow in a rapid and cost-effective way.

Unicast versus Multicast

As described in Chapter 10, streaming technology broadcasts media via either a Unicast or Multicast topology. Recall that in a Unicast mode each user makes a request to the media server to see video and that when they pull the stream they can watch the video file from start; in a Multicast mode many users connect to a single broadcast signal and join the broadcast timeline when they connect.

When broadcasting to mobile devices, you face the same concerns and problems regarding network performance and the user's ability to see a webcast. As described in detail in Chapters 2 and 10, network infrastructures and many compatibility issues (with client players, network protocols, firewalls, and media servers) define our ability to produce a successful webcast. In addition, when we include mobile users in our potential target audience for a webcast, we must address in advance any potential problems they may have, including poor training in how to operate the device for watching streaming media, wrong expectations (thinking it will be similar to a desktop experience), and the inability to see more than text and small images. Even with all these limitations, webcasting a live signal to mobile devices can be a productive experience.

A last important fact to remember when planning to invite mobile users to your webcast is the environment these users may be in during the webcast. By nature, people who use portable devices operate them in transit, while away from their base of operations, where the desktop lives, where information is stored, and where people perform work that requires concentration. We use portable devices the same way we use radios. Radios are used to receive information when we are in transit and to entertain us when we have nothing better to do; we often use them to play music or news in the background. Mobile devices have similar uses. They provide much more than a radio because we can perform many desktop-PC tasks on them, but they have limitations. To successfully attract users to listen to or watch a webcast on handheld devices, the webcast must deliver the message in a proper way and get the full attention of the users to encourage them to participate in such future webcasts.

Scheduled webcasts, regardless of whether they are delivered in Unicast or Multicast mode, can be very costly, especially if you outsource production to vendors, and can be ineffective. It is hard enough to ask people to turn on their desktop PCs for a traditional webcast; it is 10 times more difficult to ask people to turn on their portable devices and join a live webcast. Even though portable devices are much more accessible to users than their desktop computers, you must think about the user's environment. Let us use a cellular phone as an example. We carry our cellular phones wherever we go; because the device is designed to serve us on the move we treat it as a 100% portable product. When we receive an incoming call, we might be driving, walking in the street, shopping, eating dinner, or sleeping; at some of these times it is inconvenient to answer the phone. Handheld PCs are considered to have the same characteristics. I carry my iPAQ PocketPC in my pocket all the time and I can set up my calendar to alert me 15 minutes before a webcast. But what are the chances that I will stop whatever I am doing and listen to a live webcast? If I am at home, the chances are good. But if I am driving, shopping, or dining, the chances are poor.

Media on-demand are the perfect solution for streaming video or audio to mobile devices. Users maintain full control of their schedule and log on to webcasts stored on the media server at their convenience. By giving users the power to decide when and from where to watch a webcast, we guarantee higher attendance, better reception, a better experience, and potential future repeat visits. Whether you transmit the webcast using Unicast or Multicast methods is up to you and the nature of your streaming infrastructure.

Wireless Streaming Technologies

As discussed in more detail in Chapter 5, streaming over wireless networks is a challenge, both to achieve good reception between the transmitter and the receiver and to find the proper compression schema to support acceptable quality even when networks have limited bandwidths. Wireless networks, 2.5G and 3G, will support streaming video to mobile phones and hybrid voice-data devices. The emerging MPEG4 standard is promising to become the leading compression codec for the delivery of audio and video to portable voice-data devices. MPEG4 can handle new levels of interactivity. Best of all, it allows content creators to distribute the same piece of streaming video across all sorts of devices, running all sorts of operating systems. Video is the application that promises to ignite the wireless sector. All the hype surrounding 3G wireless service is based on the promise that high-speed data access and streaming applications will deliver a new wireless experience.

MPEG4 is expected to be the promising standard that will deliver video clips to mobile phones, PDAs, and other handheld devices, according to many analysts. This is true for both wireless devices and unconnected PDAs. Some of MPEG4's capabilities, such as the ability to create new content on a stored video image by transferring only a few bits to the device, are revolutionizing the way voice and data will be transmitted on the networks of the future.

Many companies that are developing streaming technologies today are planning ahead to support mobile devices. Their software is designed to play streaming files on cellular phones, handheld PCs, and PDAs. Most of these companies are developing their platforms with plans to use MPEG4 as a compression codec. Microsoft has used MPEG4 codecs since the release of Netshow version 2.0 (the predecessor of Windows Media technology). Windows Media uses an International Standards Organization (ISO)-compliant codec built into the Windows Media codec 7.0 and higher. This allows Windows Media Player to play back content encoded with MPEG4 codecs. RealSystem supports MPEG4 playback as well. Other companies such as PacketVideo have built their entire platforms on MPEG4 from start. The golden age of application development for handheld devices has just started. ActiveSky, Emblaze Research, Philips Digital Networks, RealNetworks, Toshiba, and others are developing systems to stream media to mobile devices. Some use proprietary algorithms that use Java applets to push content; some simply stream their content after it has been encoded with the MPEG4 codec (the traditional server-client relationship used in desktop streaming).

There is a strong relationship between the popularity of streaming media players and the characteristics of the mobile devices hosting them. Streaming media players are software applications residing on top of hardware and firmware equipment. Multimedia presentations require both audio and video functions that are not present in every mobile device. The success of any device relies on its ability to provide rich playback. A good example is the growing popularity of PocketPC devices. This operating system enables live or on-demand playback made possible by a built-in fast CPU, standard large memory bank, and a color display. These hardware functions are not yet present in Palm operating systems or in mobile phones. As a result, although Palm devices are more popular than PocketPC, they still cannot function as a display for multimedia content.

Palm, Inc., has been a pioneer in the field of mobile and wireless Internet solutions and a leading provider of handheld computers, but according to International Data Corporation (IDC) it is losing market share to PDAs running Microsoft's PocketPC and Windows CE operating systems. Based on the Palm OS(R) platform, Palm's handheld solutions allow people to carry and access their most critical information wherever they go. Palm handhelds address the needs of individuals, enterprises, and educational institutions through thousands of application solutions.

Palm is the most popular mobile operating system used by consumers worldwide (according to Palm sources, the operating system reaches over 75% of personal companion devices), but Palm Pilot has always been considered an organizer, not a small computer. In contrast, PocketPC has both the name and the functionality of a big computer, providing a computer-like experience for people on the move. Handspring (the company that introduced enhanced functionality into Palm devices) was the first to reveal a palm device with a color display and additional memory. Until Palm devices offer audio cards and extensive built-in memory, they will fall behind in the race with PocketPC.

When I had finished writing this book, I asked Palm representatives about any plans to release faster processors, a built-in audio card, and additional memory. The reply from Palm's official public relations firm was that Palm does not disclose its plans for future products and has not said anything specific about its future ability to display streaming content. Palm has over 70,000 developers, who are constantly working on new and innovative programs. I guess we will have to wait to see if Palm has plans to compete with PocketPC. Conflicting reports in early 2001 indicated that Palm was moving away from its identity as a handheld-computer maker and toward becoming a provider of backend enterprise systems for supporting all kinds of handhelds—including those of its rivals, PocketPC, Symbian, and Research In Motion. This was the message sent by Palm's acquisition of enterprise-focused Extended Systems, which sells middleware that connects enterprise applications with handheld devices, to make it simple for companies to manage their employees' handhelds just as they do their PCs.

One of the leading companies to introduce media playback on the Palm operating systems is ActiveSky. ActiveSky introduced an interactive media platform designed from the ground up for mobile Palm wireless users. It included authoring tools to encode media files, a server to host and stream content, and a player. The ActiveSky platform enabled additional functionality that displayed rich content through its player. Such content included interactive entertainment channels (furnished by ActiveSky's content partners), real-time data-driven applications (e.g., scores, stocks, and weather), games, multimedia messaging, and profile-based interactive advertising. Since its launch in Australia in 1999, ActiveSky has enjoyed strong sustained growth through its commitment to innovation and quality, intensive research and development, and diligent customer focus, and due to a highly talented team. ActiveSky software is available for an extensive client base across the mobile media industry throughout the world. Among the supported platforms are Windows CE, PocketPC 2002, Palm operating system, Handspring Visor Prism and Platinum, EPOC Psion, and cellular phones. In late 2001, ActiveSky changed its business model and start targeting Telco companies, offering them a server-player solution that would stream not only video or audio, but also rich animation combined with push data. Considering the slow development of 2.5G and 3G networks in North America, such an approach might not be so bad.

Microsoft and PacketVideo offer applications that have been tested and are used today on wireless networks. Other companies may close the gap in the months or years to come, but their products are not yet popular or widely available to the public. To understand how media are streamed to mobile devices, let us discuss the technologies developed by PacketVideo, RealNetworks, and Microsoft that enable content to stream over wireless networks in North America. These technologies can deliver live streaming media in real time (i.e., direct streaming, not downloadable files) to PocketPC devices and selected mobile phones.

PacketVideo

Established in August 1998, PacketVideo was created to deliver enabling multimedia software products for next-generation wireless devices and applications. In June 1999, the company achieved a significant breakthrough by delivering video over existing 14.4-kbps wireless data networks. During this time, the company also established a programming division to build commercial applications and develop relationships with content companies. At the end of 1999, PacketVideo was awarded the Wireless Communications Innovations Award at the international Consumer Electronics Show (CES), capping a remarkable year. Beginning in the first quarter of 2000, the company implemented major consumer trials around the world with wireless leaders such as Sonera, Sprint PCS, SK Telecom, and others. In May 2000, the prestigious *Red Herring Magazine* designated the company one of the 100 most important emerging companies.

The company markets its software to wireless operators, wireless device and silicon manufacturers, and content providers to ultimately enable mobile consumers to access a variety of applications, including

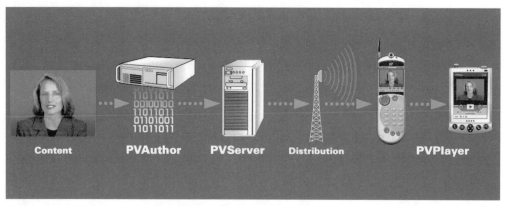

Figure 11–2
PacketVideo from production to distribution

news and financial news, music videos, weather and traffic reports, and home or work security cameras, from any location. The company is privately held; it is actively working with partners in Asia, the Pacific, Europe, and North America and has opened offices in Asia, Europe, and North America.

PacketVideo's products (see Figure 11–2) are designed to be device, operating system, and air-interface independent. (Air interface is the wireless communications protocol used to communicate data between Tags and Readers. The air interface defines such things as the antenna characteristics of the Tag and Reader, the transmit frequencies, transmit power, modulation, coding, bit rate, multiple-access scheme, interference tolerance, and message structure.) These products include:

- **PVAuthor**–This is an easy-to-use MPEG4 standards-based authoring tool that encodes video and audio for transmission over bandwidth-limited, error-prone wireless networks. Because a single PVAuthor encoding scales to simultaneously stream high-quality content over a wide variety of networks, it is a cost-effective solution for encoding both live and on-demand material. PVAuthor 2.0 supports the input of popular digital-content file formats and has interoperability with major live input sources. It is optimized for wireless carriers, content providers, and other video service providers. The system requirements for PVAuthor are:

    Windows 98 SE, 2000, or NT 4.0 (SP 5 and 6a)
    Pentium III 500 MHz, 128 MB RAM

WDM-compliant video capture card (for use with NTSC-PAL camera or other analog source)
Sound card with microphone

- **PVServer**–This is a scalable wireless multimedia delivery server application that includes services for billing, provisioning, and authorization and provides wireless operators with the features necessary to create a commercial, billable service. PVServer runs on Solaris, Hewlett-Packard HP-UX, and Linux platforms, enabling seamless integration into operators' existing infrastructure. Features of PVServer are:

  Uses an extensible modular architecture with interfaces for billing, provisioning, authorization, validation, and other services
  Allows live streaming from multiple PVAuthor sources
  Supports video on-demand from MPEG4 standards-compliant MP4 files
  Uses a proprietary FrameTrack DRC technology to provide optimum video quality over wireless networks
  Supports up to 1,000 simultaneous streams at over 64 kbps
  Streams or downloads MP4-format files to PVPlayer
  Runs on Solaris, Linux, and HP-UX platforms for high-availability and performance

- **PVPlayer**–This intelligently decodes live or on-demand digital media for viewing on wireless devices. PacketVideo's flexible technology enables high-fidelity audio, two-way audio with one-way video, two-way video-audio, and other applications. PVPlayer can be embedded in manufactured devices (e.g., silicon, SmartPhones, PDAs, or laptops) or downloaded for use as needed. Features of PVPlayer are:

  Is a MPEG4-compliant video decoder optimized for streaming video over today's wireless networks
  Supports live streaming for remote viewing applications
  Supports still-image display with streaming audio
  Supports data rates ranging from 9.6 to more than 384 kbps
  Supports from less than 1 to 30 fps
  Supports a variety of audio codecs, including GSM-AMR and others
  Supports a variety of resolutions, including CIF (352×288), QCIF (176×144), Subquarter Common Intermediate Format

(SQCIF; 128 × 96 or smaller); PacketVideo FrameTrack technology, based on MPEG4 temporal scalability; and PacketVideo Dynamic Rate Control (DRC)

Is optimized for the world's leading wireless platforms and operating systems, including ARM, Intel, Lucent, Qualcomm, Texas Instruments, Symbian EPOC, Windows CE 3.0, and others

Supports WinCE 3.0 PocketPC, Windows 98, Windows NT 4, and Windows 2000 operating systems

PacketVideo's software solutions can be deployed in a variety of configurations on a broad range of products and wireless network platforms. The company works closely with customers to optimize networks, devices, and hardware platforms for maximum throughput and audiovisual quality. PacketVideo was designed to support all major digital wireless telephone standards in use today (2G), as well as next-generation wireless networks currently being deployed (2.5G and 3G). PacketVideo's technology is air-interface independent and works across any type of wireless network, including CDMA, TDMA, GSM, GPRS, EDGE, PHS, PDC, and W-CDMA.

PacketVideo supports the MPEG4 global standard. The company believes that compliance with open standards such as MPEG4 is the only way to facilitate the growing interaction and convergence of the previously separate worlds of telecommunications, computing, and the mass media. Open standards such as MPEG4 help prevent technological dead ends. Mobile and stationary user terminals, database access, communications, and new types of interactive services will be major applications for MPEG4. For example, wireless phones are capable of receiving rich interactive digital-video content based on MPEG4 technology. MPEG4 explicitly enables wireless media, even at bit rates as low as 9.6 kbps. MPEG4 also enables digital rights management (DRM) to protect the intellectual property of content providers. PacketVideo technology is compliant with the MPEG4 global standard, which means PacketVideo technology interoperates with MPEG4-compliant hardware and software from other companies. It also means that content encoded in the MPEG4 file format will play on various MPEG4-compliant devices. Because PacketVideo is committed to the MPEG4 open standard, PacketVideo technology is an open development platform, not a proprietary deviation. The company has demonstrated the interoperability of its technology repeatedly and is committed to interoperability with MPEG4-compliant products, applications, and services. The PacketVideo standards-based solution includes compliance to the following standards: MPEG4 (ISO and IEC), H.263 baseline (ITU), 3G-324M (Third Generation Partnership Project, or 3GPP), and RTSP-RTP-RTCP (IETF).

RealNetworks RealSystem Mobile

Fearing the loss of market share as the popularity of mobile devices increased, RealNetworks announced in March 2002 the mobile version of the RealOne Player, optimized for PocketPC devices and showcasing content from more than 30 content providers, spanning news, entertainment, and sports, and available to download for free at *www.real.com/player/mobile.* In its press announcement, RealNetworks stated that with RealOne Player, PocketPC users will be able to access and play RealAudio and RealVideo programming and seamlessly transfer their personal media collections such as music from RealOne Player on their PC to their PocketPC devices. RealAudio and RealVideo content can be streamed in real time directly over a wireless data connection or downloaded from the PC to a PocketPC device for later playback. Content providers will be able to leverage their existing RealAudio and RealVideo programming, easily reaching the rapidly growing mobile audience. In addition, mobile carriers such as AT&T Wireless and the South American Telefonica will be able to try out and deliver media programming to PocketPC devices with wireless connections over future 2.5G and 3G networks.

RealNetworks had partnered in the past with Nokia to develop a player for mobile phones. In 2001, this relationship produced the RealNetworks Player for the Nokia 9210i Communicator. Under this alliance, Nokia is committed to include the mobile version of the RealOne Player as a standard feature on all its mobile devices that use the Symbian operating system (Nokia's operating system for 2.5G and 3G mobile devices). The RealOne Player, with support for 3GPP media formats, RealAudio, and RealVideo, will be included as a standard feature on the Nokia Series 60 platform, the best-of-breed mobile device software platform available for license to other mobile-device manufacturers. Nokia Networks will provide integrated media solutions to mobile operators as an authorized reseller of RealSystem Mobile, RealNetworks's standards-based media-delivery platform.

RealNetworks has always been committed to providing consumers with the best Internet media experience on the broadest array of devices and platforms. In 2002, RealNetworks announced versions of the Real-One Player for many home and mobile devices, including the Nokia 9210i and 9290 Communicators, HP Digital Entertainment Center, Sony Play-station 2, Moxi Media Center, Nokia Media Terminal, and TiVo Series 2 Digital Video Recorder (DVR).

RealNetworks services for mobile devices are consolidated under the umbrella RealSystem Mobile, which provides end-to-end solutions for delivery to mobile devices. The RealSystem Producer enables content providers to create mobile-device-ready content as part of their current content creation process. RealSystem Mobile and RealSystem Gateway work within the carrier's infrastructure to deliver content over GPRS, 1xRTT, W-CDMA, and CDMA2000 networks. RealSystem Mobile is a flexible, robust, carrier-class platform designed for broad-scale distrib-uted deployments. By leveraging over 1,000 published APIs, RealSystems can be seamlessly integrated into billing, provisioning, and customer care systems. The platform supports multiple data types, including Real-Audio, RealVideo, and 3GPP-compliant MPEG4. The products in the RealSystem Mobile family have been designed to meet the needs and ap-plications of content providers creating content for mobile users, mobile operators delivering to mobile devices, and consumers looking for a high-quality media experience on mobile devices. This product line includes:

- **RealSystem Mobile Server** – This is a streaming media server delivering a mobile digital media experience. The media server supports over 53 data types including RealAudio, RealVideo, and 3GPP-compliant MPEG4. RealSystem Mobile Server is at the heart of the RealSystem mobile delivery platform. Designed for deployment within the carrier's network, the server supports up to 2,000 concurrent users, both live and on-demand. RealSystem Mobile Server is available on multiple platforms including Solaris, Linux, and HP-UX. Surprisingly, the server is not supported on Microsoft Windows NT or 2000 operating systems.

- **RealSystem Mobile Gateway** – This is a streaming media proxy-cache that manages media at critical points in the network. RealSystem Mobile Gateway enables mobile operators to pull content from the general Internet as well as from central broadcasting locations within the mobile network and then to rebroadcast it as requested by users. RealSystem Mobile Gateway also minimizes redundant connections to the Internet for live content. Future features of this product may include bit-rate and layout optimization by device, as well as some subscriber-access functionality.

- **RealSystem Producer Plus**–This enables the creation of RealAudio and RealVideo files that can be played on a variety of mobile devices, so that content providers can create media once for delivery anywhere to any device. Parameters for video frame size, video frame rate, bit rate, and codecs are recommended to ensure the best possible playback experiences on both the Nokia 9210 Communicator and the Compaq iPAQ; these parameters can easily be set within the current RealSystem Producer Plus.

- **RealOne Player for mobile devices**–This plays both local and real-time streaming. RealOne Player is now available for the Symbian operating system and PocketPC. The media files must be hosted by RealSystem Mobile Server. RealNetworks promises in future versions to include the playback of 3GPP-mobile-device-compliant content and the advanced optimization of Internet content to device-specific constraints, a feature that will enhance content delivery to a variety of mobile phones.

Microsoft Windows Media

Microsoft has learned its lesson too—by not entering the desktop streaming arena on time, it allowed its competition to increase their market share—and the core development of Windows Media Player version 7.0 includes support for handheld devices as well as portable phones and other Web appliances. When Windows Media Player version 7.0 was released, it was able to play audio only on Windows CE version 2.0 and on the first release of PocketPC. A few months later, the official version of Windows Media Player for PocketPC was released, followed by compatible players that can now play audio and video on all PocketPC-based devices. In an effort to keep its leading position in the software market for mobile devices, Microsoft engaged in talks with the Japanese NTT

DoCoMo. At the end of 2000, the two companies offered a service in Japan in which NTT DoCoMo uses Microsoft's software to play music and video clips on cell phone devices and on the new Japanese hit wireless device, Eggy. NTT DoCoMo's Eggy currently lets users in Japan view ads and brief video clips and to capture and send video images over wireless networks.

Windows Media technology is following the path of many other Microsoft products that have made their way to mobile devices. Pocket-PC 2002 offers additional solutions that were used before only in desktops or laptops. Good examples are Microsoft's Terminal Service, which provides remote management of servers, VPN clients, SQL pocket server, and hardware that connects handheld devices to wall projectors. Because enterprises are struggling to enable their employees with portable devices that improve productivity and expand their business, it is expected that streaming applications will be part of future mobile technologies. These mobile solutions will provide one- or two-way video and audio communications over IP networks.

In a recent conversation with Microsoft executives, I learned that although the company seeks the development of software to play multimedia on Web appliances and various mobile devices, it acknowledges that the current infrastructure in North America will limit the ability to stream media to such devices for at least a few years. At the present time, Microsoft is directing its resources to continuing the support of handheld devices using 802.11b WLANs. Microsoft foresees an increasing demand for PocketPC devices in enterprises. Considering the hardware and software advantages of PocketPC devices and the large group of vendors developing applications that will improve productivity and speed up data processing, Microsoft predicts handhelds will change the way we process information at work and on the road. The big picture includes support for streaming media and full integration with NET frames.

The release of Microsoft Producer (an additional member of the Office family) provides a better understanding of Microsoft's plans for streaming media within enterprises. In past years, Microsoft Office applications have acquired over 75% of the market share among businesses. Word is an official document processor, Excel is an official spreadsheet, and PowerPoint is widely used by sales and marketing people. In late 2001, in an attempt to cash in on the recognition of these three leading applications, Microsoft included Producer in Office 2002. The application creates presentations combining HTML images, PowerPoint slides, and streaming media into compelling LAN- or Web-based presentations. The idea behind Producer is the integration of all tools into one product. Once you have installed Office 2002, you have all these tools at your fingertips. How will this affect the popularity of PocketPC? Think big. Streaming media were introduced to desktops and then migrated to mobile devices. The same is expected to happen with presentation tools. In the near future, handheld devices running PocketPC are expected to become valuable tools in enterprises, delivering information in the form of media, text, and images. This will result in increased individual productivity, improving companies' overall efficiency.

Summary

- Streaming media to mobile devices depends on the successful deployment of wireless networks supporting the 802.11b wireless protocol.
- Pilot programs in Europe and Asia prove that it is possible to stream media to mobile phones. Some of these markets offer streaming services over 2.5G wireless networks.
- Unlike in desktop PCs, in handheld devices the capability to stream media depends on hardware compatibility. To stream media, mobile devices must have proper display, CPU power, and sufficient RAM.
- The increasing popularity of WLANs indicates that enterprises are perfect candidates for portable streaming media applications.

Part III

STRATEGIES

12

Marketing Techniques

The Internet has proven its worth as a viable source for information, a tool for instant communication, and an alternative to television while we are at work. According to Pew Research, in the two days following the attacks on the World Trade Center and the Pentagon 74% of all Americans reached out to loved ones and friends via the telephone or the Internet. Eighty-two percent of Internet users used the telephone or email to make contact. Those using the Internet spent a bit more time online than usual. Following the attacks, most news Web sites with streaming media capabilities reported an overwhelming load of requests. Although it is true that over 85% turned to their television sets because the real-time reporting was available on all broadcast stations, leading news Web sites such as CNN.com and MSNBC.com quickly posted additional offline information. This information was consumed rapidly by Web surfers interested in text, images, slides, and replays of the events that were not available on broadcast television. Everything seems to have a different meaning now. From 1991 with the introduction of real-time reporting from the frontlines (national television reporting from the Gulf War) through the evolution of rich streaming media on the Internet, content media producers as well as their audience are now comfortable using a hybrid of communication tools to deliver a message.

At the end of 1999, a new type of audience was introduced to advertisers. Ad agencies called these users who watch or listen to webcasts online streamies. In summer 2000, this group represented 44% of all Internet users and 27% of Americans overall. By far, streamies are the most valuable consumer group on the Internet. Streaming media consumers are far more interactive, are more oriented to e-commerce, and spend far more time online than Internet users who do not stream. Advertisers wishing to target high-value Internet users focus their marketing on streamies. According to research performed by Arbitron/Edison Media Research Group, 61.3 million Americans have tried streaming media; 29.5 million have done so in the past month and 13.4 million have done so in the week prior to the survey. Among Internet users, 36% have listened to Internet audio and 20% have watched video over the Internet.

These results show a pattern in consumers' adoption of technology and its use in their daily lives. I like to say that everyday we learn something new. New technology affects people in different ways: Some are fascinated by it and are willing to try it immediately, and some (the majority) feel threatened by it and are overwhelmed. The second group requires more time to observe and to accept it. Most people confront technology by assimilating it to their daily needs. Once the technology has been accepted and categorized as a tool to achieve an objective, people felt more comfortable using it. To compare apples with apples let us explore two similar situations—the bombing of the World Trade Center on February 26, 1993, and the terrorist attack on the World Trade Center on September 11, 2001. In 1993, a car bomb with 1,100 pounds of explosives was detonated in the parking garage beneath the complex, killing six people and causing $300 million worth of damage. Immediately after the attack, all networks covered the event. People watched and listened to the news on their televisions and radios. The Internet was unknown then. Nobody sent email, joined chat rooms, or watched additional coverage, unless it was rebroadcast or printed in the papers. Eight years later, during the worst single terrorist attack known to modern civilization, worldwide audiences witnessed in real time the gruesome details of the most shocking and horrifying event ever broadcast over cable television, television, radio, and the Internet. The Internet had become an official medium recognized by major broadcasters as a vehicle to supplement their limited air time used for prime-time programming.

As consumers' interest in rich media over the Internet grew, the corporate appetite increased too. During the days following the World Trade Center attack, corporate America braced for the impact on an already weak economy. As a result of the attack, the NASDAQ reached its lowest level since 1929. The airline industry was the first to announce major layoffs. Others followed. Many corporations turned to the Internet and to their local internal networks to distribute fast and cost-effective video or audio announcements. Verizon Communication, which was responsible for the restoration of over 3 million voice and data lines in downtown Manhattan, webcast regular announcements stating their progress in the field. Northwest Airlines was one of the first airlines to restore flights on Friday, September 14. Their special streaming announcement was released online.

Companies use webcast technology to reach their audience and pass on important messages to them. During times of war or emergencies, these messages consist of instructions regarding public safety and other emergency-related issues delivered over fast real-time channels (television, radio, or the Internet) or over information channels for which time sensitivity is not essential (newspapers and as Internet media on-demand). In times of peace, messages reach the public in the very same fashion. What remains is to define our objectives, our messages, our target audience, and the means with which we want to reach them.

Defining Your Objectives

When defining our objectives we must separate the consumer audience from the corporate audience. The business to consumer (B2C) market is totally different from the business to business (B2B) market. In the B2C market, it is clear that a business is targeting a consumer to persuade him or her to buy a product. In the B2B market, it is clear that a business is targeting another business to persuade it to buy a product for internal use or for external use, the business to business to consumer (B2B2C) model. This scenario is simple; marketing campaigns have been written and tested before. However, targeting a client within the corporate arena is a totally different challenge. Let us say that the training department of a corporation wants to reach new employees and show them how to use the company email system. This type of relationship is called employer to employee (E2E). Or say that a corporation needs to sell an informational product (information regarding internal rules and procedures) and wants to reach its employees and ask them to review a message, absorb the information, and react to it. We must separate the B2B and E2E approaches because they use different methods to reach their target.

Business to Consumer

First, we define our objectives and how we are planning to reach our potential customers. The consumer we want to reach can be a new user of our product or a user who is familiar with our offering, and we want him or her to become a loyal customer who will use our product again. The next step is to design a strategy that will help us implement our ideas and convert them to an efficient tool to attract our customers.

Consider the real estate business, for example. Most real estate agencies have two types of customers: individuals who are asking for help in selling or renting their properties and individuals who are interested in viewing these properties to rent or buy them. In this case, our objectives are to persuade the first group to choose our company to represent them and then to reach the unknown potential customer who will rent or buy the property. To accommodate the first group, we will produce one or more videos showing our services and describing what we can do for them. To accommodate the second group we will produce many individual videos of each property we want to sell, describing the benefits and quality of life they offer. All these videos will reside on our Web site in two separate sections. Property owners will log on to the If You Are an Owner section, and consumers will log on to the Buy or Rent section. One picture is worth 1,000 words.

Employer to Employee

Large corporations with employees scattered across different states, countries, or continents have been using video to reach their employees since the early 1980s. Film had been used for training and to convey executive messages since the early 1930s. With the introduction of VCRs in the early 1980s, the means of distribution changed, along with the way corporations produced, processed, and distributed video to their employees. In the mid-1990s, many corporations traded in VHS distribution for CD-ROMs, which are faster and cheaper to produce. Complicated cable television networks (closed-caption television networks) were replaced by satellite technology. However, the cost of maintaining a satellite network is much more expensive than the cost of maintaining an IP-based distribution network. Unlike satellite technology, which requires the installation of expensive receivers at every download point and an additional air-time cost to transit the signal, streaming technology uses hardware and software that are widely available on corporate networks—the very same hardware and software used to transfer data across the company's LAN. The difference between the messages that were sent from employers to their employees five years ago and messages that will be sent next month is only the means of distribution.

There are many examples of corporations using media to address their target audiences. Each group within the corporation uses different methods to convey its message. Corporate executives address employees about corporate rules of conduct, company policies, executive addresses, and general company overviews and shareholders on a quarterly basis on the financial stability of the company and plans for future growth. Human resource departments distribute media packages to new employees describing the companies' health plans and retirement plans. Training departments rely on video to teach new or existing employees how to use applications on their desktop computers. And last, the sales task force uses media to introduce in detail new products to their overseas offices, for example, eliminating the need to travel.

Therefore, corporations are easy adopters of new media for their internal use, compared to companies that target consumers. In the corporate world, the return on investment is clear, visible, and measurable. When dealing with the public, too many facts can have a negative impact on a sale, clouding a company's ability to measure profits, thus making it much more difficult to adopt and implement new technology.

Online versus Offline

Many marketing managers are facing the decision of whether to invest resources in the online or offline promotion of their product. Before the arrival of the Internet, traditional distribution outlets included television, cable television, and radio. The term "online" referred to information available for immediate review over a mass media chain; the offline world consisted of newspapers, magazines, billboards, and other means of distribution that did not display messages in real time. With the arrival of the Internet and its impact on global distribution of information, the concepts online and offline have changed. Today "online" means to be on the Internet. When we want to pull information from the Internet, we must connect our computer to our ISP's network using a dial-up modem, DSL, or cable modem to go on the Internet. (If we have DSL or a cable modem, our computer is connected all the time.) When a computer connects to the Internet, all the links and preferences that we have set up become active links to other computers on the network. We establish these links by installing software, bookmarking sites of interest, and using media players or real time news tickers on our desktop PCs. These links connect us to sources of information. Companies or individuals that control the other end of the link we have created can send us information at will. It takes only a few seconds to deliver an email from Paris, France, to Miami, Florida. However, it takes much longer for the same message to reach us if we are tuned to our favorite news channel. In this case, the message must first be sent to the local, regional, or national office of the originator's news agency, be processed internally and sent to the agency headquarters, and then approved for broadcast. Next, it must slotted to be broadcast at a certain time. If we are lucky and we have tuned our television or radio to the right channel at the right moment, we then see or hear the message. This simplified example illustrates the power of the Internet. In a way, the Internet has given the power of choice back to the people. Before the age of television and the radio, consumers selected the information they wanted to review. People were informed by reading newspapers or by listening to other people. But news traveled slowly, definitely a drawback. The arrival of radio and then television changed people's habits. They became passive and for years relied on information that was pushed out to them. The Internet is bringing back our choice of what we want to receive. With its wide networks reaching every country, every city, and every language possible, the Internet has no borders. We have entered a new era. We are no longer recipients of pushed information but are independent-minded individuals pulling the information we want from any place we find interesting, any time we want. As a result of this cultural and psychological change, the term "offline" has been transformed to mean distribution over television, radio, cable, and newspapers.

In comparing pushed and pulled information, we must address why push technology failed in 1998. At that time, Microsoft and Netscape were engaged in a browser war, an attempt to control distribution of browsers to desktop computers. Microsoft came up with a gimmick—Internet Explorer 4.0 had an Active Desktop function supporting push technology. Users were prompted to install a desktop interface that would receive content from preselected media companies. The public rejected this effort by walking away and not activating the function. As a result, media companies who were part of this pilot program walked away too. A few months later, the new version of Internet Explorer was released with the Active Desktop function listed in the desktop preferences, not hidden, letting users choose the content they wanted to display on their desktop. Consumers tolerated the ability to make a selection from a list of options, but they did not tolerate media companies and their providers (browser software developers) gaining control over their desktop PCs. After all, I have paid for my computer and I want to be able to put my dog's picture on my screen.

Where should you promote a Web site or a product? My recommendation is to use the best of both worlds. It all depends on the nature of your business, the scope of your project, your target audience, and your financial resources. If you are a mid-size company in the construction business, the answer is obvious. Spend your budget on a good-looking Web site; include practical information about your services and perhaps add a few videos showing finished projects. Use streaming media to support your marketing efforts. If you are a corporate executive manager and you need to promote a new product, use your intranet site to show videos about the making of the product and use the medium to encourage employees to send you comments about the product. It may help you catch mistakes or improve it. Then use streaming video on your public Web site to demonstrate the product to resellers and finally to the public. If you are a programming manager of a Web site that is promoting entertainment content in the form of live or on-demand media, use streaming video. If you are using a pay-per-view model, first post short clips; teaser clips persuade visitors to buy the full package. Then post the full-length clips. Submit your short clips to media search engines to drive traffic to your site. If you are promoting interesting content, your budget allows you to do offline promotion, and you can justify the return on your investment by targeting a mass audience, buy a 30-second spot during the Superbowl. Make sure first that your streaming video files are hosted on a network that can support tens of thousands of requests at the same time.

An Arbitron/Edison Media Research study conducted last year in the United States found that the growth of streaming media over the past two and one-half years has been stunning. As of January 2001, 13% of Americans (or 29.5 million) had used either Internet audio or video in the month previous to the survey, compared to 10% in January 2000. The research also indicates that more than one-quarter (27%) of Americans (61.3 million) had experienced either Internet audio or video and 6% (13.4 million) listened to or watched streaming media each week. These encouraging findings show that more Americans are using streaming media on a regular basis despite the slower growth of broadband networks. The sudden reduction in dotcom advertising during 2000 has led to slower growth in the number of people going online and has also led to a decrease in time spent online. The interesting answers belong to the one-third of all participants who declared that they would give up television if forced to choose between home Internet access and television. It is stunning how, in a very short period of time, the Internet has become such a necessity for a large percentage of Americans. Among those who watch or listen to streaming media, nearly one-half would forsake their televisions to keep Internet access. One-half of younger Americans (ages 12–24) say they would give up their televisions in order to keep their home Internet access. The report concludes that streamies are a valuable audience for advertisers: "Compared to Internet users who do not watch or listen online, streamies are slightly younger and more likely to be male. They spend much more time online, are clicking more on banner ads and are buying more online. Streamies are much more likely than nonstreamies to have recently made a purchase over the Internet in the last week. Given that streamies are more highly educated and more likely to be employed and report higher annual incomes, advertisers wishing to target responsive and valuable consumers online should focus on streamies." (The full report is available at *www.arbitron.com*.)

Free Online Guides

If you find a good online guide, show me! Online guides for streaming content were very popular in the late 1990s. Many companies had plans to generate revenues from advertising. They offered online applications for content owners to submit entries and for Web surfers to search, find, and view streaming media content. In the early days of the Internet, everyone was excited about the possibility of launching his or her own content channel. Guerilla television was an exciting concept. Nobody needed the television networks because Web sites would start broadcasting content to any part of the world. Content owners submitted music, movies, and news content to a handful of online guides—that is, if you had access to a fashion show, a music concert, or a news event, you could just submit your content to a multimedia search engine or guide. Random visitors of these sites would watch your media and everyone would have fun. Copyrights on the Internet were never properly addressed by the legal community, and Hollywood and the music industry were late. At first they rejected any plans to launch multimedia Web sites, claiming that audiences would prefer to watch videos on their televisions or listen to music on their home stereos. This all changed when Web sites such as MP3.com and Napster introduced the concept of file sharing and changed the nature of content distribution forever. The idea of free file sharing over a network without regard to copyrights, contracts, or permissions motivated young businesses to post content online, attract visitors, and generate an income from services such as membership fees, ad revenues, and referral commissions. Hollywood realized the negative impact of Napster on the music industry and limited distribution of movie trailers to authorized Web sites only.

This online content paradise lasted approximately two years. Millions of dollars were invested in streaming infrastructures, production equipment, and highly paid executives who left their network jobs for better-paying, prestigious dotcom positions. It was nice while it lasted. In summer 2000, Wall Street realized that consumers were spending little to nothing online. Many studies were conducted about consumer behavior and spending habits and high expectations drove more investments. However, it became clear that the public was refusing to pay for entertainment. Without a valuable business model, companies such as DEN, Pseudo, and Centerseat found little support for their efforts to distribute original or licensed content. A growing number of reports about decreasing revenues from consumer Web sites, combined with hard facts showing a small or slow return on investment in dotcom businesses, started a rollercoaster that brought down the technology sector at the end of 2000. Wall Street investors, who had been competing a year earlier about where and how much to invest in dotcom companies, made a 180-degree turn and held back from any future investments. The result was chaotic. The technology sector went into a deadly spin that resulted in thousands of job cuts and, worse, hundreds of companies filing for bankruptcy. In a sense, this natural progress did encourage consolidations and cuts in spending. Dotcom companies now had to focus on generating revenues from actual sales rather than ideas. In the streaming market, three groups were eliminated: new content Web sites relying on original or licensed content, streaming guides relaying on ad dollars based on impressions, and affiliate Web sites relying on their business model of traffic (customers) driven from free ad placement on other sites. When the smoke disappeared, it was clear that the market changed. The first group no longer existed. Today, except for television, radio, and cable networks (with the exception of movie studios), there are no original content Web sites featuring originally produced entertainment or documentaries.

Atom Films was the sole survival, thanks to distribution deals; all other players merged or closed shop. Yack.com is a survivor among the streaming guides, again thanks to smart distribution deals. Affiliate Web sites are no longer in business, or their owners have completely changed their business model and now rely on hard cash deals paid for up front to support their sites.

The streaming industry evolved into a more mature and business-oriented arena. Today, not every company will launch computer farms to host streaming files, not unless someone will pay for using these streams. Online guides to streaming content will not survive the new economy unless they have a better business model than ad revenues.

True marketing campaigns are not free anymore. To be more exact, effective marketing campaigns have never been free. Listings on streaming guides will help you attract a small amount of traffic, but to create a massive amount of requests you will need to plan and to spend money. Another option is to engage in a strategic partnership, which will drive traffic to your Web site and help you offset your cost of streaming. (See the section The Buzz Word–Online Partnerships later in this chapter.)

Increasing Traffic to Your Site

Posting to Online Streaming Guides

Posting your media links on online streaming guides in the postdotcom era is a hard task. The leading streaming technology developers (Real-Networks, Apple, and Microsoft) have created powerful streaming guides that have only one objective–to showcase their streaming technology and to introduce Web sites that use it.

RealNetworks launched Realguide.com, a free service to consumers listing content covering various topics. The Web site offers a premium service (Gold Pass), a monthly subscription that grants access to exclusive content available only to Gold Pass members. This model generates revenues for RealNetworks as well as for partner sites submitting their content. RealNetworks has a strict process for selecting content for the Gold Pass platform.

QuickTime followed the Realguide concept and launched a full multimedia site available both via a browser and through the QuickTime Player version 5.0 interface. This is a free Web site with access to one of the largest movie trailer parks on the Internet.

In spring 2000, Microsoft launched Windowsmedia.com. The Web site climbed quickly to become the second most visited site on the Web (after Realguide.com). Through partnerships with several ICPs, Windowsmedia.com has managed to line up a unique and well-managed group of partners that submit almost daily fresh content to the site. Topics include entertainment news and features, music, movies, sports, educational, and news content.

Because these three sites attract most streamies, your first step is to find out if your content qualifies to be included in their programs. If you failed to negotiate an agreement with the big guys, turn to alternative sites. Here are a few examples:

- *www.mediachannel.com*–This is a Web site that lists a handful of Web sites divided by categories. Mediachannel.com has two significant areas. The Internet Video Guide section is the linchpin of the Web site. This section lists the top Web sites according to a specific category of Internet-video content. Currently, there are 18 Internet Video Guides. For example, the Entertainment Guide takes you to Web sites that contain comedy, movie, music, and television Internet video. MediaChannelTV is dedicated to Internet television. In this section, you will find Web sites that contain Internet video shows, events, and simulcast television webcasts. Use this Web site as a television guide for Internet-video. Submission to this site is free and efficient.

- *www.yack.com*–Yack does for the Internet what the Electronic Program Guide has done for television. Today, Yack's Internet Program Guide is the world's most comprehensive, steering users to over 150,000 live, on-demand, and scheduled Web events each week. Distributed through Yack's vast global network of partnerships, the guide reaches an estimated 13 million (or nearly one-half of all) consumers who regularly seek online programming. Yack was one of the first to begin cataloging Internet events, and it has continued to grow with the streaming industry. Today, 28 million people access everything from their morning newscast to full-length feature films online, and Yack's ever-expanding product line now includes over 10 content and audience-specific guides. Top companies such as Road Runner, Showtime Online, Earth-Link, WorldGate, Chello Broadband, and Line One turn to Yack to provide their audiences with a great Web experience. Submission to this site is free and efficient.

- *www.aentv.com*–Formed in 1995 Alternative Entertainment Network, Inc. (AENTV) is one of the leading producers, aggregators, and syndicators of streaming media content on the Internet. The core of AENTV's business is the production of compelling brand-driven streaming video content and its syndication to a variety of highly trafficked portals. AENTV's Content Syndication and Licensing Program brings high-quality original video programming to sites such as AskJeeves, Billboard, Compuserve, GamePro, Hollywood Reporter, Iwon, Juno, MSN, and Playboy. Unlike Mediachannel.com and Yack.com, AENTV does not accept just any content submission–your content must fit into their syndicated channels.

The Submission Process for Search Engines

The traditional search engines also include guides for streaming media Web sites or events. Yahoo! led the initiative with its Yahoo Events! Division, listing hundreds of radio stations, television stations, and garage networks streaming or downloading media. Excite, Altavista, Webcrawler, and others have their own media directories.

Submitting a Web site to a search engine is a simple process; making your link work and appear at the top listing of similar sites is almost impossible. Every search engine uses different methods to catalog the tens of thousands of submissions they receive every day. Some rely on automated systems (spiders) that surf the Web constantly to pull information about Web sites, catalog them in a main database, and make them available to the public through a search and find mechanism. Other sites rely on manual filtering of submissions; they prefer to post the submitted Web site to the proper category based on their own internal rules and requirements. What the two groups have in common are their objectives: to create a global search mechanism that will display the most accurate results of individual search actions. To achieve this goal, all search engines rely on you, the individual Web site owner, and your ability to communicate to the search engines the basic information they need to catalog your business and place it in the proper section of their site.

You are trying to bring traffic to your multimedia site. How can search engines help you? Most sites I have visited have beautiful and expensive interfaces, sophisticated databases, and nice chunks of content. I have a bad habit of looking deeply into Web sites to learn how their structures work, what technology they are using, and if they are thinking about the most important value of creating a new Web site–marketing. For example, I worked once with a brilliant Chief Technology Officer (CTO) of a company who had designed one of the most interactive multimedia sites I have ever seen. The site won awards and was recognized by the press as the first Web site of its kind to offer an ultimate broadband experience, combining streaming media presentations synchronized with contextual text, images, and e-commerce opportunities. It had beautiful architecture, smart backend support, and full press coverage, but no visitors (Web surfers) at all. With total devotion to creating the ultimate broadband site, the company had failed to address an important issue–how to bring visitors to the site to show them content and prompt them to do what they were expected to do, that is, buy products on the site. The simple process of preparing the HTML pages of the site properly and submitting the site to search engines well in advance was never done.

Rule number one in designing a Web site: Make sure you insert the proper meta tags into your HTML pages. Meta tags are HTML tags that provide information that describes the content of the Web pages a user will be viewing. Search engines have recognized that Web site owners and administrators can use this resource to control their positioning and descriptions in search engine results. Many search engines have now incorporated reading meta tags as part of their indexing formulas. Rule number two: Submit your site to search engines at least 4–6 weeks before it is expected to go live. Because search engines receive so many submissions everyday, they need at least 4–6 weeks to process entries and catalog them properly. What meta tags should you use? Here is an example of meta tags to use in a multimedia site. In this case, the site belongs to a production facility offering production services. Copy and paste these tags below the HTML tag of every HTML page on your Web site, replacing the details with your own:

```
<HEAD>
<META NAME="description" content="ABC Productions—all media production
services for entertainment and corporate clients.">
< META NAME ="keywords" content="video, productions, corporate, music,
broadcast events, industrial, tv productions, press conferences,
training, executive presentations, interactive, streaming, audio, CD-
ROM, DVD, organizations,">
<TITLE>ABC Productions</TITLE>
</HEAD>
```

Next, submit your Web site to the major search engines. Search engines are divided into two groups: local and global. Local search engines normally serve communities or regions, whereas national or global search engines have general sections offering many Web sites from many different places. The following list of global search engines is recommended by Submitcorner.com. If you are interested in submitting your Web site to a local search engine, look for the proper links in these sites to localize your submission.

- *www.altavista.com/*–Altavista currently has one of the largest Internet databases of all the search engines. Obtaining high rankings in Altavista is very difficult.

- *www.aol.com/netfind/*–AOL Netfind is a cobranded search engine powered by the Open Directory Project (ODP) and by Inktomi, the same database that powers Hotbot. Although AOL Netfind is only a branded search engine and shares the same backend system as other search engines, AOL receives a large volume of traffic each day and, just as important, it will ensure that your Web page is easy to find.

- *www.ask.com/*–AskJeeves, originally launched commercially in April 1997, has created a search engine aimed at creating a unique user experience that emphasizes ease of use and the relevance of its results. AskJeeves combines natural language questions and the use of its database of knowledge bases to best determine a suitable and targeted answer.

- *www.excite.com/*–Excite is a very popular search engine, offering a large index (over 50 million Web sites) that includes several free features such as news, stocks, horoscopes, sports, and weather. Excite opened in 1995 and acquired Webcrawler in 1996. Recently, Excite and @Home network, which form the Excite @Home network, were acquired by AT&T.

- *www.google.com/*–Google is a new contender in the search engine market and is making itself known with its very powerful and accurate search results. Google's database is smaller than some of the large search engines, but the quality of the results makes up for this. Google returns only results based on all the keywords a user has entered. In addition, Google keeps a local cache of popular sites that are requested, so if the main Web server of the destination site is down, Google will retrieve their cached copy for quick access.

- *www.hotbot.com/*–Hotbot was originally launched in 1996 by Wired Digital and has grown to become a major player in the search engine market. In late 1998, Lycos acquired Hotbot. Hotbot is powered by the Inktomi engine for their search capabilities and the ODP for their directory-based system.

- *www.infospace.com/*–Infospace, founded in 1996 with the vision of delivering real-world information anytime, anywhere, and to any device, became a major player in less than four short years. In late 1998, Infospace became a public company on the NASDAQ and continues to innovate its services and fulfill its anytime-anywhere-any device mission. Infospace licenses and uses the Netscape ODP for its primary site results and then uses a combination of GoTo and Inktomi's results as secondary results.

- *www.iwon.com/*–Iwon is a new search engine that rewards users with contest entries the more they use the search engine service. Iwon originally launched in October of 1999 and has seen significant growth into a large Internet portal, mostly thanks to its cash giveaways (over $2 million given away every month) for using its services. Many people have found this search engine an excellent alternative to the major portals. Furthermore, Iwon uses many of the same technologies (Inktomi and Direct Hit) as their rivals, making it essentially a reward-based search engine that is otherwise similar to the competition.

- *www.looksmart.com/*–Looksmart has become one of the most commercialized search engines and directory services. Launched in 1995, Looksmart was originally a free directory-based service, very similar to Yahoo! and the ODP. Recently, it took a commercial spin to its business model and now requires a payment to consider your Web site. Looksmart is powered by a large number of editors and powers several other search engines such as MSN Search, Altavista, and Excite.

- *www.lycos.com/*–Lycos is a large-scale search engine and Web portal that has increased its services beyond searching the Web. Lycos first started in early 1994 as a university project, later became a commercial operation, and has expanded into a large-scale search engine. Only in 1999 did Lycos make the shift from being an exclusive search engine to also offering directory-based listings. In 1998, Lycos acquired Wired Digital's Hotbot, which continues to operate under the same name.

- *www.northernlight.com/*–Northern Light is a large-scale search engine that indexes the Web and traditional media. Northern Light opened its search engine in late 1997, but as a late competitor in the search-engine market, it offers access to documents that are particularly popular with researchers, including access to magazines, newspapers, and other nonpublic resources, which can be purchased for a nominal fee. Regular public Web sites are searchable for free. In addition to Web searches, Northern Light offers industry, news, investment, and other types of specific searches. Recent studies have shown that Northern Light indexes over 140 million documents, making it the largest search engine.

- *www.webcrawler.com/*–Webcrawler is an old but still popular search engine that should not be forgotten. Webcrawler was originally owned by AOL in 1995 and had become the preferred search engine for AOL users until it was sold to Excite the following year. Excite continues to operate Webcrawler as a separate search engine. Webcrawler gained popularity with AOL users and has remained quite popular to this day.

- *www.yahoo.com/*–Yahoo! is the oldest and still most popular directory service for searching the Web. Originally launched in 1994, Yahoo! is one of the oldest directory-based search engines. Yahoo! does not rely on spiders or any automated tools to populate its database but instead uses people to compile large directories of Web sites. Yahoo! by far is one of the smallest databases, but its being compiled by people has served to provide fresh, quality Web sites and has made it one of the most popular Web sites on the Internet since its inception.

To maximize your position among the thousands of other companies, try to be specific during the submission process. Most search engines will let you go deep enough to specify your business in the right section. For example, if you are ABC Productions, specializing in video production services for corporations, and you want to submit your site to Yahoo! (a paid service), follow these steps:

1. Log on to the Yahoo! main page. Click on Business and Economy.
2. Click on B2B Marketplace.
3. Click on Entertainment and Media Production.
4. Click on Television.
5. Click on Production Companies.
6. Look for the Submit New Site link on the page. Follow the instructions for paying the fee and submitting your site.

Other search engines do not charge a fee for submitting a new Web site, but the submission process is similar in all search engines. Follow the steps to process as many submissions as possible.

Remember that all search engines clean out their databases on a regular basis. This process verifies the existence of old records, comparing them with the physical existence of an actual Web site on the Internet. If you have submitted an entry and have changed the domain name of your site, the search engine tools that attempt to verify your old domain record will come back empty-handed and your record will be deleted. If you have changed domain names be sure to modify your records on all the search engines. I recommend that you regularly submit your domain every quarter (every three months). This applies especially to free search engines that do not charge a fee for submission. These engines tend to clean their databases more often, clearing space for new registered sites.

The Buzz Word — Online Partnerships

The term is old, the objectives are old, but the technology is brand new. Online partnerships started in the early days of the public Internet. Companies engaged in barter deals, exchanging services and working hard to promote their products. In the early days of the Internet, when "free" was an acceptable term to Wall Street investors, online partnerships were born in many shapes and colors. My first online partnership was created out of necessity in a frantic 48 hours in March 1997. Mark Haefeli, a true visionary and the president of Second Coming Productions, an electronic publicity firm that was hired to facilitate a press conference for the Irish band U2, wanted to use the Internet to announce the band's new album and upcoming world tour. The result was the world's first Internet Press Kit (IPK). The Web site included the band's biography, video interviews, a public chat room, audio samples from the new CD, and a live webcast of the press conference. Because such announcements are normally planned and executed in secrecy, we had only 48 hours to build the site and notify our audience. A quick phone call to Real-Networks (Progressive Networks at the time) took care of the streaming video portion. Another quick call to friends in Yahoo Events! helped us with online promotion, and a last-minute call to Infinity.net (an ISP with offices in Virginia) took care of a mirror site for the duration of the event. The U2 PopMart Tour was a huge success. The site received the Intel Screamer Award for best site and was visited by more than 500,000 separate visitors during the month following the press conference. All parties did a great job, and, surprisingly, production was smooth and paperless. Today when I look back I am surprised that no contracts were signed and no money exchanged hands among the four major partners (Second Coming Productions, RealNetworks, Yahoo!, and Infinity.net). It was a first, and it will be remembered as such.

The reality today is quite different. Barter deals still exist, but most partnerships use cash. The top media sites encourage long-term partnerships, but you must first qualify based on your content and its ability to produce daily or weekly doses of fresh streams. Most readers and their companies do not fit this description. There are many alternatives. A smart marketing manager can engage in an online partnership that will serve his plans and, at the same time, offer added value to the company's new partner. Marketing managers or corporate executives can adopt this strategy to their daily plans to promote a project or an event to potential audiences.

For example, a producer of a fashion show wants to promote a live or on-demand show in streaming format. The producer should contact one or more of the leading streaming sites and ask them if they are interested in the show. In addition, the producer should contact one of the streaming syndication sites and ask it if it is interested in syndicating the content and offering it to its existing clients. A reasonable question is: Who will pay for the cost of streaming? The answer depends on the type of relationship the producer manages to establish between the Web site that owns the content and one or more of the potential content aggregators and on their interest in the media. In the corporate world, situations vary, but most cases are generally similar.

For example, a corporate executive in charge of a new product wants to train the company sales force in how to better sell the product to their list of clients. The executive talks to the IT department and the corporate video department and asks them to facilitate a live webcast with an option of posting the media on their servers later. The executive calls the sales and corporate communications departments, asking them to help him or her promote the event and to make sure all sales representatives tune in to the event. Corporate communications posts an announcement on the company intranet site. The sales department reaches all its representatives in advance and asks them to join the live webcast. By planning ahead and sharing information with all parties involved, the executive maximizes exposure and achieves his or her goal.

These two examples illustrate the proper way to promote an online event. Online partnerships do not necessarily mean contracts and cash transactions. These financial transactions are an essential part of every business, but in some cases the benefits are not immediately visible to all sides and they tend to be deal breakers. My suggestion to you, the reader, is to evaluate every case on its merits and to try to make the best out of existing or future relationships with external parties or fellow managers in your organization.

Summary

- Define your objectives before planning a marketing campaign.
- Maximize the impact of your message by combining distribution over online and offline channels. Remember that online solutions are different than offline outlets because they provide access to information on demand.
- Online guides to streaming sites offer a limited presence. The majority of Web surfers and streamies visit the large media portals, where they get extensive coverage of news, music, and entertainment content streamed mostly by the traditional radio, television, and cable networks.
- Submission of your Web site to search engines and proper coding of the Web site are essential to generate random traffic to your site. Four to six weeks are needed for search engines to process new entries.
- The Internet introduces powerful tools to communicate with audiences of all types. Be smart in using it.

13

Case Studies

How to Measure Success

The three examples presented here illustrate different approaches that were taken to implement streaming media solutions. The common ground for all these case studies was the need to deliver a rich experience to end-users, an experience that traditional media such as television and radio could not deliver. In all these cases, the Internet provided a broad and more efficient platform to convey a message. Streaming media was used to express what written words or static images could not. Additional applications were combined to support e-commerce (Centerseat.com), measure user response (enterprise multimedia archives), and create interest in a new product (U2 PopMart Internet Press Kit). Streaming media proved to be an innovative cost-effective way to deliver a message from one to many.

We have entered a new millennium and the use of new technology helps us shape our lives for the better. To deliver messages properly, we must first decide on the proper technology and method. How can we achieve such a difficult task in a fast-paced changing world? The solution lies in education–by exposing ourselves and those around us to new technologies, we maintain an advantage over our competitors. This applies to local enterprises, small and large, as well as to governments and countries. We live in an information age. The advantage we have over our competitors no longer lies in the amount of arms or vegetables we produce but instead in our ability to share, manage, and deliver information. It is hard to evaluate a success story, but by reading the following case studies you will be able to analyze the methods used and judge for yourself whether the means were justified. Learn from these examples as you plan your next project.

Case 1—Centerseat and Broadband Channels on the Web

Solution Overview

Founded in 1999 by Scott Harmolin, Lee Haddad, and Mark Haefeli, Centerseat was the first company to use streaming video in an untraditional way. Until the appearance of Centerseat.com, video and audio were displayed either as stand-alone applications, that is, Web users could select a live or on-demand video feed and watch the feed the same way we watch television or listen to radio; or if there were content-related images or text these were displayed as the primary source of information and the video or audio was a supplement. News sites led the market with news articles that included video clips delivering a visual representation of the text. RealNetworks introduced SMIL to transform RealPlayer into a browser, adding text and image elements corresponding to the video.

But Centerseat was the first site to incorporate all the elements in one browser, adding e-commerce-targeted opportunities and giving users full control over the information displayed. The three founders of Centerseat promised to revolutionize the users' experience when they watched video on the Web. Centerseat revised the long-awaited concept of interactive television and introduced a new platform that delivered to the Web rich media (video) synchronized with contextual text, images, and e-commerce opportunities. In September 2000, Centerseat received the *Ad Week Magazine* award Best Interactive Site in 2000.

Situation

When the plans to develop Centerseat.com were underway, it was clear that the site was about to introduce a new environment in which users would not just be watching videos in a passive way but would be encouraged to participate in a rich interactive experience. Additional components were added to the mix. The business plan behind Centerseat.com was to target visitors in a smart way, so they were presented with the possibility of purchasing items related to the video content they had selected to watch. For example, if users watched Britney Spears in her first online webcast, they would be prompted to purchase Britney's last CD or other products such as signed autographs or T-shirts. To achieve this, it was imperative to bring users to the product offerings with a limited number of clicks. Many studies show that visitors to a Web site tend to leave the site unless they are presented with both appealing and interesting content. Centerseat.com succeeded in bringing visitors to the point of purchase in only three mouse clicks:

1. A navigational page helped users select a channel, such as a music or movie channel.
2. Users selected from a list of available programs, displayed on the second page.
3. Users watched the program, viewed synchronized text and images related to the videos, and were given the opportunity to browse through selected products that fit their video selection.

All of this was executed by assembling video, all related text and images, and a shopping environment in one single window.

The core team that designed the functionality of Centerseat.com included Scott Harmolin (CEO), Jason Poley (CTO), Andrew Rosenman (Director of Web Architecture), and me (Media Processing and Streaming Architecture). Scott Harmolin had an extraordinary ability to define technology and implement it in business models. When he invited us to join the team, we brought our experiences in different fields, and together we developed the first true interactive broadband site. Andrew Rosenman was a wizard in Web technologies and had a very good sense of the details; he was responsible for designing the Centerseat Web infrastructure. Jason Poley had an extensive knowledge of networks and contributed to implementing Andrew's plans. He was also responsible for all the components of Centerseat's backend. I helped establish a production flow to process media, archive it on the network, convert it to different formats, and serve it through multiple platforms.

Business Solution

In March 2000, after 10 months of aggressive development, Centerseat .com version 1.0 launched. Centerseat (the company) was one of the first entertainment networks to produce original and acquired content targeting the broadband Web audience. Centerseat (the Web site) included videos combined with interactive elements that were divided into six content-categorized channels offering entertainment shows in the areas of film, music, sports, lifestyle and travel, and family and kids (see Figure 13–1). The programming included live action, fictional, and animated series; talk shows; news; special-interest profiles; and documentaries covering the day's biggest stars, hottest topics, and most happening trends (see Figure 13–2).

Centerseat's business plan was to provide leading consumer brands, retailers, and large community sites with an easy method to add integrated rich media content, commerce, and advertising to their Web presence through the creation of cobranded Web sites. The programs presented on these B2B2C sites, drawn from Centerseat's library or specifically produced for business partners, were targeted to the partners' specific audiences and communities. This content was contextually linked to ancillary information and e-commerce. Centerseat's technology platform prompted consumers to explore and purchase online at the point of peak interest, while the relevant content was being viewed.

The Centerseat platform allowed the highly targeted delivery of brand and advertising messages and e-commerce opportunities based on an individual user's behavior and interests. It provided a range of different advertising and sponsorship vehicles, from video spots and programs to static and interactive banner ads and billboards.

Figure 13–1
Centerseat.com main Web page

Figure 13–2
Centerseat.com hot spot channel page

A significant benefit to the company partners was Centerseat's network of cobranded sites that gave partner companies the ability to enhance their overall exposure and relationship with consumers, as well as increase e-commerce opportunities. This simultaneously provided broader exposure with the capability to narrowly target niche audiences. In short, the process enabled marketers to increase sales potential and new opportunities in a simple plug-in-and-play manner, offering a direct link between integrated content and communications solutions and targeted commerce.

Benefits

With the appearance of RealNetworks SMIL technology and the introduction of interactive rich media systems by multiple companies at the beginning of 2000, it was clear to technology analysts and Wall Street investors that the Web was no longer a text and image platform. Centerseat created an interactive platform that encouraged visitors to explore a new experience. Its unique platform provided many benefits, including:

- The ability to use media for new purposes for multiple outlets, creating additional revenues. Using an old syndication model, the client had to pay for licensing content created by Centerseat.
- A faster, more efficient content production line. Media were used for multipurpose channels. The same content was prepared for

Centerseat's Mall programming, for Centerseat's own site, and for Centerseat's cobranded partners' sites.

- A smart Web interface that generated associations among videos, text, images, and e-commerce opportunities and brought together points of interest with points of purchase.

- Additional components (not just video presentations) expanded the length of visits to the Web site. Both investors and advertisers were in agreement that the longer they could attract and keep a visitor at a site, the better the chances that the visitor will make a purchase.

- Platform used for new purposes, with minor branding changes (Fubu Y2G, Click2Asia, and Borders), brought the cost of production (to the client) down. Short video clips that included an interactive treatment were used by clients in a syndicated model. Each platform displayed the content in a different skin. As a result, the client did not spend capital creating content from scratch.

- The creation of customer loyalty by providing reliable cutting-edge content, updated on a regular basis.

Software Used

- Web server–Apache UNIX
- Streaming technology–Windows Media
- Platform–proprietary HTML, XML, and Java
- Database–Oracle
- Video production gear–BetaSP, DV, and DVCAM
- Editing equipment–AVID Media Composer 1000 and Final Cut Pro, both operating on Macintosh operating system

Case Study

Centerseat.com (the site) received extensive coverage in the media. Centerseat (the company) hired a staff of more than 90 people, including ex-network executives, top public relations personnel, and a video production staff of over 35 devoted to producing original programming for the site. This massive recruiting effort was covered by articles printed in top magazines and televised interviews with Centerseat executives. One month after its official launch, the site was rated the fourteenth largest broadband site on the Web, topping brand names such as NBCi.com and Launch.com.

Centerseat's (the company's) streaming infrastructure had been designed a few months earlier. Centerseat's production capabilities relied on the strength of its acquired production arm—Second Coming Productions, acquired in April 1999. In eight months, the production team grew from 15 to 60 inhouse producers, editors, and support staff. Most personnel had strong video-production backgrounds and the process of producing new media was new to them. David Levine and Terry Baker, former ABC and NBC veterans, were hired to supervise the massive production process that was expected to create 10 new original programs per week to feed the future channels of Centerseat.com. Production teams were assigned to projects and news. In addition, Web designers and programmers were hired to build Centerseat's backend Web infrastructure and to produce individual Web components of future shows.

Because Centerseat's production arm continued to perform video-production services for old and new clients, the company saw revenues from this part of its business, as well as from additional content that could be used for new purposes on its broadband channels. Lee Haddad, president of Centerseat, led the business development team and signed distribution agreements with various partners to make use of Centerseat's content on their broadband sites. Centerseat created for its partners branded portals that used the same content available on Centerseat.com. Among its partners were Borders Bookstores (the second-largest bookstore chain in the United States), Click2Asia.com (one of the largest Asian portals), and Fubu's Y2G.com (a site dedicated to hip-hop culture). Through its partnerships with Mill Malls, CyberExpo.com, and Skytron Networks, Centerseat reached to traditional media outlets by producing and delivering a biweekly one-hour show available to over 110 million viewers per month through an in-mall network of televisions, onsite computers, and food-court jumbo plasma displays.

For media-savvy professionals, it is interesting to learn how Centerseat processed its video content with a view to fit it into different media. All video content was recorded on BetaSP, DV, or DVCAM formats. Video production projects that created content planned for broadcast clients were recorded on BetaSP. Low-budget programs aimed at Web audiences were recorded on DV or DVCAM.

Here are the steps used to process and create video content for the site:

1. Senior executives decide which topics to cover.
2. A production coordinator assigns shows to both video producers and their Web producers' partners.
3. The video producer and Web producer meet to agree on traditional script (video) and a Web script (for the creation and timing of Web components).
4. The show is scheduled on production time line (for the Web).
5. Video producers plan and execute the shoot.
6. Tapes arrive from the field in boxes.
7. The library team catalogs each tape (labels it and creates an entry in an automated network database) and stores it.
8. The video content is encoded to low-resolution (300-kbps) streaming files and posted on an internal media server. The production team can review low-resolution content on the internal network.
9. The producers screen the content and prepare the editing list.
10. The final script is passed to Web producer.
11. The video producer and video editor edit the content.
12. Still images or captured images from video are submitted to Web producer. Images are processed by the Web designers.
13. The content is outputted to a master tape and returned to the library.
14. The Web components are created and fit into channel templates.
15. The encoding engineer works with preassigned templates to create media and prepares the necessary media for multiple outlets.
16. AVI files are created and stored on the network and the encoding team creates streaming files for 28-, 56-, 100-, and 300-kbps modems. (Centerseat selected Microsoft Windows Media as its preferred streaming technology due to its low operational cost and absence of licensing fees. For a startup with a limited budget, the cost of RealNetworks technology was too high).
17. More streaming files are prepared for 28-, 56-, 100-, and 300-kbps modems and placed on cobranded partner broadband portals. These files are different than the other streaming files–they always start with the cobranded site logo.

18. Additional files are prepared for Centerseat portable-device-distribution outlets through ActiveSky (media for Palm and PocketPC devices) and Windowsmedia.com (media for Windows CE PocketPC devices) partnerships.

19. Media are transferred to hosting vendors on the Internet. (Centerseat used both iBeam and Akamai to host its streaming content on the Web. The company saw about 1 million unique visitors each month and needed to rely on a reliable streaming network that could handle high load.)

20. MPEG1 or MPEG2 files were prepared from the AVI files (see step 16) for distribution to in-mall partners.

21. Additional copies are made to deliver BetaSP tapes to in-mall partners.

22. The Web interface for the new show is uploaded to the Web servers and tested. This includes cobranded shows prepared for the Web partners.

23. All parties are notified that the content is available to go live.

This amazing process was established in late 1999 and drew a lot of attention from video professionals. As the industry matures and other Web portals and interactive television channels are born, I am confident that many will adopt the production flow that was first established by Centerseat. The characteristics of this process will remain a unique example of a proven production flow that created, processed, and distributed digital media to multiple outlets.

In the beginning of 2001, Centerseat changed its business model. The company shifted from content creation and distribution to software development, offering components from its proprietary platform to companies interested in building interactive media applications.

The slow growth of broadband networks caused by the failure of DSL and cable vendors to provide customers with high-speed Internet access created a domino effect. Dotcom companies failed to deliver the revenues promised to investors simply because the technology grew too fast, before consumers had a chance to absorb and adopt it. Failing consumer confidence scared off advertisers who were the main source of revenues for many Web companies. In the streaming media arena, broadband content distributors such as Pseudo and Digital Entertainment Network closed their doors when advertisers withdrew. The fall of the dotcom companies started a snowball effect, damaging the technology sector badly. Downsizing among many Web companies and the events following September 11 brought the American economy into an official recession that lasted well into 2002.

Case 2—The Fortune 500 Company and Developing a User-Friendly Mediacentric Corporate Web site

Solution Overview

This case study involves one of the Fortune 500 companies. I was not able to get permission to use the company's name and therefore I refer to it here as "the company." The company created an interactive internal platform to support the webcasting of live events in real time through its corporate intranet. The application was intended to store the same video events or other prerecorded events on an easy-to-use video on-demand database interface that was accessible in a number of ways. Various departments in the company were assigned to create and input content into the new system. Only individuals within these departments had access to the content creation section. These departments used the internal platform to publish live and on-demand presentations that included training sessions, sales presentations, human resources information, and corporate communication announcements. A special unit that processed streaming media for the company's internal network owned the publishing part of the solution and the company's IT department owned the equipment and methods to access the media.

Situation

In the early 1980s, most enterprises started using video to train their staff, record corporate events, or distribute important announcements to their employees. Cable television networks were very popular, but costly to transmit when a broadcast had to reach different cities. Companies shifted to the duplication of tapes and sent those tapes to their branches. In the early 1990s, videotapes were replaced by CD-ROMs that played on employees' personal computers. Satellite technology was the next corporate fad. When prices dropped and small dishes were introduced, many companies launched satellite networks, uplinking from a central location and downlinking to their branches. The term "satellite office" came from the use of satellite transmissions to communicate with branches in other cities or states. When streaming technology was introduced in 1995, few companies understood the potential in savings from using streaming video on their existing Ethernet networks.

Realizing the hidden potential in streaming media technology, the company decided in summer 1998 to explore the possibility of creating some streaming-related products to be used internally and then, after testing (on the company's own network), released to the public.

Business Solution

First, a team was put in place. The vice president in charge assigned a project manager to identify the appropriate groups in the corporation and ask them to join the task force. Representatives from various departments were identified. Among them were developers who had developed similar products for the company, representatives from the company's IT department, the group that owned the company's intranet Web site, executives from the sales department, personnel from human resources, representatives from the legal department (because deployment would require contact with external vendors), personnel from the training department, and executives from the CEO's office. All participants were notified about their roles and a timetable for executing the project was established.

Second, the project manager asked the group that was assigned to create the Web interface (of the application) to write out a plan describing how the system would operate. The proposed system was a digital archive designed to live on the corporate network. The archive had two interfaces: the administration interface and the end-user interface. The first created the records and maintained them, and the second provided a search mechanism and the option to display selected entries using streaming media. My job was to identify all the components, list them, and specify how the system would function.

Benefits

A centralized digital media archive deployed on a corporate network properly has many benefits. Enterprises with many branches normally adopt a universal policy regarding the use and distribution of information.

A message that is not conveyed properly to employees can cause miscommunication and result in the loss of productivity and eventually in the loss of revenues. Because of this, companies spend a lot of time on properly planning systems to deliver information.

The company selected RealSystem as its streaming technology because it had a strategic partnership with RealNetworks to develop products together. RealNetworks helped the company build the digital archive system and used it later as a case study showing how to deploy a successful mediacentric streaming solution in the enterprise. The digital archive system offered the company many benefits:

- A centralized location from which to distribute streaming media to company employees
- A way to measure the costs of production and billing related to the creation and distribution of streaming media content; the group responsible for managing the system billed various departments in the company for the costs associated with encoding and serving media files
- A way to measure costs of production and billing related to the creation of Web content related to streaming media content; the same group responsible for managing the system designed the necessary pages to point to the media on the archives
- A way for the IT department to deploy the software necessary for users to experience streaming media content; the IT department was responsible for both deploying the proper media players on every workstation within the enterprise and establishing a help desk to support employees with streaming problems
- A way for the IT department to measure network use and to upgrade access according to the estimated peak use of streaming media content flowing through their controlled and supervised network
- A way for the company's help desk to troubleshoot calls related to streaming media in a consistent way
- A centralized educational platform dictating to departments how to embed content (i.e., players and related content) on their individual departmental Web sites
- A one-time investment in a system that served multiple departments

Software Used

- Web servers for digital archive interface–AIX
- Host server for actual database–AIX
- Host servers for the RealSystem servers–Windows NT 4.0
- Backup software–the company's own developed system
- Backup media storage–the company's own developed backup solution

Case Study

We started with graphic elements. Corporations must be conservative about the way they deploy new technology; each individual responds differently to new tasks. To avoid a rejection of the site (which represented a change in the way employees received information), we used a clean and simple layout. The general design captured the attention of the visitor and made a bold statement that this was a media-based Web site. The interface incorporated elements of the ongoing merger of television and computer screens, but at the same time looked exactly like the main page of the corporate intranet site.

Visitors to the multimedia site found the content in a fast and reliable manner. Their understanding of where items were located (in the navigational bar) reflected their past experience using television remote controls or browsing through a printed magazine. The pages were not overloaded with information; they used visuals rather then text to convey the message, which was short and to the point. Primarily, this was a video on-demand interface, designed to accommodate the end-user. A library of prerecorded video files was used that included a short description of the content and a small thumbnail image of the subject. Information was organized in a table-style format or summary-line items, with a short description of the selection found. The suggested graphic interface included:

- Main page–This showed a visual teaser of the main events last posted to the site. It used small images with title text linking to the actual subject and had a visual link to a user-guided tour to accommodate new visitors.
- Navigational bar–This provided immediate information on and included links to Search, Post Video, Tour (the digital archive

system), Download Media Player, Help, and so on. The navigational bar was posted on every page within the site. It was kept consistent on every page to make the general look of the site match the general look of the company's intranet site.

- Digital media archive—This served as an application for internal company use. The graphic design matched the general look of the company's intranet site, with standard masthead and footers according to the company's publishing guidelines. There were three options: find videos of interest, submit an event, and take an interactive tour of the application.

The company used a distributed architecture. Media servers were located at multiple points and were load balanced to support peak use. The proposed technical architecture of the company's digital media archives relied on the following components (see Figure 13–3):

- A data entry interface for the content provider and maintenance office

- A database to store content submission data

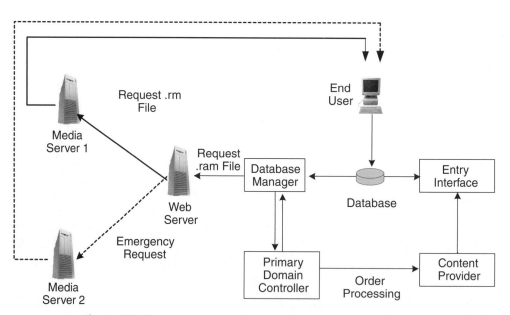

Figure 13–3
Content provider / end-user interface

- A database manager
- Load-balanced Web servers to store media links and the site (in HTML format)
- RealSystem servers hosted on Windows NT stations

We were launching a new product, or a revised product that would use new technology (the streaming application used RealVideo). Our objectives were first to gain user confidence and then to provide users with the tools we were offering. Users had to feel comfortable when they logged on to the site; the site had to be user friendly, providing ease of use that included proper navigation, a clean layout, step-by-step guidance for new users, and immediate access to information for repeat users.

The content on the site included the following options:

- A Find Video page with the following options to locate video:
    Find video by keywords
    Find video by browsing the entire selection
    Find video by viewing recent titles
    Find video by topic
- See Streaming Video/Listen to Streaming Audio File and Download Video or Audio File (to the user's computer), which were crucial so that the company's sales force could use some of the digitized video in their presentations and so that employees could use some of the digitized video to learn about a certain company's product or policy
- A Submit Event page where selected individuals could add content, such as:
    A brief description of what the digital archives does, explaining how this online solution could more effectively reach target audiences at a fraction of the cost compared to other means of communication such as satellite and videoconferencing
    Help on which application would best suit a user's needs, with an invitation to take a tour of the digital archive
    An explanation of how to submit an event, with online forms, prices, and procedures
    A contact-information page for questions and general comments
- The Digital Archive Tour page to guide visitors unfamiliar with the site or with streaming technology and to demonstrate the site's functionality and benefits, such as:

A general overview of what this new application can offer users and their departments

Specific answers to users' questions, found by browsing the interactive tour pages

A Frequently Asked Questions page listing new ideas about how to improve productivity and increase savings on communications

Content providers submitted information through the data-entry interface on the site. The content was reviewed by the department that was assigned to handle all media content. The content was processed and actual video-audio material was loaded onto the host RealVideo server. A link was sent to the content provider for future use. The content was also posted in the media archive.

A backup mechanism was established. To avoid server failure as a result of excessive use, it was recommended that the company develop an automated backup mechanism. The automated backup system lived on the external Web server where the site resided and included a connectivity agent that verified the status of the host video server 24/7.

The company assigned the task of maintaining the operation to various groups. The interactive group was responsible for preparing media for different departments and creating Web pages linking to content. The IT department was responsible for equipment installation and maintenance and for the installation of media players on all client computers. The company help desk was trained by the interactive group to be able to support streaming technology. The corporate communications, human resources, and training departments were responsible for notifying their employees about the availability of the new system and how to use it.

Case 3—U2 PopMart Tour and the First Internet Press Kit

Solution Overview

IPKs are used today to supplement or complement press releases in the form of video, images, and text that are normally distributed to traditional media outlets. Press kits contain information about a product and event or any type of news that individuals or companies want to release to the public or to a selected group of recipients. In the past, press kits were released in three forms: text and images were distributed to print outlets;

video clips, text, and images were sent to television stations and syndicated or cable operators; and audio clips were sent to individual or syndicated radio stations. With the arrival of the IPK, distribution took a new turn. The Web provides a platform that includes all the components of a press kit, adding advantages such as:

- Reaching a wider audience on a local or global scale
- Displaying all presentation elements (print, audio, and video) on one platform
- Cutting the cost of producing a press kit
- Enabling fast publication and last-minute changes
- Adding audience participation through interactive elements such as chat or incoming audio or video feed

This is the IPK as we know it today. In March 1997, all these components did not exist yet.

Situation

One of only a few bands to achieve consistent commercial and critical success across two full decades, U2 has charted its success on its own terms on both the artistic and business sides of the music industry. From the band's earliest days in Dublin, Ireland, to the present, U2 has broken free from the traditional limitations of what a rock band—and rock music—could and could not do. By combining an original sound with honest lyrics and a challenging social message, U2 has earned the respect of their peers and critics and an almost fanatical following of fans around the world.

In February 1997, U2's public relations firm contracted Second Coming Productions, a New York–based company recognized in the area of electronic publicity, to produce all video aspects of an unusual press conference that was scheduled to take place in a downtown Manhattan Kmart superstore. Mark Haefeli, president of Second Coming Productions and a wizard of electronic publicity productions, assigned his youngest producer, David Ragsdale, to add another aspect to the event: the distribution of the press conference on a new emerging medium, the Internet. Ragsdale contacted Yard Productions, Second Coming Productions's Web vendor, notifying them of the event. All this happened only 48 hours before the official press conference. At the time, I was working for Yard Productions, and the production of the U2 press conference Web site was assigned to me.

There were no rules or guidelines for how to create a site that would serve the role that a traditional press kit served on national television. It was clear that we would have to create a product from the ground up–an IPK that would present to journalists (representing the media) and fans worldwide information about the band, their new album, and an up-coming world tour.

Business Solution

My team had two designers and one network administrator who had knowledge about encoding video to streaming format. The public relations firm supplied some relevant text, but had no images of the band. We had to grab screen shots from the videos we received. Fortunately, we received a copy of U2's new CD and got permission to use its artwork for the site. During a stressful and exhausting two days, we designed a Web site that included text information describing the band's plans to release an album, the group's updated biography, tour dates, exclusive video clips recorded behind the scenes during the recording of the album, audio samples, a guest room where visitors could post notes, and a chat room for fans to exchange information regarding the band and their tour.

Benefits

A special interface had to be created to provide easy navigation and fast access to information on the site. In the beginning of 1997 the majority of Web sites on the Web were created to look like brochures because most Web designers came from print backgrounds. Text and images were aligned, and entire pages had to be downloaded with navigational links built into each page. Eran Bendheim, the designer at Yard Productions who worked with me on the site, and I together came up with a solution. The U2 PopMart site introduced one of the first navigational bars that worked in a frame environment. What has become a standard used by most site developers today was a ground-breaking technique in March 1997. Figure 13–4 shows the navigational bar at the left, which displays all the links to available pages on the site. By clicking on the link on the left side, users could display the proper page on the right side.

The easy navigation, the lineup of unique content, and the fact that all the related information was available in one place helped the U2 PopMart press conference site win Intel's Screamer Award, given to selected sites recognized for their use of innovative Web solutions.

Figure 13 – 4
Videos page in U2 press conference site

Software Used

The U2 PopMart site was created with traditional Web tools.

- HTML pages–Hand-written
- Image creation–Adobe Photoshop
- Animated images creation–Macromedia Director
- Streaming video files creation–RealSystem Producer
- Streaming media playback–RealPlayer version 4.01
- Host server–UNIX
- Web server–Apache (in 1997, computers running Windows NT 4.0 server and IIS version 2.0 were not as popular as Apache servers)

- Host server for streaming on-demand media files—RealSystem Server with a license for 60 concurrent streams using UNIX (we chose RealVideo because the technology was the most popular streaming technology among Internet users at the time)

All media files were encoded as video files for 28.8 and 56 kBps dial-up modems.

Case Study

As we were designing the different elements in the site, I realized that it would not help us to just put the site together—we also had to notify the public about its existence (marketing) and provide a stable platform to accommodate a large number of visitors (scalability). And we had less then 36 hours before the press conference was about to start. In the early days of the Internet, companies pioneered different solutions, evaluating business models along the way. Because most Web events were happening for the very first time, we participated in those days in many firsts. Because many companies had to create a portfolio showcasing their strengths, many companies were willing to donate their services and expertise for the recognition and the ability to use these events in their technology showcase. Taking advantage of this, we placed calls to a few major players and asked for their help. David Ragsdale called Progressive Networks (known today as RealNetworks, the maker of Real-Video) and got their support to carry the webcast in real time on their network. That solved the problem of producing the live webcast. We still had to attract an audience and provide a stable connection to the site. Yahoo! was the largest search engine on the Web and launched during that time Yahoo! Net Events, a section of Yahoo! Events listing live webcasts using various streaming technologies available on the Web. In exchange for listing Yahoo! as a preferred search engine partner, we were scheduled to appear on the search engine every time visitors typed the keywords "U2", "Pop", and "PopMart." (We got around the four-week lead time with a phone call and manual posting.) In addition, we contacted the U2 Web ring administrator and emailed him a banner we created (see Figure 13–5), asking him to keep the news secret until the official release. Sonicnet.com, Liveconcert.com, and Island Records Web sites also joined us by posting the banner we created.

Next we had to find an ISP that would mirror the site and help us load balance the heavy traffic that our fast marketing campaign would

Figure 13–5
Web advertising banner from the U2 press conference site

generate. David Ragsdale's cousin worked at the time for Infinet, a Canadian ISP that had a data center in Virginia. We called and got a verbal commitment from Infinet to host a mirror site for the next 90 days. When the site was ready, we sent our contact a copy of the site. We had no time to load balance the two sites, so we used a basic left-and-right-door approach, in which visitors select which site to enter based on their geographical location. The New York server was called East Coast and the Virginia server was called West Coast.

After 12 a.m., on the morning of the day when the press conference was scheduled, all the site members posted our banner, and, most important, Yahoo! activated the keyword redirection technology and started directing traffic to the site. The rest is history. U2 turned Kmart in Union Square into a media circus and, thanks to the fabulous job done by Second Coming Productions and a live satellite transmission, millions witnessed the press conference all over the world and on the Internet. Statistical reports provided by both servers indicated that close to 2,000 unique visitors accessed the site during the live webcast. In the 30 days following the press conference and thanks to the visitors that Yahoo! redirected, we measured a little over 500,000 unique visitors to the site. These were pretty impressive numbers in April 1997. The number of visitors declined as the U2 tour continued and other sites started displaying images and videos from other U2-related events; but, until the site shut down recently, 2,500 unique visitors per month were still accessing the site. The site statistics were measured by Webtrends software, a popular traffic-measurement software used by many ISPs. Island Records (U2's record label) launched an official U2 Web site only in 1999. Before that, the band relied on dozens of unofficial fan Web sites presenting information in the form of video, audio, images, and text and even selling tickets and merchandise.

When we launched the site we provided visitors with what they wanted. We gave them access to media over the Internet that was not available on television. We gave them a platform to express their thoughts and love to the band. There was no financial model in place to generate revenues from the site. All the participants volunteered their services to create the first IPK.

As I look back on this project, what strikes me most is that we managed to create such a successful site with superb content with no financial investment at all. Despite the fact that we launched a simple site with only a few pages, a worldwide audience found the site and left its mark on it. The diversity of visitors is most visible on the site's guestbook page. Even today, when I mention to people that I produced the U2 PopMart Web site they remember visiting it. This is an example of the true power of the Internet.

Summary

- For new technology to be successful, the product must offer a solution to a problem or provide a way to achieve a goal in a more efficient way, consumers must have time to absorb it, and a financial justification must accompany the product from the start.

- A true Web interactive experience is possible only on broadband networks. DSL and cable-modem customers will have a better experience while watching and interacting with rich media presentations on their high-speed Internet access.

- Lack of proper infrastructure was one of the main reasons consumers failed to use broadband channels.

- Digital media archives on corporate networks can offer a cost-effective and more efficient way to publish media.

- The true power of the Internet lies in new ideas and the way we use them to improve our lives. The Internet is and, I hope, will continue to be a global web of networks that helps us exercise our right of freedom of expression.

Glossary

Analog A signal that varies continuously over a range of amplitudes. By contrast, a digital signal can have only two values for amplitude, representing either 1 or 0.

Analog-to-digital converter (ADC) A chip that converts analog video signals to digital signals. ADCs are used by video capture cards to convert video into a format that the computer can manipulate and store.

API Application program interface. A tool that enables users to retrieve and update all data elements in an integrated system.

ASCII A universal, standardized code for text and numbers used by computers and word processors.

ASD Microsoft's Advanced Streaming Format (ASF) Stream Descriptor. ASD files specify encoding parameters for the Windows Media Encoder.

ASF Advanced streaming format. The standard file format of Windows Media files.

ASX Microsoft's active stream redirector file. ASX files provide the Windows Media Player with instructions on how to find media (server information) and which titles to display when the media plays.

AVI Audio Video Interleaved file. A sound and motion picture file that conforms to the Microsoft Windows Resource Interchange File Format (RIFF) specification. AVI files (which end with an .avi extension) require a special player that is included with some Web browsers or may be downloaded.

B to B Business to business. A term used to indicate a business offering its products to other businesses.

Bandwidth The amount of information that can be passed through a given circuit in a given amount of time. In the case of video, the larger the bandwidth, the greater the picture detail can be. Bandwidth usually measured in bits per second.

Betacam An analog videotape format using 12.5 mm tape, developed by Sony and derived from the earlier Betamax. Betacams available include Betacam SP, Digital Betacam, and Betacam SX.

Binary A system of representing data based on two possibilities, 0 and 1, used by computers and other digital equipment.

Bit A binary digit, a 0 or a 1, representing a "no" or a "yes" answer to a question. A bit is the smallest piece of information a computer understands.

Bit rate The amount of data transported in a given amount of time, usually defined in megabits per second (millions of bits per second, or MBps). Bit rate is one means used to define the amount of compression used on a video signal. For example, DV has a bit rate of 25 MBps; uncompressed D1 has a bit rate of 270 MBps.

Bluetooth A new short-range wireless initiative for connecting wireless phones, mobile PCs, and other mobile computing devices to one another.

BNC A network cable or connector. Stands for Bayonet Neill-Concelman (the inventors), British Naval Connector, Barrel Nut Connector, Bayonet N-Type Compact, and Bayonet Nut Coupling. Also referred to as Coaxial, Thinnet, 10base2, and RG 58 cable. Often used for baseband video (a type of system in which only digital data is carried on the cable).

BRI Basic rate interface. An ISDN phone line with two 64 kbps channels and one 16 kbps channel.

Broadband A term describing the information capacity or bandwidth of a communication channel. The term "broadband" generally refers to channels with bandwidths higher than 2 MBps.

Byte Eight bits. The combination of 8 bits into 1 byte allows each byte to represent 256 possible values. (*see* Bit, Megabyte, Gigabyte, Terabyte)

Cable modem Device that connects a computer to a cable-TV source to transmit data quickly to an Internet service provider.

Capture If the source footage is analog, "capture" refers to the act of digitization (conversion to a digital format) to make the video usable on a computer and, usually, the simultaneous compression of data to reduce the video to a manageable data rate for processing and storage. If the source video is digital, "capture" typically refers to its transfer from an external device, such as a digital camcorder or tape deck, to a computer hard drive.

CCIR 601 The standard for digitizing component video. Also sometimes called D1 after the VTR (Video Tape Recorder) format that first used this signal. For NTSC, this standard calls for an image of 720 by 486 pixels sampled at 4:2:2 with a depth of either 8 or 10 bits. (*see* 4:2:2)

CDMA Code division multiple access. Code division technology originally developed for military use more than thirty years ago. CDMA is a multiple-access technique for transmitting data that uses code sequences as traffic channels. The data is transmitted within common radio channels and is compatible with CDMA One (IS-95) air interface.

Cell The basic geographical unit of a cellular communications system. Service coverage of a given area is based on an interlocking network of cells, each with a radio base station (transmitter/receiver) at its center. The size of each cell is determined by the terrain and forecasted number of users.

Circuit switching A core network transmission technique in which an entire channel or circuit is used to deliver a data transmission. Even when no information (voice, data) is being transmitted, the circuit remains open throughout the entire session. Circuit switching is being replaced by packet switching.

Client The user-side software or computer used to display streaming media.

Cluster servers An array of servers functioning as a single entity. Data and media on each server is replicated on all others, creating a fail-safe environment.

Codec Compressor/decompressor. A software component that translates video or audio from an uncompressed form to the compressed form in which it is stored. Sorenson Video and Cinepak are common QuickTime video codecs. Also called a "compressor."

Color bar A vertical bar of color used to test cameras and other video equipment.

Component video A video signal in which the luminance and chrominance signals are kept separate. Component video requires a higher bandwidth than composite video but yields a higher quality picture.

Composite video A video signal in which the luminance and chrominance signals are combined in an encoder to create video signals (e.g., NTSC, PAL or SECAM), allowing video to be broadcast economically.

Compression ratio The ratio of the amount of data in a file before compression versus the amount after compression. The higher the ratio, the more the data has been condensed.

Content Information or knowledge managed and shared over the Internet.

Content providers Industry leaders in the business of gathering or creating content or information of interest to library users; book reviews, book jackets, author biographies, and first chapters are examples of the types of content provided by these companies.

Coupler A device that connects analog or digital devices to one another.

CPU Central processing unit. The heart of a computer, a single circuit chip with millions of transistors programmed to interpret and carry out commands.

Crossplatform Describes software that works on multiple computer platforms (e.g., on both PC and Macintosh).

Data rate Amount of information per second used to represent a movie. The data rate of a 2X speed CD-ROM movie is about 200 kbps; the data rate of uncompressed NTSC video is about 27 MBps.

Data stream Information or knowledge that is "pushed" to users through an electronic library; this information should be maintained by the e-library vendor, not its end-users.

Datagram *See* Packet.

dB Decibel. A measure of the ratio of the strength of one electronic signal to another. The higher the decibel of a signal, the greater its strength.

Deinterlace To remove the artifacts that remain when a video is interlaced (*see* Interlacing).

Delta frames Frames that contain only changes from previous frame. Delta frames are created by codecs that use temporal compression. Also called "difference frames."

Depth of field The span of distance from a lens within which both objects that are far from the camera and those that are near appear sharp in the printed picture.

Desktop video The integration of several video capabilities (e.g., titles, graphics, switcher, editing) into one or several computers. Except for gathering the original footage, which must be done using cameras and microphones, most of the production process can take place on a desktop computer.

Digital A system in which everything is defined by a series of numbers, usually 1s and 0s (*see* Binary).

Digital media archive A system for managing, preserving, and providing on-line access to a digital collection. Digital media archives can include data in a wide variety of forms, from documents and images to sound and video files.

Digitizing The act of converting analog video or audio to digital form.

DNS Domain name system. The DNS identifies each computer as a network node on the Internet using an internet protocol address system to translate domain names to IP numbers and vice versa.

Download Send data from the main machine (e.g., a digital camcorder, VCR, or mainframe computer) to a secondary machine (e.g., a personal computer).

DSL Digital subscriber line. A technology for bringing high-bandwidth information to homes and small businesses over ordinary copper telephone lines.

DV Digital video. A digital tape-recording format using approximately $5:1$ compression to produce Betacam quality on a very small cassette. Digital video originated as a consumer product but is being used professionally. Some examples of DV cameras are Panasonic's DVC-Pro and Sony's DVCam. These cameras use a 25 MBps data rate and $4:1:1$ sampling. A variation, DVC-Pro 50, uses a 50 MBps data rate and $4:2:2$ sampling.

DVD Digital video disk (or digital versatile disc). A format for putting full-length movies on a 5″ CD-like disk using MPEG2 compression. Produces the highest video quality in a consumer format.

Edit decision list (EDL) A list of edit decisions made during an edit session and usually saved to a floppy disk. Recording edits in an EDL allows the user to redo or modify an edit at a later time without having to start all over again.

Electronic library (e-library) An electronic library is accessible from anywhere via the Internet and can deliver personalized, library-caliber knowledge directly to its users without being confined to the contents of a physical library; information from any online source can be managed and shared by e-librarians with their users, making more knowledge available to users than ever before. The goal of an e-library is to perform online all the functions of the traditional library, in addition to many more available in today's digital world.

EMI Electromagnetic interference. Any electromagnetic force that interrupts, obstructs, or otherwise degrades or limits the performance of a computer or related equipment.

Encode In multimedia, this term means compressing a file.

Firewire Apple's trademarked name for the IEEE 1394 standard, a very fast external bus often used to connect DV cameras to computers. Some other companies use different names to describe their 1394 products (e.g., I-Link).

1G, 2G, 3G First generation wireless, second generation wireless, third generation wireless. The term *first generation wireless* refers to analog wireless phones; *second generation wireless,* to digital wireless phones on circuit-switched networks; and *third generation wireless,* to digital wireless devices on packet-switched networks.

Fixed wireless network Also called fixed cellular network. This seemingly self-contradictory term signifies a cellular network that is set up to support fixed rather than mobile subscribers. Fixed wireless is increasingly being used as a fast and economic substitute for modern telephone services because it avoids the need for fixed wires.

Flattening Final pass applied to a QuickTime movie to ensure that the data has been laid out in a completely linear fashion and that all external references have been removed.

4:4:4 color A sampling ratio that has equal amounts of the luminance and both chrominance channels (*see* 4:1:1 color). Can also be used for red, green, and blue (RGB) sampling, the color space used in most computer programs.

4:1:1 color The sampling ratio most frequently used in the DV signal. For every four samples of luminance there is one sample each of the color-difference signals, red minus luminance (R-Y) and blue minus luminance (B-Y). This sampling ratio is used by most DV formats, including mini-DV.

4:3 ratio The aspect ratio of conventional video, television, and computer screens, 4 units by 3 units.

4:2:2 color Mildly compressed video color subsampling in which the luminance channel is not subsampled, but the chrominance channel has half the resolution. Commonly used in professional video formats, such as Beta-CamSP.

4:2:0 color A sampling system used to digitize the luminance and color difference compnents (Y, R-Y, and B-Y) of a video signal. The "4" represents the 13.5 MHz sampling frequency of Y, while the R-Y and B-Y are sampled at

6.75 MHz—effectively between every other line only (one line is sampled at 4:0:0 luminance only, and the next at 4:2:2).

fps Frames per second, a measure of the frame rate of video or film. NTSC video is 29.97 fps, PAL video is 25 fps, and film is 24 fps.

Frame One complete video image. A frame contains two fields. There are 30 frames in one second of NTSC video.

Frame rate In a movie, the number of frames per second.

Gigabyte 1,073,741,824 bytes.

GPRS General packet radio service. A GSM data transmission technique in which data is transmitted and received in packets rather than through a continuous channel. GPRS uses a portable terminal for the transmission and reception of data.

GSM Global system for mobile communications. Originally intended as a pan-European standard for a digital cellular telephone network to support cross-border roaming, GSM is now one of the world's main digital wireless standards. GSM uses TDMA air interface. It can be implemented in 900 MHz, 1800 MHz, or 1900 MHz frequency bands.

GUI Graphical user interface. A graphics-based user interface that incorporates icons and pull-down menus that provide an easy-to-follow guide to using a software application.

HDTV High definition television. Any of several TV formats capable of displaying on a wider screen (16 × 9 as opposed to the conventional 4 × 3) and at higher resolution than standard-definition TV (SDTV).

Hinted files Term used in Apple's QuickTime architecture for video files that are formatted for true streaming.

HTTP streaming *See* Progressive download.

ICP Internet content providers. *See* Content providers.

IEEE 1394 *See* Firewire.

iMode iMode is NTT DoCoMo's mobile Internet access system. Technically iMode is an overlay of NTT DoCoMo's ordinary mobile voice system. While the voice system is "circuit-switched" (i.e., you need to dial-up), iMode is "packet-switched."

Interlace A process in which the picture is split into two fields by sending all the odd-numbered lines to one field and all the even-numbered lines to second field. This was necessary when there was not enough bandwidth to send a complete frame fast enough to create a nonflickering image.

IP Internet protocol. Specifies the format of packets, also called datagrams, and the addressing scheme used to route a message to a specific network or sub-network. Most networks combine IP with a higher-level protocol called transport control protocol (TCP), which establishes a virtual connection between a destination and a source.

IPK Internet press kit. A term used to describe the release of news-related content to the media or to the public via the Internet.

ISDN Integrated Services Digital Network. A switched network providing end-to-end digital connectivity for the simultaneous transmission of voice, data, video, imaging, and fax over several multiplexed communications channels. ISDN employs high-speed, out-of-band signaling protocols that conform to international standards.

ISP Internet service provider. A service company that, in cooperation with like companies, provides co-location of servers, dial-up access to the Internet, or other IP base transport services.

JPEG Joint Photographic Experts Group. A standard for compressing still pictures and video images in a form suitable for frame-by-frame editing.

kbps Kilobits per second (8,192 bits per second). The standard measure of data rate and transmission capacity.

Key frame A frame at the beginning or end of a sequence of frames selected for use as a reference for any of a variety of functions. In interframe video compression, key frames typically store complete information about the image, while the frames in between may store only the differences between two key frames.

Kilobyte 1,024 bytes.

Knowledge management (KM) The use of computer technology to organize, manage, and distribute electronically all types of information. With the right KM, information can be customized to meet the needs of a wide variety of users.

Live video Video that is captured, compressed, and distributed in real time; the opposite of "on-demand" video. Live video systems must use fairly "symmetric" codecs to compress the video in real time (*See* Symmetric codecs).

Lossless A compression process that reduces the bandwidth required for transmission of a given data rate without loss of the original data.

Lossy A compression scheme or other process, such as duplication, that causes degradation of signal fidelity. Lossy compression can compress to any level, but the more the data is compressed, the more quality is sacrificed.

Mbone Multicast backbone. A live audio and video multicast virtual network superimposed upon the Internet.

MBps Megabits per second (8,388,608 bits per second).

Media on-demand Video that is not broadcast "live" as it is filmed, but is compressed and made available on a server for people to watch when they wish. A Webcast would be "live," whereas an online movie trailer would be "on demand." Most audio and video on the Web is "on demand."

Megabyte 1,048,576 bytes.

Meta tags Tags that describe various aspects of a Web page. Meta tags may be used for a wide variety of metadata—data that describes other data—but in recent years the term has been used to describe preprogrammed data associated with media content. For example, meta tags are used to index video, making it searchable in streaming media archives.

MHz Megahertz (1,000,000 hertz, or 1,000,000 cycles per second). Used to measure band and bandwidth.

Mini plug Stereo audio plug most common in consumer audio devices.

MMS Microsoft Media Server. Network protocol used by Microsoft Windows Media Server to communicate with Netshow players. The actual multimedia data in ASF format may be delivered using HTTP, TCP, or UDP as available.

MOV Apple QuickTime movie file extension used to name both movie redirect files and actual QuickTime media files.

MPEG1 Format that produces high quality video and audio streams at approximately two times CD-ROM data rates. Standard MPEG1 is full frame rate (24–30 fps, depending on the source) with a quarter size screen (352 × 240 pixels).

MPEG2 Format that produces files with a high data rate and full broadcast quality. MPEG-2 playback requires either an extremely fast computer and video card or a hardware accelerator card. MPEG2 is the format for DVDs and many home satellite dish systems. Standard MPEG2 is full frame rate (24–30 fps) and full screen resolution (720 × 480 pixels).

MP3 MPEG1, layer 3. MPEG audio format. Generally used in audio-only files (.mp3 files). A lower-bandwidth format than MPEG layer-2 audio, but still not ideal for modem streaming. MP3 became very popular as a format to store and deliver music on the Internet.

MPEG4 MPEG4 is utilized in three fields: digital television; interactive graphics (e.g., applications, synthetic content); and interactive multimedia (e.g., distribution of and access to content on the World Wide Web).

MPEG7 Formally named "Multimedia Content Description Interface," MPEG7 is a standard for describing multimedia content data. This data supports some degree of interpretation of the information's meaning and can be passed onto or accessed by means of a device or a computer code. MPEG7 is not uniquely suited to any single application; rather, the elements that MPEG7 standardizes support a broad a range of applications.

Multicast An efficient way to transmit the same media stream to many recipients simultaneously. The media stream is replicated at router hops where the path to different multicast group members diverges. Multicast end-users experience the same portion of the media at the same time (in contrast to Unicast, which allows each end-user to control his or her own experience when accessing prerecorded, on-demand files). The infrastructure to handle multicasting, known as the Mbone (multicast backbone) is still emerging; the Internet is not yet ready for the popular proliferation of multicasting. The terms "multicast" and "narrowcast" are sometimes used interchangeably, although "multicast" more specifically refers to the actual technology inherent in the process.

Multimedia In the context of mobile communications, the term "multimedia" is used to describe a service that may combine voice, data, graphics, and video information.

Narrowband A term describing the information capacity or bandwidth of a communication channel. Bandwidths less than 65 kbps are generally considered narrowband.

NTSC National Television Systems Committee. Also the name of the television and video standard in use in the United States. NTSC consists of 525 horizontal lines at a field rate of 60 fields per second (two fields equal one complete frame). Only 486 of these lines are used for the picture; the rest are used for sync and extra information such as VITC and closed captioning.

Packet Although computers and modems can send data one character at a time, it's more efficient to send information in larger blocks called "data packets," or "datagrams." Packets used with the standard Internet protocol, TCP/IP, are typically around 1,500 characters. Packets consist of the data being transmitted plus the IP address information of the sender and the recipient.

Packet switching A core network transmission technique that involves splitting information into "packets" of data that are organized in a specific way that includes control information (e.g., destination, origin length), the data, and error correction and detection bits. Packet switching is attractive for mobile access because radio spectrum is used only when data is actually being transmitted. The technology is an improvement on circuit-switched data.

PAL Phase alternate line. The television and video standard in use in most of Europe. Consists of 625 horizontal lines at a field rate of 50 fields per second (two fields equal one complete frame). Only 576 of these lines are used for the picture; the rest are used for sync or extra information such as VITC and closed captioning.

PDC Personal digital cellular. The digital wireless standard used in Japan. PDC uses TDMA air interface.

Personalization Capability for electronic library users to choose the specific information to be "pushed" or delivered directly to them.

Phono plug *See* RCA plug.

Pixel Short for "picture element," the basic unit from which a video or computer picture is made. Essentially a dot with a given color and brightness value. D1 images are 720 pixels wide and 486 pixels high. NTSC images are 640 x 480 pixels.

Progressive download Term referring to online media that users may watch as it downloads. Also called "HTTP streaming" because standard HTTP

Web servers can deliver progressive download files without using special protocols.

QuickTime Apple Computers' crossplatform multimedia architecture.

RA RealAudio. The file extension used for RealAudio files. With the introduction of RealVideo 6.0, .rm (RealMedia) became the file extension used to indicate both audio and video files.

RAID "redundant array of inexpensive disks," a system of using multiple hard disks to enhance the reliability of server system. RAID system configurations include non-RAID, RAID 0, 1, 0+1, 3, or 5.

RAM RealVideo reference file that is placed on the HTTP server and gives the RealPlayer the location of the movie file on the RealServer.

RCA plug Also called a phono plug; a type of connector used for consumer video or audio signals. Designed to self-clean when removed and reconnected.

Real-time communication Communication (usually two-way) in which the information sent is received instantly by the other party in a continuous stream. Telephone calls and videoconferencing are real-time; database access and e-mails are not.

RealSystem RealNetworks's streaming architecture.

RFI Radio frequency interference.

RGB Red, green, blue, the primary colors of light. Computers and some analog component devices use separate red, green, and blue color channels to keep the full bandwidth and therefore maintain the highest quality picture.

RISC Reduced instruction set computing.

RM RealNetworks's RealMedia streaming file extension.

Roaming Ability of a mobile phone user to travel from one cell to another with complete communications continuity. Roaming is supported by a cellular network of radio base stations. The term "roaming" also refers to Internet work operability—moving from one network provider to another (internationally).

RTP Real Time Transport Protocol.

RTSP Real time streaming protocol, an application-level protocol for controlling the delivery of data with real-time properties. RTSP provides an extensible framework to enable controlled, on-demand delivery of real-time data such as audio and video. Sources of data can include both live data feeds and stored clips. This protocol is intended to control multiple data delivery sessions; provide a means for choosing delivery channels such as UDP, multicast UDP, and TCP; and provide a means for choosing delivery mechanisms based upon RTP (RFC 1889).

Sample rate The number of samples per second used for audio. Higher sample rates yield higher quality audio than lower sample rates. Common sample rates include 11.025 kHz, 22.050 kHz, and 44.100 kHz (CD quality).

Sampling frequency The number of sample measurements taken from an analog signal in a second, generally expressed in megahertz. These samples are then converted into digital numeric values to create the digital signal.

SCSI Small computer system interface. Pronounced "scuzzy." An intelligent interface device that expands a microprocessor (CPU) bus to facilitate connections to communications buses with greater width and speed. SCSI exchanges data with the peripherals over a separate communications bus rather than the multiple peripherals (e.g., CD-ROM drives, hard drives, or scanners).

SDK Software development kits.

Server The machine hosting the media and acting upon request from clients to display media.

Signal-to-noise (SNR) The ratio of the amplitude of the desired signal to the amplitude of noise signals at a given point in time. SNR is usually expressed in decibels and in terms of peak values for impulse noise and root-mean-square values for random noise.

16:9 ratio A wide-screen television format in which the aspect ratio of the screen is 16 units wide by 9 units high, as opposed to conventional video, television, and computer screens, in which the aspect ratio is 4 units by 3 units.

Smart phone A cellular phone that can connect to the Internet for tasks like Web browsing and sending and receiving e-mail. Smart phones typically include a personal digital assistant.

SMIL Synchronized Multimedia Integration Language. A markup language developed by the World Wide Web Consortium (W3C) that would enable Web developers to divide multimedia content into separate files and streams (audio, video, text, and images) and send them to a user's computer individually. They would then be displayed together on screen as if they were a single multimedia stream.

SMPTE Society of Motion Picture and Television Engineers. A major standards-setting organization for the motion picture and television industries. Established the standards for time code and for all the major videotape formats.

SSH Secure Shell. A UNIX-based command interface and protocol for securely getting access to a remote computer. It is widely used by network administrators to control Web and other kinds of servers remotely. SSH is actually a suite of three utilities—slogin, ssh, and scp. These three utilities are secure versions of the earlier UNIX utilities, rlogin, rsh, and rcp. SSH commands are encrypted and made secure in several ways. For example, both ends of the client/server connection are authenticated using digital certificates, and passwords are protected by encryption.

Streamies Internet users who frequently consume streaming media content.

S-Video A video signal in which the luminance and chrominance are separated from one another when the signal is processed for more effective processing.

Symmetric codec Codec that encodes and decodes video in roughly the same amount of time. Live streaming systems use symmetric codecs in order to encode video in real time as it is captured.

Syntax The grammar, structure, or order of the elements in a language statement. (Semantics is the meaning of these elements.) Syntax applies to computer languages as well as to natural languages.

TCP/IP Transmission Control Protocol/Internet Protocol. These two protocols were developed by the U.S. military to allow computers to talk to each other over long-distance networks. IP is responsible for moving packets of data between nodes. TCP is responsible for verifying delivery from client to server. TCP/IP forms the basis of the Internet and is built into almost every common operating system.

TDMA Time division multiple access. The new name for the "Digital AMPS" (D-AMPS) mobile standard, now called ANSI-136, used in the Americas, the Asia Pacific, and other areas. TDMA services can be delivered in the 800 MHz and 1900 MHz frequency bands.

Telecine A device that creates video from motion picture film.

Terabyte 1,000,000,000,000 bytes.

Tunneling The use of specially designed paths to carry multicast traffic over the Internet.

UDP User Datagram Protocol. Like TCP, UDP runs on top of IP networks. Unlike TCP/IP, UDP/IP provides very little error recovery; however, it offers a direct way to send and receive datagrams over an IP network. It is primarily used for streaming over the Internet.

URL Uniform resource locator. The "address" used to find a document or resource on the World Wide Web. The first part of the address specifies the protocol (typically HTTP for Web pages, FTP for files not residing on a Web server, or RTSP for streaming files); the second part specifies the IP address or domain name; and the remainder specifies the directory structure for finding the discrete file on the host computer.

USB Universal Serial Bus. A standard bus type for all kinds of devices, including scanners, digital cameras, printers, and hot swappable devices (devices that can be connected and disconnected while computer is on). USB supports a 12 MBps transfer rate.

Unicast The technique whereby a single stream is transmitted to a single end-user (i.e., each end-user gets a unique stream). Bandwidth-hogging unicasting is not as efficient as multicasting.

User A person using a computer to access information on a network of other computers.

Variable bit rate (VBR) Two-pass process of analyzing and then compressing movies or audio to an optimal data rate. Produces movies with data rates that vary from second to second instead of having uniform, flat data rates. The

Developer Edition of Sorenson Video provides VBR, as do certain MP3 audio encoders.

VCR Videocassette recorder.

VHS Video home system. A consumer videocassette recorder using ½-in. film.

VPN Virtual Private Networking. Networking that uses the public network to transfer information using secure methods; for example, a VPN could be set up between a home office and a business office using the Internet as a transfer pipe.

WAP Wireless Application Protocol. A global, open standard for online service access from small-screen mobile phones.

WCDMA Wideband CDMA. The air interface technology selected by the major Japanese mobile communications operators, and in January 1998 by the European Telecommunications Standards Institute (ETSI), for wideband wireless access to support third-generation services. This technology is optimized to allow very high speed multimedia services such as full-motion video, Internet access, and videoconferencing.

Webcast A broadcast of live video or audio on the Internet.

Wizard An interactive utility that leads a user through all of the steps required to complete a complex task. Wizards produce a step-by-step guide for the user with each possible alternative displayed. If a condition that prevents a step from being completed occurs, methods for resolving the problem are presented. When the problem is resolved, the user is returned to the next step in the process, until the task has been completed.

WMA Windows Media Audio. Windows Media audio file format. This is yet another Microsoft streaming file format.

WML Wireless Markup Language. The markup language used in the Wireless Application Protocol (WAP).

WMV Microsoft's Windows Media Video name extension. WMV replaced Active Streaming Format (ASF) and separated streaming media files into audio (WMA) and video (WMV) categories.

WWW World Wide Web, Web, W3. A global, virtual network–based hypertext information system that uses the Internet as its transport mechanism to display computer screens (i.e., Web pages) of graphical, video, textual, and even audio information. Created in 1989 at a research institute in Switzerland, the Web relies upon browsers and the hypertext transport protocol (http), an Internet standard that specifies how an application can locate and acquire resources stored on another computer on the Internet. Most Web documents are created using hypertext markup language (html), a coding system for WWW documents. The Web, with its ability to incorporate hypermedia (graphics, sounds, animations, video), has become a popular medium for publishing information on the Internet. With the development of secure hypertext transfer protocol (shttp), the Web is now a commercial medium where consumers can browse on-line catalogs and purchase merchandise using secure, encrypted credit card information that is protected from unauthorized interception.

XLR plug A three-pin audio connector used for microphone, line, and snake connections.

XML Extensible Markup Language. A specification developed by the World Wide Web Consortium. XML is designed especially for Web documents. It allows designers to create their own customized tags, enabling the definition, transmission, validation, and interpretation of data between applications and between organizations.

Vendor Support

Use the following links to receive vendor support for hardware and software mentioned in the book.

QuickTime
www.apple.com/support

RealSystem
service.real.com

Windows Media
support.microsoft.com

Sorenson Broadcaster
www.sorenson.com/content.php?cats=5

Viewcast Osprey cards
www.viewcast.com/osprey_support_contacts.html

Winnov cards
www.winnov.com/support/index.htm

Companion Web Site Support

To contact the author, download software updates, or receive free technical support in implementing some of the guidelines mentioned in the book, log on to the Streaming Media Handbook companion Web site at www.streaminghandbook .com.

Index

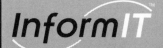

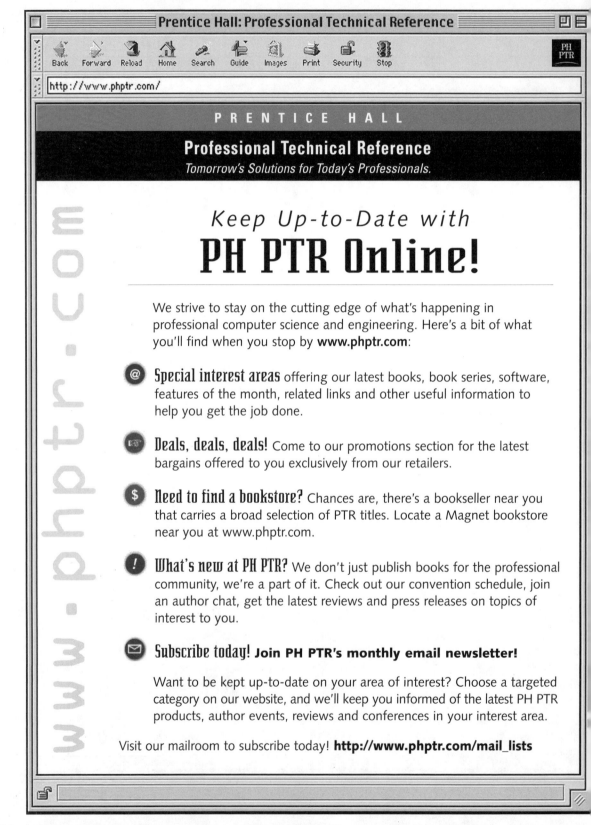